Photograph by Blank-Stoller
FRANK A. VANDERLIP

FROM FARM BOY
TO FINANCIER

By
FRANK A. VANDERLIP
in collaboration with
BOYDEN SPARKES

D. APPLETON-CENTURY COMPANY
INCORPORATED

NEW YORK   *1935*   LONDON

Copyright 1935 by Frank A. Vanderlip
All rights reserved.

*REPRINT EDITION AND COVERT ART DESIGN
DAUPHIN PUBLICATIONS 2017*

ISBN 9781939438560

CONTENTS

CHAPTER		PAGE
I.	ON THE FARM	1
II.	FACTORY OVERALLS	14
III.	ESCAPE FROM OVERALLS	23
IV.	WHITE-COLLAR WORKER	31
V.	VANDERLIP, THE YOUNG REPORTER	38
VI.	FINANCIAL EDITOR	51
VII.	EX-NEWSPAPERMAN	62
VIII.	A JUNIOR CABINET OFFICER	66
IX.	THE SPANISH-AMERICAN WAR	79
X.	AN INVITATION FROM WALL STREET	93
XI.	"STILLMAN'S MONEY TRAP"	99
XII.	THE MASTER OF THE CITY BANK	110
XIII.	THE BANK'S YOUNGEST VICE-PRESIDENT	121
XIV.	TAKING ROOT	131
XV.	MEN BEHIND THE BANK	141
XVI.	A FOREIGN INVESTMENT	156
XVII.	1907	161
XVIII.	THE NEW PRESIDENT OF THE CITY BANK	178
XIX.	THE ELDER MORGAN AS AN ALLEY	190
XX.	AN ADVENTURE WITH E. H. HARRIMAN	197
XXI.	A CONCLAVE ON JEKYL ISLAND	210
XXII.	MILLIONAIRE	220
XXIII.	RECRUITING FOR THE CITY BANK	228
XXIV.	WALL STREET ADJUSTS ITSELF TO WAR	233
XXV.	FRESH FIELDS TO CULTIVATE	249
XXVI.	NEW PLANS FOR THE BANK	259
XXVII.	TROUBLE WITH ROCKEFELLER	272
XXVIII.	THE BURDEN OF A BANKER	281
XXIX.	DOLLAR-A-YEAR MAN	291
XXX.	I LEAVE THE BANK	298
INDEX		308

ILLUSTRATIONS

Frank A. Vanderlip. . . . . *frontispiece*
FACING PAGE

Mr. Vanderlip's father. 13

Mr. Vanderlip's mother and father. 13

Home of Harmon Vanderlip, Frank A. Vanderlip's
    grandfather, near Madison, Ohio. 22

A family group on Harmon Vanderlip's farm, taken by
    Frank A. Vanderlip about the time of his trip to
    President Garfield's funeral. 22

Frank A. Vanderlip as a reporter on the Chicago *Tribune*. . . . 61

Charles T. Yerkes, Chicago traction magnate. 61

Richard Green, chief messenger in the Treasury
    Department. 78

Dr. P. N. Barnesby as a young man. 78

Lyman J. Gage, Secretary of the Treasure, and his three
    Assistant Secretaries. Left to right: General O. L.
    Spaulding, William B. Howell, Frank A. Vander-
    lip, and Mr. Gage. 78

Lyman J. Gage, center, and Mr. Vanderlip, second from right, on
    board a revenue-cutter in 1897. 92

War-bond activity in the Treasury Department during
    the Spanish-American War. 92

James Stillman as President of the National City Bank. . . . 120

E. H. Harriman. 155

William Rockefeller. 155

H. C. Frick. 155

ILLUSTRATIONS

	FACING PAGE
Jacob Schiff.	155
Frank A. Vanderlip after he became President of the National City Bank.	189
Frank A. Vanderlip soon after he went into the National City Bank.	189
J. P. Morgan.	196
Marvin Hughitt and Julius Kruttschnitt.	209
Henry P. Davison.	248
Andrew Carnegie.	248
Mr. and Mrs. Frank A. Vanderlip.	297

CHAPTER I
ON THE FARM

IN THE garden of my home, Beechwood, at Scarborough, there is a bronze statue by Rudulph Evans of a collie dog. The model, a beautiful creature, was a gift graciously made long ago by the elder J.P. Morgan who bred these animals as a hobby at kennels maintained at his country home on the other, the western, side of the Hudson River. The dog was perfectly made; and a so richly talented sculptor as my friend Evans certainly fixed in metal the accurate shape of this vanished companion of my eldest son. Yet the statue, which has the magic property of exciting an almost ancient recollection of mine, comes subtly into conflict with the past by putting my memory slightly out of drawing; that is until I close my eyes and the vision comes into focus. Then I can see again, satisfyingly, myself and Snap on our way to the pasture to bring up the cows.

I was a farm boy and going for the cows was one of my earliest duties; to go along was all I was required to do for the dog did the work, showing admirable intelligence at his job, rounding up the cows and nipping the heels of any that were lazy. In our part of the world two miles from Oswego, Illinois, Snap was indexed as a shepherd dog, but he was really a collie although not like Mr. Morgan's gift, a show dog. Snap was black with a white collar, a white stripe down his back and at the end of his tail a plume of white. It was an exquisite sensation on a Summer morning to feel with my bare feet the smooth, cool cow path in the prairie sod, to inhale the fragrance and to see the flowers, the yellow blossoms with black centers on tall stems that I knew as resinweeds; the pink ones which were called prairie pointers and now have cultivated descendants called cyclamen in many carefully tended gardens; but they were wild flowers then and all the more charming for that reason. On a frosty day when my feet still were bare I would scamper along that path to take a warm stand on a piece of pasture where a cow had been lying; a place surrendered to me at Snap's command.

I deserve no patent; on every square mile of the prairies, I supposed, some other boy was doing that and possibly they are still doing it; yet I was astonished years afterward when Leslie M. Shaw while he was secretary of the treasure brought such a recollection out of his memories of his boyhood on a farm. Snap found plenty to do on our farm, where he was rated by my father as half a man. If a pig got out of the pen he would round it up; a young pig he would bowl over and hold to earth with his open mouth, never hurting it, although from its squealing you might suppose it was being slaughtered. If a chicken was wanted for the dinner-table all that was necessary was to point to a selection in the flock pecking about the barnyard and Snap would get it; but he would never but it, just hold it on the ground with his open mouth until you came and took it. I remember all those things of Snap, and yet just as vividly I remember when my father on a cold day in our kitchen took from his overcoat picket the black-and-white puppy that became the understanding dog I tell about. He would follow my father behind the walking plough, before we got a riding plough, all day long and any snake he saw was killed on sight. He would grab and bite and shake them until they stopped writhing. That was his method with the ordinary green snakes; but if he came upon a big one or a poisonous snake, he would bark and circle out of reach until my father or the hired man could come and kill it.

I had a very perfect companionship with my father and mother. Physically I resembled my mother; her people had come from a rather distinguished line of pioneers. They came out of Salem, were settled for a time at South Lee, Massachusetts, and at Cleveland. Moses Hoyt, my mother's grandfather, had a powder factory. In Aurora other relatives had a machine-shop and my mother was, so to speak, the daughter of the wagon factory there. My father had been born in Ohio of pioneer farmer stock, then drifted West, learned the blacksmith trade and became superintendent of the wagon works of the Woodworth family; when he married Charlotte Woodworth, my mother, she was only sixteen. Because of poor health he had been rejected from service in the Union Army. He had more education than the average farmer. I know as I got into algebra he was able to help me with it and I always looked up to him as being well informed. He wore a dark beard so long it seemed to accentuate any movement of his head. I would turn the handle of the grindstone for him when he was sharpening the mowing-machine sickle. That blade was four feet long and notched with teeth so that it required a lot of grinding. Sometimes, bent over, I would become so enthralled by his drudgery that even when he stopped to examine the edge of the blade I would keep on turning. Then he would say: "Are you trying to get a few turns ahead?" He had a great deal of that capacity for forming sound rules of conduct which we call common sense. For example, there was the advice he gave when I was sent into that entrancing place, our cellar, a store-house of food, with bins of apples, squash, pumpkins; with cider barrels, and rows of hanging sides of pork and ham; mother would sometimes caution me to select apples with bad spots so that they would not be left to contaminate the sound ones; father would say: "If you do that, you will be eating bad apples the rest of your life: Pick out the best ones."

One of the first things my father did on the farm was to construct a blacksmith shop. He was such an ingenious mechanic that I believed there was nothing beyond his powers. I recall now with what admiration I watched him build a two-seat sleigh mounted on light runners made of oak planks cut out in a graceful pattern and bound on the bottom with iron. When the woodwork was finished and naked in its newness I helped to paint it, but it was my father who with sure hand and a finer brush put the fancy stripe of blood carmine along the edges of its glossy panels. When we rode in it on winter days the bottom would be deep in straw and buffalo robes; to cover our laps on special occasions there was a souvenir of my father's courting days, a fine robe of white fox bordered with long, thick tails. That white fox robe was what kept me warm and snug in my bed at the top of the house on arcticly cold nights. My father built an ice-house and then, acting on advice in the *American Agriculturist*, we packed the ice in buckwheat straw, which proved the editor wrong by heating so that all our supply of ice melted; we should have used sawdust or shavings. He built the milk-house, too; a half-subterranean structure with masonry walls two feet thick of carefully mortised roundheads, which was our word for the glacial boulders that were strewn about the farm when we first came. In the first year my father, planting corn, cut the raw prairie sod with a stroke of his ax, and then dropped into that earth-wound a seed. He built the cow-barn; a great shelter that held fifty head. It was almost cathedral-like in its vastness to me then. From the wide central alley I could look straight up to the beam which was the ridge pole; on either side in the lofts the hay was stored. The cows in two long rows confronted each other. Each through a corridor that followed the outer wall entered her stall to be secured within stanchions made of two-by-six boards held by a bolt at the bottom and fastened across the cow's neck by a button of wood. The edges of the boards were rounded and the inner surfaces were as glossy as

ON THE FARM

varnish because of the polishing received from the movements in these stocks of cows' necks.

We milked thirty to forty cows; they were reddish-brown or cream and white, and if it was not a blooded herd, at least there was a queen whose chief prerogative of which we were aware was to go first into the barn. This I saw one time: Two other cows impatiently entered ahead of her. She waited outside, the other cows like outraged court ladies standing behind her. There was no sound apparent to my ears but presently the two rude cows emerged in a kind of fright and as they went wide of her she entered, full of milk and silent indignation. To keep the rats and mice under control in the cow-barn a cat was domiciled there and he rated for his work a kind of milk tax; but I would never give it to him in a saucer. He had learned that no amount of mewing would gain his breakfast, but that if he say up, held his forepaws off the floor and opened his mouth I would squirt milk into it.

A few years later, I was made, one summer, the herd boy, cook and tutor of thirty-six calves. They had to be taught to drink. The way you did that was to cup milk in your hand from a pail to the calf's mouth, gradually overcoming his inclination to put his head up for milk; but even when one was induced to lower his head into a pail a contrary impulse to bunt would frequently result in the upset of a pail. The pails contained a fluid that was made of milk and hay tea, and infusion of hay boiled in kettles suspended over bonfires in the yard. Each calf had a name that was entered on a ruled page of a patent medicine almanac and each name was checked as that calf was fed. At the end of that summer for my work my father gave me a calf for my own and when it was sold I was richer than I had dreamed of being; I had twelve dollars.

I marvel today the way I spent that money. I might have bought an air-rifle big enough to kill gophers and small birds, but I was never able to find sport in killing things. It seems to me now that I was extraordinarily sensitive to all the afflictions of the creatures on our farm. When I was quite young a visitor on the farm shot a bird. I ran as his retriever to pick it up and when I discovered there was blood on my hands I was greatly disturbed and could not forget. Long years afterward I was induced to go hunting, shot at a deer, missed it and was delighted for a suddenly remembered my youthful prejudices against killing creatures. Even on that gala day of farm life, the first cold spell when we would butcher our hogs, I would absent myself to avoid the sight, the scent of blood and the wretched cries of the animals I had known. When their piggish screams ceased then I might return to help a little with the bristly scraping. A bob sleigh with its low, plank bed became the mortuary table and close beside it was the barrel of scalding hot water into which the carcass of each hog would be soused. Their sudden lifelessness oppressed me. I remember, too, my extreme sadness when our finest horse, an extraordinarily beautiful animal, was involved in a runaway. The team was hauling a heavily loaded wagon when the thing happened and in the final smash-up the tongue of the wagon struck the foreleg of that lovely horse. I saw it then, lying in a tangle of dusty harness, saw it lift its head until its neck was iridescent in the sun, and felt its despair when it fell back and the soft black muzzle was in the dirt, the buried nostril blowing an explosion of dust with each exhalation. I saw a man lift its hoof to demonstrate the shattered leg was limp as rope and then I started off so that I might be far away before a gun could be brought from the farm-house.

What I did buy with my twelve dollars gained from the sale of the calf was a six years' subscription to the New York *Weekly Tribune*, with a premium of Wester's unabridged dictionary. That offer was advertised to me by a sign hanging on the wall of the village post-office in Oswego. I have the dictionary yet and I suspect that rooted in my mind are some of the *Tribune's* prejudices planted there by the fierce things printed during the Hayes-Tilden controversy. I would explore the dictionary at random and I know I got my calf's worth. That calls to mind a later thing. I was associated with Woodrow Wilson for a good many years when we were trustees of the Carnegie Foundation. I have been from the inception a member of the executive committee and for a while he was a member, also. All the other members were college presidents, but there was never a resolution written or anything drafted that would not make Wilson itch to change a word or two; invariably he improved any statement he altered. One day I asked him how he accounted for his clarity in the use of words. He said he attributed it to the fact that his father had made it a rule of their household that everyone had not merely to consult but to read the dictionary. It was a volume to be picked up every day.

I have no slightest recollection of any stern family rules at home. There never was compulsion in the family and there never was resistance; but there were kindnesses every day. One night when my father came from attending an auction sale of the possessions of a German farmer he spoke to me mysteriously, suggesting that I look out in the kitchen which was a kind of lean-to addition on our red-painted house. It was after lamplight and difficult to see, but I could hear a strangely exciting, an incredible clattering upon the boards of the kitchen floor. Then I saw what was there. A pony! It was a sorrel with a tail, a mane, a forelock and face silvery white. I can't believe there was ever a boy more delirious with joy than I was then, or afterward for that matter. I named the pony Dutchman. It was a grand thing for me to have; to feed that animal before I fed myself, to make its coat shine and to ridge it, to ride off along swelling with pride and wishing for people to observe me were riches for my soul. But that was not all of the joy of owning Dutchman. He was no longer young but he had been a circus pony!

My devoted father brought me from Aurora a boy's size saddle and, what nicely fitted the pony, a bridle ornamented at the brow band with notched discs of leather, one upon the other in a narrowing succession. The saddle had a horn and was elaborately embossed. Think what it was like for me to ride that pony two miles to the Oswego schoolyard and there to have an audience of boys and girls Dutchman, you see, was a trained pony. At my command he would rear up on his hind legs and show the whites of his eyes and paw the air as for so many years he had done in sawdust rings of a circus. Oh, that was not all; if I asked him, "What did you do in California?" he would paw the ground and even the dullest child would know instantly that the pony was saying he had dug gold out there. He had other answers for other questions and was altogether one of the finest things in which I have ever taken pride. Is it any wonder I loved my father?

My knowledge of the Civil War was derived from *Harpers' Weekly*, from the illustrations in a file of back numbers—the war issues—kept in our house. What I saw and read there I rehearsed with an old Civil War cavalry saber that destiny had brought into our stock of farm tools. The end had been broken off and, sharpened on a grindstone, it was used as a corn knife. By the Fourth of July corn ought to be knee-high to a man; but the later growth Nature hurried like a stage magician so that on still nights the expanding, lengthening plants could be heard faintly crackling and the stalks eight and even ten feet high ridged hilt and slashing valiantly I would proceed from one end of a corn row to the other, unaware that I was working. I who could not bear to see hogs or chickens die, I was slaughtering regiments; in the same way I assaulted the pumpkins that must be reduced to small bits before they were placed in the feed troughs lest a cow choke on too big a piece. Such gory fancies of military prowess made my work lighter but did not by a tissue thickness callous my sensitiveness. Sometimes, at the end of a corn row close to the road, I would find myself trading looks with those who rode on the front seat of a covered-wagon, their faces framed in the canvas gathered over the foremost wagon bow. I watched such passages many times, and in my memory usually a cow is walking behind haltered to the tail-board. The western migration did not catch my imagination; I never longed to join the procession; there was pioneering enough for me on the section where I lived.

I read a great deal whenever I set out on Dutchman to herd the cows on some unfenced field I would have tucked inside the bib of my overalls a magazine or book. Arthur Young, a school-mate who lived in Oswego and who was to be envied because he could play tunes on a violin, had a set a Louisa Muhlbach's book; historical novels. One by one I borrowed and devoured them at home we had a set of Shakespeare and a lot of James Fenimore Cooper's works. I would sit in the saddle reading, with the strong sunlight beating on the pages, until I more or less ruined my eyes. There in the saddle I experienced vicariously all the adventures set down by Jules Verne. When I read his stories first they were being published by the Franklin Square Library in a format slightly smaller than that of the *Saturday*

ON THE FARM

Evening Post. We had back numbers for years into the past of a magazine called *Saturday's Own*; we had old copies of *St. Nicolas, Hearth and Home, Harpers' Weekly* and the *Youths' Companion*. Magazines were never thrown away but were traded around. They contained a lot of instruction. In *Our Young Folks* (which published the "Peterkin papers") a series had been printed called "Lessons in Magic," so that I learned how to slap an apparently solid right of iron onto a walking-stick held horizontally before me; when I made the bran disappear from a goblet by passing a cloth over it my spectators were not supposed to know that the bran was glued to a sheet of paper cut to the shape of the glass. That practice in prestidigitation, I hasten to add, was not any part of my training for a banking career. From the premium list of *Youths' Companion*, which was my Rue de la Paix, I elected to purchase a fret saw, and on the wall of a room of my home today is a newspaper-rack of walnut intricately patterned y my sawing.

I remember one incident that almost became disastrous. I had sent money to the *Youths' Companion* for Christmas gifts for my parents, my little brother and baby sister. The packages were handed to me in Oswego on a day when I did not have my pony. I caught a ride on a stranger's bob-sleigh traveling toward our farm; then, when the man turned at an angle away from my route, I jumped out hurriedly only to remember, within a few minutes, that my precious Christmas bundles in a stranger's sleigh were vanishing across the prairie into the

ON THE FARM

snowy twilight. Desperately, yelling shrilly, I ran across the fields and by some miracle of the season I made the driver hear me so that I intercepted him a regained the packages. Glad I was, too, for even with gifts it promised to be dismal holiday in our house.

MR. VANDERLIP'S MOTHER AND FATHER

MR. VANDERLIP'S FATHER

CHAPTER II
FACTORY OVERALLS

WINTER in Illinois then meant frosty window-panes for weeks upon weeks. My tall and bearded father had what was spoken of as a heavy cold. He coughed a great deal. We did not dream then that in such a bland fluid as milk there might lurk so dreadful an affliction; today, of course, in most states a great deal of money is spent to destroy infected cattle. One day in the yard when it was deep with snow my father had a severe coughing spell, and when he straightened up I saw on the whiteness at his feet a scarlet stain; a death warrant.

At intervals through the winter the doctor came from his home eight miles away, driving his horse and buggy over bad roads to leave a bottle of useless medicine to be administered with a teaspoon. Galloping consumption it was called in those days. For a time my father was in bed, his eyes getting bigger daily; and then he died. Time passes so slowly when you are young and small that the drive behind a hearse in a procession of neighbor's buggies has lasted, far back in my mind, through all the years. My mother's face was hidden from me behind a veil of heavy black crêpe; I heard the dreadful sound of frozen clods thudding on a box and somehow knew my boyhood was at an end.

FACTORY OVERALLS

My grandfather came and tried to help my mother run the farm, but he did not do it very well; the seeds of tragedy were in that soil. The little brother, ten years younger than I, grew thin and gaunt and then died of tuberculosis. It was tragedy, too, when with all our hopes centered on a flock of young turkeys, their legs would begin to curl up with a fatal ailment we called turkey rheumatism. A whole year's work was wiped out in visitation of cholera; by twos and threes and even fours the hogs would lie down and die; they died quickly from cholera. It was a great strain for us to meet all the responsibilities. There was a mortgage for $5,000 on the farm and the interest rate was 10 percent. An old gentleman in Aurora named Budlong owned the document and I remember being sent to him once with the interest, for half a year, in cash, pinned in my pocket. We never saw bank checks and had no bank account; consequently we had to hoard carefully any cash we got. Curiously, I can remember the price we got for butter; thirty-six cents a pound. We were proud to get so high a price. In the summer we would sell the bull calves to the Oswego butcher and they were eaten there in the village; occasionally there was a beef animal to sell. After the milk factory was started, an enterprise of tremendous importance to us, there was a monthly check for our milk and cream; but there was uncertainty and little peace in that existence for my mother. I remember some money I made of the farm by gathering husks for a mattress factory between Oswego and Aurora. I was thirteen and with the six dollars bought an ulster overcoat I needed to wear to school.

Christopher Duffy, an easy-going young Irishman who had been in the Civil War, was the schoolmaster in Oswego. Once when I was about twelve, I think, I ran away to Aurora to see General Grant. As the train rolled into the station I crowded close to the platform right among some who had been his soldiers, and I saw him get his hand badly pinched when someone closed the door on it. He took it rather simply, but we learned from the papers that he had to stop shaking hands with his admirers.

There was no complaint at home because I had abandoned school for such an expedition; my mother thought I had been very enterprising. It was a great thing to have seen General Grant.

I was a pretty good scholar I guess; at least pretty studious. I could write a little better than the others and could certainly spell worse. Then, when I had gone about as far I could in the country school, the farm was sold at an auction held at the county-seat; the land brought forty-six dollars an acre if I remember rightly, more than enough to satisfy the mortgage. Then there was another auction, a country sale such as I had always been eager to attend when they were held on other farms; but this time the things to be sold were our own. I was not eager that time, I can tell you.

The nasal voice of Dave Hall, the auctioneer, standing in a wagon so as to be above the heads of the crowd, grated on my ears when he began describing things that belonged to us; parts of us, really. The cattle, haltered, one by one were led up to the wagon where he stood. The farm machines were clustered in the yard; likewise piles of dishes and rows of furniture. Vividly I remember the gesture of parting with it all. From a pine tree my father had plated I cut some branches and carried those to Aurora where mother, bringing me and my young sister, joined her household with that of her mother and two maiden aunts of mine. I became the man of that household then; the year was 1880 and a job and had been found for me.

I can feel even now a flush of embarrassment as I think of my first appearance in the machine-shop where I became an apprentice. I was aware of a continuous scrutiny by the men who worked at the lathes, the benches and the planers. They were making, there and in the foundry, large woodworking machinery; big planers and enormous circular-saws. The factory was owned by the Hoyts, cousins of my grandmother, but that faint distinction did not lessen my blushes. As the morning slowly wore on I learned how to make the bolts that were used to fasten the knives on the planers but I also learned that there was a connection between the grins of the men and the fact that my trousers were tucked inside of farm boots, the canvas pull-ons projecting untidily above the tops at the hinges of my knees. Even Ambrose Higgins, the foreman, who was an excellent man but something of a dandy, let his eyes fix themselves on those boot-tops which labeled me as from the country; farm boots were not worn in the great city of Aurora. Well, the next day I was comfortably concealed in the herd; my trousers hung as curtains around my boot-tops at least to the level of my ankle bones, and to that extent I had made social progress.

It was in that big factory chamber with its system of overhead belts flying about in response to the fall of Fox River water on a mill-wheel that I learned, eventually, enough of the trade to be rated as a journeyman machinist. I learned with the others to sense by the feelings in my stomach when it was time to expect the shrilling of a steam-whistle at the railroad shops on the other side of the river; that whistle regulated my life six days a week for about three and a half years. I started at my lathe when it blew at seven o'clock in the morning; when it blew at twelve with the others, and like them grease-blackened, I rushed for the stack of tin basins in the wash-room; at one I started work again; and at six I stopped.

Saturday was different; we worked only nine hours, until five o'clock on Saturdays, but that was payday and I stood in line with the other machinists slowly progressing toward the office window through which the bookkeeper handed out the sealed, yellow envelops. I was being paid at the rate of seventy-five cents a day, but, of course, there was that short nine-hour day on Saturday to be calculated when the payroll was made up, so my envelope contained not $4.50 but $4.43. I must say, though, for quite a while that sum seemed like an awful lot of money to me; indeed, it was not so long after I began making that much I decided I could afford to go to a theater. I saw George C. Miln, a preacher who had become an actor, in "The Fool's Revenge." That must have been in 1880 and I recall now that as the gas-lights flared before the curtain I had such a thrill as repaid me for all my hours at the lathe. But now I am making it sound as if the machine-shop was drudgery, when actually it was not. Why, I could read and study there and never be rebuked. I suppose I am talking about forgotten processes, but when a wood-working machine was ordered from the company it was first drafted in the drafting-room; then the complete drafts would be sent to the pattern-maker where the patterns were made out of white pine, and these would be sent to the foundry where the casting was done. The rough casting eventually appeared among us machinists. There were, for instance, great rolls of steel a foot or more in diameter and three feet long. In the completed planer the function of such rolls was to draw a board into contact with the swiftly revolving knife.

On the occasions when I have been in machine-shops in recent years and seen the speed at which the lathes are run with their hard-steel tools I stand amazed; such speeds would have burned the point off a tool in the days when I was running a lathe. A lucky thing, too, for me. If the task was to cut the outer surface off one of those rolls, I would set it, start the lathe and sometimes have half an hour during which I need do nothing more than glance at the job occasionally; that was when I read and studied.

I found my greatest pleasure at that time in the Aurora Public Library, and then quite like an adventurer, I traveled to a city upon which the country's minds were focused. I went to Cleveland.

The astonishing hat I wore to the funeral of President Garfield plagues me for an explanation I cannot give. As I made ready for the trip I was sixteen, but soon to be seventeen. For a boy whose life had been restricted to home, the farm and a machine-shop, it was going to be a thrilling and a dignifying adventure to travel on railroad trains from Aurora all the way to Cleveland to see pageant of the journey was a substantial, pre-Civil War receptacle of black leather and heavy brass fastenings, and while my mother and grandmother were busy making enough sandwiches and other refreshments as nearly to fill it, I made the important purchase that crowned my wardrobe. I bought this hat that had caught my fancy, a soft black felt, low crowned, with an extra wide brim, a thing clearly designed to be fixed on the head of a villain. It was from a block that had become stylish during the months that Garfield lingered. The hat was made in the likeness of the one worn by his assassin and it was called a Guiteau hat. That was what I lifted in farewell as I stood on the platform of a Burlington railway coach, observed by the ladies of our house.

From the Burlington station on the West Side of Chicago I walked, according to directions given me at home, toward the Lake Shore railroad station, but at the end of LaSalle Street I became confused. The old Board of Trade Building was then being built. It is only in the United States that men outlast their temples; that one has vanished to make place for a taller market. Eventually I found my way in what seemed to me then to be a labyrinth and came to the station. Aboard my train I was full of hunger, but I firmly resisted from eating until the train was rolling southward through Englewood. Then began a struggle that lasted throughout the night. There was some kind of a trick catch on that hand-bag and I could not get the darn thing open. I was using fingers that had become strong extracting milk from cows and yet I had not the slightest success; the bag remained closed. With so much food in my custody I could not waste any of my sharply limited funds to buy a meal, consequently I went supperless. Ever and again during the long night I renewed my efforts to solve the puzzle of the bag's lock, but because it was borrowed I never dared attack the thing with the violence I sorely wanted to use upon it. Impishly it cheated me of breakfast, too, and only when I had at last reached the comparative plenty of my relatives' home in Cleveland did the perverse metal fastenings of that bag unlatch.

On the rainy day of the Garfield funeral I stood on Euclid Avenue as part of a living corridor through which the cortège passed. Guiteau hats were numerously worn, the most perverted symbol of respect that ever I have seen; yet it was respect. I cannot imagine a more awesome spectacle for such a boy as I, a youthful Republican to whom "horse-thief" was no more opprobrious and epithet than "Democrat." The canopied and heavily draped catafalque on which the coffin was hauled through the streets was as large a platform and as carefully arranged as a Mardi Gras float; but not even the gloom of its blackness could spoil for me so rich a show. Cadenced by dirges, by fifers and drummers, companies of bearded heads under heavy leather shakos marched past my wide eyes. Slanting over shoulders and up past the forage caps of companies in blue I saw the rifles with which, not so many years before, they had been killing men in gray. I saw former President Rutherford B. Hayes. I saw Arthur, the successor of the president who was in his coffin. I saw Blaine and Windom and the other members of the cabinet. These men were as deities to me. I came back to Aurora somewhat distinguished by my experience. The men in the shop were eager for the details that I could give them.

HOME OF HARMON VANDERLIP, FRANK A. VANDERLIP'S GRANDFATHER, NEAR MADISON, OHIO

A FAMILY GROUP ON HARMON VANDERLIP'S FARM, TAKEN BY FRANK A. VANDERLIP ABOUT THE TIME OF HIS TRIP TO PRESIDENT GARFIELD'S FUNERAL

CHAPTER III
ESCAPE FROM OVERALLS

IF I could have lived my life according to a program of desire I would have been engaged in pure science all my days; physics interested me intensely when I was in Aurora. I had a chum named Wynn Meredith. His enthusiasm for electricity infected me. When we saw a design for a dynamo in the *Scientific American* we determined to make one. I had the castings made in the shop. The project took us several months. I got a real lesson out of winding the armature. I learned that if you missed doing a thing right at one turn you never could cover it up with the next. If I failed to spool the wire on with every strand snugly in its place the hump of the flaw would show in spite of everything until I unwrapped enough wire to make it right. Our dynamo worked, and years afterward I heard that it was still being used in a little silver-plating factory in Aurora. I even tried to get a job with the new electric company which had put arc lamps on steel towers one hundred and fifty feet high in order to light the city. They offered me work inserting carbons in the lamps, but I decided I was not sufficiently interested in electricity for that; every lamp was to be reached only after a hazardous, dizzy climb; I had too much caution. I figured I might learn more about electricity at college and began sending for catalogues. In the

ESCAPE FROM OVERALLS

meantime, I was earning a little extra money teaching algebra to some of my shop-mates at fifty cents an hour, but I was spending the money taking German lessons; and from Myron Stolp, and inventor of uncommercial devices and son of one of the towns' big men, I was taking mathematics, descriptive geometry. I was determined I was not going to spend the rest of my life in overalls at a lathe in a machine-shop. But how was I to get out? Looking backward now I am amazed that in six moves I got out of overalls and became the president of the nation's biggest bank. Then, of course, I was not even thinking of banking.

Wynn Meredith had decided to go to the University of Illinois, but I wanted to attend a college that could increase my understanding of electricity. Cornell, the only one that offered such a course, was, however, too far away for my purse, so I also went to Champaign. There at Illinois I was told I would have to take an entrance examination and shuddered outside the door of the professor who was, first of all, going to test my knowledge of English.

"What have you read?" he asked me and it seems to me now that his eyes rested understandingly on the bruised and broken finger-nails, the grease-etched lines on my hands that were fluttering about my clothes in search of pockets to hide in.

"Shakespeare," I blurted.

ESCAPE FROM OVERALLS

"Well," he said very gently, "tell me about some one of his plays that you have read."

Romeo and Juliet was the one I chose to tell about, and that kind gentleman listened as intently, with as much genuine interest, as if Shakespeare himself were standing there telling it for the first time. When I stopped talking he nodded and smiled upon me with real friendship and made me understand that I was thenceforth a member of the student body; I was "in" college. Well, even today I think it was a sensible examination, though I realize that the modern curricula require proofs of wider knowledge, of more solid foundations.

Pledged to be roommates, Wynn and I went looking for the least expensive living accommodations we could find, and so we entered the establishment of a boarding-house lady right out of Dickens. She looked like her name, she behaved in keeping with it, and whenever she spoke I felt Mrs. Scroggins was as perfect an example of onomatopoeia as ever I encountered.

I have somewhere in my archines my account-book of that year and the expenditures total $226. It had been money saved out of my $4.43 a week; none of it was borrowed, but with the end of the school year when it was all gone there was nothing for me to do but to go back to the shop, to put on my overalls and take my place again at a lathe. The general superintendent of the plant found time to tell me that they planned to put me at other jobs, and I was given to understand that someday I might rise to a position like that of Ambrose Higgins, the foreman. Somehow the knowledge that Mr. Higgins's job was what was in store for me settled the thing, stiffened my spine. I made up my mind right then and there that I would not have my career in that shop. I was getting $1.25 a day; a journeyman machinist able to work at my trade at lathe or bench. I might have gone anywhere with such a passport, but I knew I had to get out of overalls and do something, anything else. I think I was really desperate then. I yearned as much as ever to go to college, but it seemed out of the question since I was the only man of a family of women; and I had no one with influence to smooth a path for me. That was when my eye was caught by an advertisement of a course of shorthand taught by mail. Tachygraphy it was called. I subscribed. With a piece of chalk I practiced making the shorthand characters on the tail stock of my lathe. I worked diligently because I had persuaded myself that those cabalistic signs were going to be the wizard formula by means of which I was to be released from the enchantment of overalls and a factory. Just thinking and wishing fervently was like a chemical change in the situation, and when word was passed around that the shop was going to shut down for a few weeks I swelled with eagerness. In those days when business was slack the euphemistic explanation was given that the factory was going to "take inventory."

That was when I saw the chance to make my first move; to get out of overalls. The very day of the shutdown I read in the Aurora *Evening Post* an item of news that probably had been written and set in type by the person concerned; it was an announcement of the departure of the city editor to another city and another job. I had never written anything and can recall now nothing to explain the nerve, the daring that carried me, after a sleepless night, into the office of the publisher of the newspaper to ask him for the job of city editor.

His name was Constantine; he owned the paper and he ran it, but how well he ran it you may gather from the fact that he gave me what I asked for. Six dollars a week was the pay and quite often I had to go out and collect the amount from delinquent subscribers or advertisers, for rarely was there that much money in the till. The paper was housed in a one-story wooden building of two rooms, and which was the most gummy with a deposit of chewing tobacco it would be hard for me to say with accuracy. The year was 1885 and I was twenty-one, but my soul was inches taller because I was now a personage. Calling myself city editor meant more to me then than to have suddenly discovered that I possessed a patent of nobility and might call myself baron.

City Editor! It was there in the lower left-hand corner of the cards that were printed for me in the job-room which was the same room that sheltered the hand-press from which came all copies of the Aurora *Evening Post*, when someone, generally me, turned a big wheel; but I was strong. I learned to set type, too, so that as we got close to the end of our day and the back room was noisy with rowdy carrier boys, I could stand at a case and put my information, never my thoughts, into shape for printing. I really ought to report, though, that my work was half done in the morning when I met the Burlington train from Chicago and got a long, heavy box that contained our ration of boiler plate; lead-cast feature stories, fashion notes and other filler material that came to us ready to go into the forms with further treatment except sawing for length. I went to the police station, I went to the city hall, and to the other sources of routine news and although the expression was not then in use I was in Aurora, at least within the person of Frank A. Vanderlip, a big shot. Actually I was, too. Not many people in Aurora had an annual pass that would carry them free anywhere on the Burlington Railroad. That little reddish piece of cardboard made me seem important to myself and railroad conductors spoke, I fancied, a little more considerately to me than to ordinary passengers who had to pay for tickets. On a Saturday afternoon with a clear conscience I could catch a train to Quincy or run up to Chicago. One night up there at the Chicago Opera House I saw Booth play Othello and Lawrence Barrett play Iago, and then the next night I returned with thousands of others and saw Barrett play Othello and Booth play Iago. I saw Booth play Hamlet, too, and put a little piece about it in the paper.

Once I went to Geneva, the seat of Kane County, to cover a murder trial. A farmer, in what was a not infrequent occurrence in pioneer farming, had been involved in a controversy over a line fence; he had shot and killed his neighbor. The defendant's name was Hope and his lawyer was a man named Elbert Gary. Hope was given a fairly light sentence. A long, long time afterward when I mentioned that trial to Judge Gary, of the United States Steel Corporation, I had a feeling that the corporation lawyer was not particularly interested in the fact that I had believed, that day in Geneva, that he had made a brilliant defense and a poignant appeal for jury sympathy for the murderer. All too quickly we began to talk of other matters, of corporation affairs.

But the big, the significant thing that happened to me while I was working on the Aurora paper was a friendship I formed with a man named Joseph French Johnson. If a man's life, as a chemical solution, may have the rate of its reactions accelerated by a catalyst, then this friendship was for me just such a changing force. He had been born in Aurora, the son of a grocer, had gone to Harvard, then to the German university at Halle. He had come back to the United States and worked on the old Springfield *Republican* under Same Bowles. This man, Joe Johnson, returning to Aurora, had married the sister of Myron Stolp who had continued to tutor me in mathematics. To me this tall, blond man of the world who made me quite comfortable by being not too tidy in his habits of dress, was the most exciting individual I had ever encountered. At this time he had a job in Chicago with a firm which represented, I think, the very beginnings of a craft, a business, the members of which speak of themselves now as investment counselors.

I used to go shyly to see Johnson at his house in the evenings when he had returned from his day's work in Chicago. I knew that he worked for a man there names Moses Scudder, but I had only a vague idea what Scudder did. Then Johnson proposed to me that I might, in view of my shorthand accomplishment, Tachygraphy, take a job in Chicago as a stenographer. I took the job and I had made my second move. I was paid $15 a week; in the present as I gaze out across my sloping lawn to the far side of the Hudson River and think of all that I have had, I realized my wage was much, much larger than $15 a week; but Moses Scudder, of course, knew nothing of that. When he found out that I would have to learn how to run his typewriter my fate, for a minute or two, was back in the balance; but he nodded and I was hired.

CHAPERT IV
WHITE-COLLAR WORKER

THE elevator in the office building where I worked was to me a starting contraption. In the course of its flights between the ground and the ninth floor the cage swayed alarmingly in the shaft and the walls of my stomach fluttered with it. A rope that appeared through a hole in the floor and vanished through another superimposed in the roof was the means of its uncertain control by an operator whose behavior I watched as tenderly as today I might watch the manipulations of a balloon pilot in whose custody, far from earth, I found myself. For me the elevator was an expression in motion of all that bewildering and fascination modernity which was totaled in the word Chicago. Really it was modern because almost, one might have said, the oldest parts were younger than Vanderlip.

The proof of that was a recollection of my very first trip away from home in 1872 when I was "seven, goin' on eight"; a memorable trip. My father and mother took me for a day in Chicago. We went to the Exposition and then, so that I might appreciate what had happened the year before, in '71, my father took me for a ride on a street-car that was drawn by horses through the ruins of the South Side to the stock-yards. Out there in the volcanic-like mounds that had been grain elevators before the fire, the wheat, the corn and the rye were still smoking; occasionally the sodden piles would nourish visible flame. That great fire which had seemed to destroy Chicago had simply cleared a significant area for men with fresh ideas.

Two of my early memories are germane. When I was perhaps five or six, on the first cold days of the season I would see at the railroad freight station in Oswego a line of farm wagons serval blocks long; each was piled with the frozen carcasses of hogs intended for shipment to Chicago. The farmers talked and joked in clusters as they waited their turns at the loading-platform. Then, all that changed and thereafter the hogs were shipped alive to Chicago. The packing plants had been built. I remember also the peddlers who came to our kitchen-door when I was small. The tin-peddler with his big, red coach with its enormous trunk behind was an institution to be patronized; but there were also pack-peddlers, bearded Jews who trudged from farm-house to farm-house with their wares done up in oil-cloth coverings. They wandered on year after year sleeping sometimes in farm-house beds and sometimes in barns. In time their spines took on a pathetic curvature and their minds, too, were shaped by the endless bargaining with people who did not easily part with money. Some of those fellows transmuted their packs into big establishments and themselves into great merchants. I like to think that one of the packs that was spread upon the floor of the Vanderlip kitchen was that of the man who became the founder of the great packing-house firm of Morris & Company.

The ninth-floor office of Moses Scudder, who became my employer in 1886, was in a building gone long ago, one that stood at the northwest corner of LaSalle Street and Jackson Boulevard. Across LaSalle Street was that palace of Victorian elegance, the Grand Pacific Hotel. Its famous cuisine was something that occasionally tempted the almost regal Marshal Field to come for luncheon, but I could enjoy its food in those days only by the tantalizing process of inhaling the odors that drifted into my nostrils as I passed along the street beside its kitchens. Across Jackson Boulevard was the smoke-blackened temple of the Board of Trade, with windows of stained glass and imitation marble interiors stained at the base-boards with tobacco juice. In the streets of that region at any time I was apt to rub shoulders with a millionaire of the pork or grain trades; but when I took my place at my desk I was feeling pretty far removed from the rich adventures of commerce. I was no longer eligible for a pass on the Burlington Road so I had to pay for my daily journeys between Aurora and Chicago. The price of my ticket took quite a big bite out of my $15 a week; yet I was two jobs removed from overalls.

Scudder was chiefly concerned with the brokerage firm of W. T. Baker & Company, of which he was member, and this other, The Investors' Agency, an investigating enterprise, was a side issue; he gave just a part of his time to it and his only employees were Joseph French Johnson and myself. For a time Johnson did all the important work and I was the office drudge. I took letters and reports dictated sometimes by Scudder and sometimes by Johnson. I took letters not brilliantly but with rather ponderous accuracy in the characters of my correspondence-course Tachygraphy, then by laborious, forefinger peckings, I transcribed my notes. The typewriter I used was of a species, the Caligraph, which has assisted the commercial development of the United States by vanishing with the buffalo and the Indian. It had a double bank keyboard and for days the upper and lower case letters afflicted my memory as a kind of double jeopardy; and then, almost before I expected proficiency, my two forefingers were able to clatter up and down the face of that machine at a gallop.

I looked upon Scudder as a great Mogul; he was a man of wealth in my young eyes. He was plump, well-groomed and quite good-looking man, but he was pretty distant and never admitted me to a closer relationship with him than that of his employee. There was in him a certain narrowness that is inherent in the suspicious, investigating type, the kind that rejects everything at first approach and only afterward detects worth. Yet, through Scudder, I was given my first look into a citadel of success; he sent me on an errand to his apartment. The starched costume of the Irish servant girl who opened the door for me, the feeling of costly rugs under my feet, the bric-a-brac and the too ornately gold-framed oil paintings on the walls and their misty reflections in the polished, parquet floors, remained for a long time fixed in my mind as a vision of what riches meant in Chicago.

Then I began to study mortgages as a part of my work, making written reports of my findings. Most of Scudder's clients were insurance companies; as investors they would engage Scudder to give them a report on some bond issue concerning which they were feeling dubious. It was become my job then to read the mortgage that secured the bongs and to hunt for the holes. I was learning as a young kitten learns to hunt mice, by practice, how to hunt for legal flaws in mortgages. It was a good thing for me to have it etched upon my mind so early that the most handsomely engraved security may be the mask of a piece of financial trickery. I was discovering, too, the meaning of a balance-sheet, learning ways to appraise the prospects of a property based on its past performances. For days on end I might be engaged in making up the income account of a railroad over a series of years. I was getting my first training in finance, and as I look back upon it I wonder at my good luck in stumbling in to situation that offered me such an unparalleled opportunity to learn. There are great organizations nowadays which undertake to do this sort of thing for any investor, but in that time Scudder had gone into an uncharted sea of commerce. If only he had altered his procedure so as to put less emphases on the hunt for flaws and had employed the same technique to hunt out the money-making properties, I can see that his business would have flourished as it did not then; his salesmanship should have been on how to make money rather than on how not to lose it; everybody wants to make it.

I was required to build up our files. Every time there was a new bond issue I would write for a copy of the mortgage. I got copies of the annual reports of all the big corporations. Expanding this information and indexing it gave me an understanding of the sources of financial information that was far from common 1886. I know that I was completely absorbed in the work, too; if I had not been I should never have worked out by myself the notion of plotting on a map in different colors the various mortgages of a railroad property. Today that sort of thing is highly developed, but it is still a source of pride for me to remember that I did it first. Naturally I composed reports on the results of my research into the affairs of various companies and I tried earnestly to make those reports readable, somewhat less obscure in their phrasing than the documents from which the information was abstracted.

Once it was my job to write a history of a strike of locomotive engineers and firemen against the Burlington. There was turned over to me a great mass of correspondence and transcripts of meetings. This was back in the dark ages of American industry, and railroad officials who refused to deal with the representatives of organized employees were persuaded they were doing right. It was a revealing thing to discover that stubborn pride on both sides was the force that had tied up a railroad system for weeks, blocking commerce, blighting the lives of thousands who should not have been involved, and causing accidents. Violence in strikes is not a new thing in our history. I can life a curtain in my mind and see, back in '94, whole freight trains ablaze from the torches of incendiary strikers. I can see back there in the past not only the burning trains but the Federal troops encamped on the Lake Front. But considering all that I learned in those first years in Chicago, I think my richest source of knowledge was my friend Joseph French Johnson. He was a natural teacher.

We met each other in Aurora at the 7:15 train in the morning. It took an hour and a quarter to ride the thirty-nine miles into Chicago; in the afternoon we caught the 5:25 back to Aurora. Going and coming, Johnson talked with me; he was my preceptor in economics, in journalism, in living. Others riding in the same dust-and-cinder-laden atmosphere of a Burlington Railroad coach saw in us, I suppose, just two more commuters. Yet I know that in our particular plush-seat we two represented all that Leland Stanford, Jr., meant when he defined a university as Mark Hopkins at one end of a log and a student at the other. I never knew Mark Hopkins, but on any spot where I sat down to learn I would want to have my old friend Johnson, for then the learning would be easy and delightful. He was absorbed in economics, but heart and soul he was a newspaperman. That was how it happened that my career was guided back into the strong current of journalism.

CHAPTER V
VANDERLIP, THE YOUNG REPORTER

JOSEPH FRENCH JOHNSON went to the Chicago *Tribune* as financial editor and about a year later, in 1889, he induced John Wilkie, who was assistant to Fred Hall, the city editor, to give me a try-out as a reporter. Wilkie was a fine fellow, with a fresh, rosy complexion and a dark mustache tightly curled at the ends. I know the day of my first appearance in the reporters' room was May fourth because for years afterward anyone who found himself suspect in some small matter was sure to hear propounded the question: "Where were you on the night of May fourth?" It was the night of the Cronin murder. My first assignment, however, was to go to the court-house and attend the sheriff's sale of the Wabash Railroad; it had been in receivership. Naturally, in my work for Scudder I had acquired a thorough understanding of the background of events which came to a climax there on the sidewalk and steps of the court-house. I turned in my copy, supposing myself to be a young man on trial; then I went to a theater, since it was Saturday night, and saw Rosina Vokes in "My Milliner's Bill." She was a light actress of great charm and I guess I thought more about her than I did about anything else on my way home Aurora. On Monday I returned to the

Tribune for the purpose of asking what conclusion they had come to about my try-out effort. I knew it had been printed; all my friends and relatives knew it had been printed.

I got a profane greeting at the desk of the city editor. Where in Hell, I was asked, had I been on Saturday night? Mildly I explained that I had supposed I had been expected merely to produce a sample of my reporting skill on Saturday. Well, I was mistaken. I was on the staff and my salary was twenty dollars a week. Long afterward in Wall Street, when reporters came into my office in the National City Bank, sometimes they must have thought I was pondering rather long over my answer to a question, but I may say now that actually I was often wondering if they could feel in their work the same excitement with which I had approached mine in those years when I was a reported in Chicago. Make no mistake about it: I was a reporter. My deity was the *Tribune*. The sacrifices laid upon the altar were scoops; none of us in those days knew the meaning of the word hand-out because we were reporters.

Soon after that time, I think, Fred Hall abandoned the city desk to Wilkie and himself became an editorial writer, but he was my boss long enough to create a feeling of awe that time has not dissipated; it stays along with the rest of the spell of enchantment that is fixed upon those of us who get into our nostrils while we are young the smell of printers' ink.

Hall was a little, dried-up man who in the office seemed to wear always upon his enormous head, summer and winter, as if it were a charm that preserved his powers, the same stale, fly-specked straw hat. In my experience that head of his is without analogue, and when I was a young reporter it was breath-taking to see Hall tap himself for knowledge as a lesser person might have done with an encyclopedia. His brain was an enchanted mirror in which he could reflect at will anything that had ever happened within the circumference of the *Tribune's* circulation. He seemed literally to feed upon scraps of information, but by some extraordinary system of mnemonics, each scrap as the need for it recurred boiled obligingly to the surface of his mind. In effect he was an ambulant newspaper morgue; he could tell you off-hand the dividend rate of the street-car company, the address of the saloon I Kenwood, the back room of which was the hand-out of the alderman; and tell you, too, the name and address of the lady who had the year before sued a certain millionaire for breach of promise. Hall lived for work and never unbent. Once, I remember, a fresh new-comer on the staff lifted himself to a seat on Hall's desk and addressed him as "Fred."

We who waited for any angry outbreak saw the boss lift his big head. When he looked up at one through thick spectacles the magnification of his eyes made the encounter seem like a meeting face to face through the glass of a fish bowl. This time we saw Mr. Hall's slight frame swell with a deep inhalation and then he said:

"Don't be so formal! Call me Freddie."

Nowhere in a long career in business have I ever found anything to compare with the atmosphere of a newspaper shop in action; there is a feeling, an esprit in the reporters' room that I believe is a too rare element in our world. I believe that even in the small victories of newspaper reporting there is a flavor that is exquisite. When I find myself aware, on the banking side of my mind, that a counting-room is rather too conspicuous in the identity of some journal that I want to admire, I long for the means to prove what I feel to be true; that if a newspaper were to concern itself first and last with the various phases and editors might be so richly paid as never to desert their calling even though in importance the business office people shriveled to mere shadows of their present selves. If only some genius could be born and developed who would establish that as truth this would be a better world and I would rephrase what I have always said: The newspaper field is the greatest in the world to have been in.

In my day the Chicago *Tribune* was housed in an old building at Dearborn and Madison streets. We had a reporters' room where we wrote our stories and waited around for something to happen, "to break." There were no typewriters for us at that time and we wrote on a copy table using pencils. It would have been easy then to persuade me that the darkest shadows in the corners of that big room were really clouds of romance. I was completely a *Tribune* man. How can I show that? Well, there was that Cronin murder, a phase of which was assigned to me for investigation.

It was a big story which received rather more space in the newspapers than would be given to the best of murders even today. Dr. Cronin, a member of the Clan-na-Gael, an organization of Irishmen, was reported to be missing. A man, it seemed, had come to the door and begged the doctor to go with him to attend some poor old man; they had driven away in the stranger's vehicle, a buggy with red wheels drawn by a white horse. After a body discovered in a sewer basin was found to be that of Dr. Cronin, a couple of amateur detectives who went painstakingly from one liver-stable to another succeeded in locating the very white horse and buggy with red wheels in which the victim had been lured away. The two who did that competent tracking were *Tribune* men; my associates in the reporters' room! Aye, that was a thrill for me.

But the assignment I got was an unpleasant thrill. I hated it, but because I was a *Tribune* man I obeyed. Late one night I told to go to the tough region back of the stock-yards to ask a question that not all the diplomats of the world could have phrased in tactful form. With distaste in my heart and tremors in my knees, I made my way across streets deep in slime and rubbish, past saloons that echoed brawling curses, and came at last to a parish house next to a Catholic church. I knew that the scowling Irish immigrants, stock-yard laborers, who had eyed me as I passed their squalid frame tenements, were the members of this parish to which I had come, and as I waited after making the door-pull jangle the bell I fancied all of them creeping closer and closer upon me from the darkness so as to overhear my dreadful question. Then the priest came and received me into a little room bare of furniture except benches against the wall. I stammered out the words that required him to say whether he was mixed up in the murder of Dr. Cronin. No lightning flash broke about my head; instead that gentleman's white teeth were revealed in a grand smile; he perfectly charmed me. The delightful man kept me there, young cub that I was, for half an hour as his guest, and when I started back for the office my heart sang because I had no story to write; of course he had known nothing of any such foul scheme. Out of a month of general assignments I recall another that made me cringe; I was sent to ask a banker for some details of his daughter's elopement.

After that I was detailed to come in the morning to the city editor's office, to mark our paper to show who had written the stories and which were scoops; also to identify our humiliations, the scoops in the other, the rival newspapers. I answered the telephones and in a variety of ways was the faintest shadow in authority of the city editor himself. I would write an obvious assignment on the book; one that was routine every Saturday, I remember, was for a man to go to the South Side to get from the Rev. Dr. George C. Lorimer a copy of his Sunday sermon which we would publish Monday morning. Then the staff would arrive, fifteen or twenty as I remember them; Bismark, Leo Canman the railroad editor, Elliott Flower, one of the star reporters whose cigarette-yellowed fingers made him seem to me almost Oriental in vice; afterward for years I was encountering his short stories in magazines and reading them with envious pleasure. Another who was like a fellow club-member there was Teddy McPhelan. I remember the night he was dashing off sheet after sheet of pencil-written copy about the opening of the Auditorium and the singing of Adelina Patti. It was Jim Keeley, according to my recollection, who after reading Teddy's copy congratulated him, remarking that the interior of the Auditorium must have presented a great sight.

"My dear boy," said McPhelan superciliously, "I haven't been down there." Personally I shall always believe that he had been down.

It was I who was sitting on the desk the morning Keeley, who had been a London foundling, came in looking for a job and that alone is distinction, even though all I could tell him was to come back later when the boss, the managing editor, Van Benthuysen (afterward managing editor of the New York *World*), would be around. Keeley was great! But he was without compassion. I remember the prematurely spring-like occasion when he wandered into the office on his day off; violets in his buttonhole, his suit pressed, a light top-coat on his arm; just killing time before going to keep a date with a girl.

"Keeley!" That was Van Benthuysen shouting. "Catch a train for Wyoming. Troops have been called out...." I have forgotten whether it was an Indian uprising or a cattlemen's war, but I remember Keeley's violets. Even before he caught up with the troops he had run into snow-storms, but he kept on as a matter of course and when he had his story he felt that he must make a scoop of it in spite of the fact that other reporters were there and possessed just as much information as he did. What could he do? The disturbance was quelled, and so, with its errand accomplished, the column of soldiers was marching out of the hills back toward the railroad and the telegraph lines that paralleled it for many hundreds of miles, across the prairies, across state boundaries, into Chicago. Those cavalrymen were real horsemen, more careful of their mounts than of themselves. Alternately they walked and trotted. For companionship, for security and possibly for further news the reporters, all on horseback, rode with some of the officers. Now, what Keeley did was this: One the pretext of adjusting a stirrup leather he dismounted. When the column had dwindled in his eyes until it was no more than a dust cloud on the horizon he mounted again and thereafter rode hard on a line diagonal to that of the troopers. At a point farther east than the station where the commander of the soldiers planned to strike it, Keeley reached the railroad. There he climbed a telegraph pole and cut the telegraph wires. Then he rode on to the next station east and wrote and filed his story. Behind him was a dead telegraph wire and frustrated rivals.

Ahead? Well, ahead of Jim Keeley there stretched an astonishing career in journalism. I remember that when the words of his story had been written out at the end of clicking telegraph wire in the *Tribune* office and were printed in the paper we exulted; again our Deity was supreme, had scooped her opposition. Why marvel at that? We see something akin to it when we watch young men risking their necks on a football field; yet, long after the college spirit would be dormant this other force is to be encountered alive, throbbing in the hearts of newspapermen.

In the afternoons I was a reporter, too; my job was to write a column of interviews with people in the different hotels and I did my hunting with a pack; Finley Peter Dunne of the *Herald* with eye-glasses and one little finger projecting stiffly from its fellows; also a tall, very trim, blond young man with a mustache named Charles Dillingham who represented the *Times*. Sometimes George Ade of the *News* was in our company, although he was not concerned with hotel news. What a trio of wits! And how kind they were to me! Even the heavy beard on my young face was treated by them as if it were normal. The tradition of the time that it was always open season for faking on the hotel beat would, at first, have complicated my life but for the generosity of Dillingham. If he conspired with a hotel clerk to write upon the register the invented name of a Russian concerning whom he had concocted a story and interview, at least he would give me enough of the invented facts to spare me the consequences of being scooped; and thereafter if any suspicious person inquired for the Russian the hotel clerk ally would say: "Mr. Sonofagunsky has just left town."

A stock of plain white cards was kept on the desk of each hotel for the convenience of those calling on guests, and on these we would write our names and the names of our papers when we were seeking an interview. Several times after Dillingham obligingly had written cards for all of us we were chagrined. Word would come down from a man like Senator Depew: "I'll see Mr. Dillingham." It was a long time before we discovered that when he had prepared our cards Dillingham under Dunne's name had written *Police Gazette* and on my card *Salvation Army War Cry*. Another time when some Oriental potentate declined to talk to reporters Dillingham adopted some high-faulting' title of his own and sent word that with his secretaries he desired to pay his respects to the Maharajah. That worked and gleefully the four of us marched upstairs to be received in state.

Nothing ever awed my companions; once when we were trying to get the details of a proposed flour-milling combine a very bumptious multi-millionaire was refusing to assist us but did say something disparaging of Jews.

"Oh," protested George Ade, "I don't think you ought to speak that way before Mr. Dillingheimer."

The man was so conscience-stricken, perhaps frightened, that he gave us the information we wanted.

If there were dull afternoons I have forgotten them because the hotel doors that swing open to any knocks in my memory always expose something exciting. There was one occasion when the four of us received permission to enter the Palmer House suite of a visiting duchess or countess and when we confronted her we gasped.

In 1934 as I mulled over these adventures of our mutual pasts, Dillingham died. Otherwise I would say to ask Dillingham if she was really beautiful! Dillingham, who became the entrepreneur of the stage talents of Julia Marlowe, Mrs. Leslie Carter, Fritzi Scheff and Elsie Ferguson; he would have said to you as often he has said to me, that she was the most beautiful creature he ever saw in his life. That day all he could think to utter was the current banality, "Where were you on the night of May fourth?" And then we proceeded with our interview. Just to see and hear the voice of such loveliness was precisely the sort of experience that could make me aware that I wanted polishing. I remember, too, when for the first time I saw a great company of ladies and gentlemen in evening clothes; I saw champagne for the first time that night and though the mayor, the elder Carter Harrison, was not deterred by his responsibilities from drinking his, I left the glass at my elbow untouched: I had work to do! I was there to report the closing banquet of a convention of hotel men. My instructions were to write at the table where I sat and send my copy by a relay of boys to the office. I did not drink then and very little afterward. What I am trying to express is some of my wonder that, exposed as I was every day to beauty, to hotel luxury, to free champagne, to the delightfulness of being irresponsible, I should have gone on working earnestly, much of the time solemnly.

I think I almost never played. Really, I never have learned to play and now that I am old the lack does not seem to be virtue. What held me fixed to work and duty in my young manhood was my terrific load of responsibility; my mother, my sister, my grandmother, two maiden aunts looked to me for support. I am honestly, deeply grateful for that responsibility. It was a valuable heritage. They were all so sweet, so worthwhile that I was glad to keep sober and on the job, nourishing such talents as I had. Oh, I had some ability; that was established to my satisfaction a couple of months after I went on the *Tribune* when there was a decimation of the staff and though older, more expert reporters were dismissed, I held my job. What I wrote I wrote carefully, lovingly, and without being rewritten it got printed.

We dreamed of scoops; our reporters' rooms occasionally echoed details of the exploit, possible apocryphal, of someone who was on his way home in the early morning after the last edition had been run off and who found the body of a man who had been murdered. This was before the streets had been graded, so that there were convenient hiding-places under the sidewalks in weed-grown areas. Our man, with a fine journalistic economy, dragged the body out of sight, keeping it, and without ice, so as to have a scoop the following morning. Neither that sort of scoop nor the bar-room of McGarry's saloon captured much of young Vanderlip; yet at that bar Finley Peter Dunne found that which made him famous. The natural philosophy of the bartender there was the priming that set going in Dunne's mind the machinery of Mr. Dooley. 'Tis an old story but I cannot desert it now for his account of it was the start of Pete Dunne's fame:

A *Tribune* man, finding a new man behind the bar of McGarry's place, cajoled him into serving a drink of find brandy and then told him to put it on the book until pay-day. Then the bartender called out:

"Is Smith good for a drink, Mr. McGarry?"

"Has he had it?"

"He has!"

"He is!"

Why should I not have gone on forever laughing in the company of John McCutcheon at such jests? The thing becomes dramatic only now that I look back upon it.

CHAPTER VI
FINANCIAL EDITOR

I HAD gone to the Richelieu Hotel which was a small but very swell hotel in Michigan Avenue; the mere fact of staying amid its luxury made a man important. A man from Spokane had registered and I sent up a card on which I had written a request for an interview; I have forgotten his name but when he opened his door to me that man, in effect, opened the long corridor through which ever since I have been passing. We had a general conversation during which he developed the idea that his town needed a good morning newspaper. I was greatly impressed and, returning to the office, talked it over excitedly with Joseph French Johnson. Dillingham was on the *Tribune* by that time. For a while I was tempted to set out for Spokane, too; but in the end Johnson went and founded a paper which Mrs. Johnson named the Spokane *Spokesman*; Watson of the Chicago *Mail* went with them to handle the business side and Dillingham became the city editor of the new paper. But I remained in Chicago and took over Johnson's job. I became the financial editor of the Chicago *Tribune*; eventually my salary was $45 a week.

When one starts to pick out threads in the embroidery of recollection unsuspected patterns are revealed; there was, for example, my first experience as an investor, an adventure with far-reaching consequences to my life. Some $3,000 was left to my mother from my father's estate. It had been guarded ever so carefully but not that I was financial editor of the *Tribune* I felt quite competent to invest it. Indeed, I think I must have been looking for a likely thing to buy on that day when in search of news I went into the bank of which Lyman J. Gage was president, the First National. The bank was offering the bonds on the Central Market, an enterprise then building in Chicago. Anyway, I decided to buy some of the Central Markey stock; that seemed to me to be the ideal shape into which to transform my mother's tiny fortune.

Really, I must have been feeling big then because it was not long afterward that I went home to Aurora on Saturday night and caused my mother to gasp by announcing to her that we were going to Europe; as Cook's tourists. We had a day or so in New York before our boat sailed and so we went aboard a steamer for a cruise up the Hudson. Across the Hudson River from where I now sit on most pleasant days there is a palisade of stone, always changing its dark color, the perfect theater in which to see again all that lingers in my mind; but when I close my eyes and hear the chunking of some actual old river-steamer it is on the river itself that I seem to be with my mother on that day when we sailed to West Point. It is strangely confusing to have my memory cruise with its cargo of the past so close to where I find myself in the present, seated in the very midst of the gorgeous scenery which delighted us many, many years ago.

My mother did not see Europe really for the first time on that trip because she went abroad with a rich background of literary associations, and so did I. The fare on the small Red Star boat was $79; we went to Antwerp, saw Belgium and Holland, then up the Rhine, on to Paris, London, up into Scotland, then to Ireland; and on very little money. How young my mother was and how glad I am we could go then! Thanks to my beard, I suppose, each time we approached the desk of another hotel we were mistaken for husband and wife and there were always, on the Continent, compliments to make my mother blush when the fact was explained that I was, after all, her son. But our homecoming was sad enough. The Ventral Market Company had gone into bankruptcy; the little family fortune was gone and with it practically all the pride and dignity of the financial editor of the *Tribune*. Well, I was not just a hick by any means and I began to bore into the matter with the determined enthusiasm of a genuine *Tribune* reporter hunting a scoop.

I found out I was one of a very few persons who had ever paid anything for the stock of the company; I had paid $100 a share for stock that had been passed around to influential insiders as a bonus. By digging I learned there was a law in Illinois which required that stock had to be paid for in full and armed with that fact I went to a meeting of creditors that was presided over by President Gage of the First National. That was the day, I think, that he became aware of me as a person; previously I had only a slight acquaintance with him; but at the meeting I told those gentlemen who were full of reorganization schemes that they, the creditors, were going to have to pay in full for my shares of the stock which had been issued free to them. There were some conferences with lawyers in which I was politely stubborn and finally I got back my mother's money and my self-respect.

I became, as financial editor of the *Tribune*, almost the equivalent of a daily stroke of apoplexy to a masterful financier of the city. He was Charles T. Yerkes who had a sort of Monte Cristo background to make him recklessly daring in his ambitions. Control of the North and West Side street railways was his; likewise he had control of the gas companies, but he was overweening ben on extending his power and not particular in the means he employed. As for me, all I wanted was a minimum of one first-page financial scoop each week. Even gentle-mannered managers in that dark age withheld from the public all that they could of the financial facts of their corporations and anyone who tried to pry out some financial news about his companies was to Yerkes no better than a spy. Thanks to my work for Scudder I was one financial reporter who really knew how to collate the financial facts of a company. To get all the available published information of a corporation over a series of years, the annual reports, if any, the balance-sheets, and then to follow these through was the sort of picture-puzzle game I like to play; especially when the end of the trail brought me to a piece of information worthy of Page One.

FINANCIAL EDITOR

An early escapade of mine was to buy a share of stock in each of Yerkes's corporations, using a few hundred dollars I had saved to make the purchase. I made sure that each share was registered in my name, too. Well, the ownership of a share was just like having a legal ticket of admission to the annual meeting of the company's stock-holders. The first time I made use of that device was in attending the meeting of the West Side Street Railway Company. Mind, I was a stenographer, too, so that literally I missed nothing.

I got all the figures of the earnings and the number of passengers that had been carried. Then Yerkes spoke to the gathering and complimented himself before them by making it clear to the stock-holders that they really made their profits out of the strap-hangers. Naturally, that was my lead.

I took no one into my confidence as to the means I was using to get my facts and so it was more than a year before the rival newspapers began buying shares of stock for their financial editors. After that the lid was off; we were admitted even if we happened not to be stock-holders, but there was less information presented. However, I had spooned the cream from that pan of milk. I suppose I had become as a familiar with the corporate affairs of those Street Railway companies as anybody other than the high officers. I would construct income accounts and publish them before there was any thought of making them public. Once as I stood outside the rail at the desk of an officer in a trust company I noted something peculiar about the number of the bonds he was signing. Each number was preceded by a letter, as A-1000, and with that clue I began an investigation which revealed that these bonds were secured by an open-end mortgage; additional bonds were being certified of which the public at that time were unaware; but they were not unaware long. I discovered a trick those companies employed when buying land on which to build a power-house. The company would buy through a subsidiary or some individual a piece of land. Then there would be recorded, quietly, a large mortgage on this property. Subsequently the land would be transferred to the street railway company. That secret mortgage would have precedence over the lien of bonds which the company issued and which the purchasers supposed were secured by a first mortgage. I unearthed a great deal of the financial skullduggery of that period. Afterward, when Yerkes was branching out socially, he provided himself with a family crest having a device of three wolves. He used to point to one of the most viciously fanged wolves. "This one," he would say, "is Vanderlip."

I remember that I carried out during the course of weeks an investigation of secret rebates by the railroads. I did a lot of traveling and to accomplish my purpose, which was good, I resorted to some obnoxious methods. In that time it was still the practice to wholesale railroad transportation at a price lower than it was retailed. The Interstate Commerce law had made it illegal to give a lower rate to the big shipper but the means used to evade

FINANCIAL EDITOR

the law was to collect the full rate from a favored shipper and then secretly send him a rebate. The scandal was largely in connection with the packers who shipped train-loads from Chicago to New York every day. The trouble was with the railroad men themselves; they would not keep rate agreements and each freight man was trying to outdo his rivals in the matter of rebating sums sufficient to hold for his line the tremendous transportation business of the meat-packing firms. My job was to build up a case that would if necessary stand up in court; we had to have evidence. The New York correspondent of the *Tribune* had enlisted a man who could through some means produce veritable letters and canceled checks of the New York Central Railroad. I never knew how he got them and I did not want to look into that abyss of shame; but I wanted the facts, or, as we said, the story. He would bring me the documents each evening and I would have them photographed if they seemed to be worthwhile. I dare now to suppose that all the material was returned to the files before morning; but then the less I knew about it the better I was suited. Long ago I discovered that black is not black; never.

Well, finally I was ready and wrote my story. It was to cover considerably more than two full pages in the Chicago *Tribune*, but so that the full impact of it might strike in Washington, the management of the paper for the occasion took over the plant of the Washington *Star* and with its machinery, in conjunction with a prodigal use for telegraph lines, produced in the Capital a complete edition of the

Chicago *Tribune*, one that was the twin of that which at the same time was being sold on the streets of Chicago. When Congress assembled that morning every senator and representative found on his desk a copy of the day's Chicago *Tribune*.

I shan't moralize about the method of accomplishing that scoop; in my heart I am now and always have been a newspaperman; at least I think so. Old Joseph Medill helped to make me one for all time on an occasion when I was inclined to feel just a trifle sick at my stomach; scared, if you want to know the truth. Marshall Field, the greatest merchant and the most prodigal advertiser in Chicago, had let it be known that he was much put out by the way I was dealing with financial news. He had come to headquarters with his kick and I was sent for, to come to the sanctum sanctorum where I never before had been, the office of the editor, Joseph Medill; indeed, I had traded greetings with Mr. Medill only once or twice before this occasion. He was old, deaf, and shuffled in his stride. This day, treating me with nice dignity, he explained that Mr. Field was objecting to something I had written for the financial page. Regrettable I have forgotten now what the point of dispute was; but it does not matter because the real issue was whether the largest advertiser could make the editor of the *Tribune* knuckle down and accept his point of view.

Mr. Field was a beautifully groomed man; his mustache was gray. As I listened to his complaint I was well aware that he was no ordinary person. Then

FINANCIAL EDITOR

I expressed my viewpoint, gratefully aware that the dim-eyed old man behind the desk was listening as judicially to me as he had listened to Marshall Field. I salute him across the years that intervene. If he had truckled then, even a little, all his power would have been gone as was Samson's when Delilah cut his hair; but he did not truckle. There was no ranting, no scolding; Joseph Medill simply stood up to the situation. The *Tribune* was the *Tribune*. Mr. Field had the right of any reader to make a protest, but Mr. Field was mistaken. The *Tribune* would proceed. From that day on I think that for the *Tribune* under Joseph Medill I would have hidden bodies, too, had that been necessary to make us greater.

One thing I had done that stands as a point of differentiation was to join the Union League Club; some banker friend proposed me and I was elected. Possible the road divided for me there; the others in the reporters' room were finding much of their diversion in McGarry's saloon. Nevertheless, I was the president of the Press Club. I got the honor, I fancy now, because it was calculated that I would be best able to pilot it into safer waters. It had a terrific load of debt. We were housed on the third floor of a building which had no elevator at the northeast corner of Clark and Madison; Opie Read was usually around the sometimes Dr. Frank Lydston; to my same I have forgotten most of the others. My biggest contribution was to get Colonel Robert Ingersoll, whom I greatly admired, to give a lecture at the Auditorium; we packed the house and if a few more members had paid their dues the Press Club would have been almost solvent. During my administration the Whitechapel Club, much more, even extravagantly, Bohemian in character, merged with us. We needed their dues! but as president I was always somewhat fearful as to how they might carry on in our clubrooms. I could not forget that only a year or so before when one of their members had died they had taken his body to the dunes at the lower end of Lake Michigan and there had burned it on a funeral pyre of railroad ties. There was no widow about, as I recall, to commit, if that is the word, suttee. Well, that was a first-page story, too; and would be again if any one cared enough to do it.

How can I say, with any hope of accuracy after so long a time, precisely what it was that persuaded me I ought to take dancing lessons? I had experienced no social life. I had moved my mother and the other ladies of our household to Chicago and we were established in Englewood; but outside of home all my contacts were with men. Then I became a pupil, a bearded pupil, of Bournique's Dancing Academy. I knew I needed sand-papering and the Bournique's treatment included instruction in the waltz, two-step, polka, schottische and quadrilles. I had a dress suit and when I did not wear white gloves I carefully, in accordance with instructions, kept a folded handkerchief on the fingers with which I touched the back of any partner. That was required of me as a rule of etiquette, I was told, so that if my fingers perspired the lady's dress would not suffer. I put none of my dancing instruction into practice in Chicago.

I have revealed the dancing lessons first, but actually the most important instruction I was getting then was at the University of Chicago. It opened its doors in September, 1892, and I was one of the first students enrolled; since I was on a morning paper I could devote my mornings to work in classrooms. For three years I went faithfully. One time I arranged to spread my two weeks' vacation over fourteen weeks so that I could attend a course of lectures by a great constitutional law man, Von Holtz, a German; I took seminar work there also from J. Lawrence Laughlin, a professor of economics. My first professor of economics was Adolph Miller, who for a great many years has been a distinguished member of the Federal Reserve Board. He was a great inspiration to me during those years I studied at the University of Chicago. He had a perfectly developed ability for accurate definition, and accurate definition of words is most important thing in expounding Political Economy. The friendship I formed with Adolph Economy. The friendship I formed with Adolph Miller then has endured as a precious thing in all the years that have followed.

When the World's Fair Columbian Exposition came along I studied it as something designed for my special benefit. If I had been simply a college youth in that time I suppose my fellow students would have referred to me as a grind and, as I have shown, even at the Press Club I was managing to work rather than to play.

Culver Service

CHARLES T. YERKES, CHICAGO TRACTION MAGNATE.

Photograph by Stevens

FRANK A. VANDERLIP AS A REPORTER ON THE CHICAGO "TRIBUNE."

CHAPTER VII
EX-NEWSPAPERMAN

ON of the former financial editors of the *Tribune*, Clinton B. Evans, had established a weekly, the *Economist*, and made a fair success of it. Near the close of 1894 I left the *Tribune* to become editor of this publication. Although I ceased to be a newspaper reporter I continued to be a reporter; nevertheless, there was an alteration in my relations with financiers in Chicago; a notable instance was, I think, in 1896. I was called out of bed to the telephone and asked to come to the house of P.D. Armour. I got there just before midnight and found the presidents of most of the banks and the governors of the stock exchange. There had been a financial collapse; Moore Brothers had failed. They were a couple of lawyers who had been running a big operation in Diamond Match Company stock. When it was discovered they would be unable to pay back their borrowings a very dangerous situation was seen to exist. One of the bankers put the matter before me.

"We want you," he said, "to handle this story so as to minimize its effect. We have decided not to open the stock exchange tomorrow but unless the news is handled with discretion we will have runs on all the banks and savings institutions."

"I'll do it," I said, "on one condition. Every man here must pledge himself not to see reporters or answer any questions tonight."

With their assurances given I went directly to the *Tribune* office and told the city editor to telephone the city editors of the other paper that I had a financial story of first-class importance, that I could be obtained nowhere else, but that I would give it to them provided they pledged themselves to print it exactly as I wrote it and gave me permission to inspect their headlines. All the papers except the *Interocean* agreed to the proposition and I proceeded to write.

The end of my story was a curious sort of afterthought, a kind of—"by the way, The Stock Exchange will not open today." From a newspaper point of view I had written a story that was as badly done as possible; yet I was proud of it. In a cab I went from one newspaper shop to another until I had inspected all the headlines and satisfied myself that the men who had committed the papers to the policy I had laid down were keeping faith; then to bed, happy.

Now what had happened to me? Some years afterward in a similar situation following the failure of the Walsh banks James Keeley was invited to the First National Bank to such a conference as I had gone to at P.D. Armour's house; only that one was behind locked doors and none attending it was supposed to leave. They were trying to "sew him up"; to get from him the sort of help I believed it was my duty to give. For precisely the same reason, because he believed it was his duty, Keeley eluded that gathering, took up a tray of coffee cups in order to fool the guard at the door, and soon afterward was supervising a re-plate of the last edition, getting a sensational scoop onto the streets of the Loop. Clearly there had been a change in me.

Possibly Lyman J. Gage had appraised that change. At any rate, when I went to offer my congratulations after it became known that Mr. Gage was to become Secretary of the Treasury in the McKinley Cabinet, he invited me to sit down for a conference.

I had been seeing him from day to day during six or seven years. He knew what I had been writing; indeed, he had been conscious of me as a person since I had taken a stand about the Vanderlip stock in the Central Market. What he suggested on this occasion was that he would like to have me go to Washington with him as his private secretary. We only had a tentative agreement because at first he was not sure whether he had the power of appointment. For my part I was ready to go without quibbling for the chance of taking a year, perhaps, of postgraduate work in finance in the Treasury Department.

We went to Washington together on the third of March, 1897, neither of us knowing our way about town, much less about politics. Well, I found out that the private secretary's job was to sit in a small room outside the big room of the Secretary of the Treasury and be a sort of reception-clerk. He was expected to be polite to callers and to take in the name of any important visitor to the Secretary. I did that for just one day, a day of many people coming in to say a word out of politeness; there was no business transacted. I thought over the situation rapidly. I knew I was not going to spend my time carrying cards to Mr. Gage's desk.

The second morning I sat myself down opposite Mr. Gage on the other side of his broad table-desk, and drew up my swivel-chair, close. Neither of us had any idea what my duties were to be nothing was said when I took it upon myself to change my desk. However, I kept busy.

One morning about six weeks later Mr. Gage returned to his office after a visit to the White House.

"I had a talk with the President," he said.

I looked up to show my interest.

"I told him I wanted to ask just one favor of him and I said it would be the only one I would ask during his administration."

"Yes, sir?"

"Well, the President said: 'What is it?' and I said: 'I want Vanderlip made Assistant Secretary of the Treasury.'"

I cannot say honestly whether I spoke aloud but I know that every fiber of me was asking what Mr. McKinley had said. Even now I can remember Mr. Gage's eye-glasses held delicately between his thumb and forefinger as he fanned them in a narrow arc. He was watching me with quiet joy as he told me.

"The President said: 'All right. Send him over.'"

Suddenly I remember that an Assistant Secretary rated a carriage and a pair of horses.

CHAPTER VIII
A JUNIOR CABINET OFFICER

ON a Sunday evening, perhaps the first Sunday evening I was in Washington, I committed my great social *faux pas*. The invitation was not for dinner; I was to come at nine o'clock in the evening to the home of James Stanley Brown, whose wife was Molly Garfield. My family never were church-goers, but somehow I had received an impression that church social customs would rule the day from end to end; consequently I put on my morning-coat. In that costume I was a figure suited to relieve from its stone pedestal any monument of a non-military statesman within the District of Columbia. I felt grand and not at all uncertain until I had passed the portals of the Brown residence. Then my faint perception of the butler's surprise at my appearance became the detonating cap that set off the dynamite of my confusion as he ushered me into a drawing-room where there were many ladies and gentlemen, all in evening dress.

The trouble with me was that I had gone about socially in Chicago almost not at all. A morning newspaperman simply could not adjust night work to the playtimes of polite people. It is significant, though, that after my first tidal wave of embarrassment that Sunday night at the Browns' residence I proceeded to have a nice time. The chief difficulty then, and for a long time afterward, lay in the field of small talk; I had none, not a word. Where another young man upon being introduced to a lady would engage at once in a conversation that would appear to keep them both animated and at ease, and more, thoroughly established as acquaintances for the future, such meetings were for me experiences in futility. The dinners were less painful, yet because I was a bachelor assistant secretary of a department and a handy man for such entertainments I had many dinner invitations and generally found myself placed between ladies who were complete strangers to me. I do not wonder now that generally we remained as strangers. But then I was taken, so to speak, in hand. Three of my rescuers were women. There was Cornelia Gage, the wife of Secretary Gage, who was enormously helpful. There was Lucy Page, an elderly Southern woman of great distinction whose family was deeply rooted in the social life of Washington. She saw to it that I had invitations to the worthwhile balls and entertainments. The other was Edith Newlands, the wife of Senator Newlands and a niece of Ward McAllister. I still regard her as about the most charming woman in the world. I, who never went to a real ball in Chicago, found myself early in my career in Washington dancing at a cotillion given by the rich a socially elegant Leiters of Chicago. It was well enough to go to such entertainments and to acquit myself acceptably, but what were the obligations? How was a young man such as I to perform the rituals when I was so ignorant of many things which the people I was meeting seemed to know as young fish know how to swim? There was a most bewildering card etiquette and there were other tactical problems confronting me every time I went out or returned to my quarters. From the peril of such things I was saved by a colored man, an ex-slave.

Richard Green was his name and when I came into the treasury department he had been for many years the chief messenger of the Secretary's office; a man tall, black, handsome, wise and tenderly considerate. In every function of a servant he was thoroughly competent and with a sincere wish to avoid even the semblance of condescension I report that I formed a friendship for that man, as did most persons who came in contact with him. In our relations we were as two men encountering each other at a masquerade; our places in life, the color of our hides were but part of the scene in which we found ourselves. Not even Lucy Page and Edith Newlands were better informed about the social customs of Washington. My old affection for him fires up afresh as I think how tactfully Richard guided me in the way I should go.

As he placed some mail on my desk or performed in my vicinity a chore that probably he had invented for the opportunity it gave him, he would ask me, perhaps, if I had yet called on somebody at whose home I recently had dined and in that way he would reveal to me that after dining one paid a dinner call, that after a party there should follow a party call. I

A JUNIOR CABINET OFFICER

cannot now recall even a small part of the things I learned from Richard Green, but I cannot forget his kindness, his delicacy in all human relationships. His day never was ended as long as there was anything he might do for you. At big dinners at the White House he was always asked to serve. He was the major domo at all the dinners given in Washington by Mr. Gage, and when I sat down in what was for me the unusual rôle of dinner-party host, I was as much at ease, knowing Richard was running the affair, as if he had been, in disguise, that master of the rituals of polite society, Ward McAllister himself. When I see him now, in memory, clothed in evening dress, his finely modeled skull the very shape of sensitive intelligence, I know him for what he was, one of the greatest of gentlemen, a black Admirable Crichton.

Richard, who knew nothing of his forbears and for that very reason set the more store by the family he was rearing, experienced a shocking tragedy before my advent in Washington. His little son went one day with some boys into the yard of a woman who had been annoyed by trespassers who stole her fruit. She fired a shotgun at that band of small colored boys and the one struck by the charge, and killed, was Richard's boy. Richard has been dead now for a decade, but many times he came to see me here at Beechwood and always it was fine to know he was under my roof. Once I went from New York to Washington to attend the wedding of his grandchild. Then, as when I went to his funeral, I found myself in the company of cabinet officers and of other important men who had discovered that Richard Green was a grand character whose like is only to be encountered once or twice in a lifetime.

Thanks to Richard and to my three social preceptresses, I went about more and more; indeed, for pretty nearly the first time in my life I had a girl and, of all places, she lived in the White House! What I mean is that I had met a niece of President McKinley, that I sought her company on all possible occasions, that she permitted me to call on her and that I was privileged to escort her to parties and to the theater. I tell you, that was a sensation for me, to go calling on a girl at the White House. In the darkness of my Government carriage with my thoughts cadenced to the clop, clopping of the horses' hoofs as I approached the iron gates and the graveled live, often I experienced a Cinderella-like qualm. Suppose the spell were to be broken and I were to find myself grease-blackened and once more in the thralldom of overalls!

I never mounted the steps and crossed the stone porch to the front door of the White House without a feeling of awe; Lincoln's feet had trod those steps where mine were walking; beyond the door, possibly in corners, I like to fancy, there still lingered atmosphere that he had breathed. Well, romantic feelings could survive even such notions, but there was a more difficult matter every time I became the escort of the lady to a ball or a theater. We were chaperoned by a White House military aide! If that convention now languishes be sure it was I who withered it with black thoughts. I had cause enough because many a time as I sat or stood listening to our chaperone, in his handsome blue and gold uniform, gaily conversing with my companion, my civilian drabness ached right through to my bones. This was beneficial; it prevented me from becoming vain.

Naturally I played only a small part of any day for there was a prodigious amount of work to be done. To the farm and the machine shop I owed a toughened, sinewy body that renewed its energy again and again through a long day. I had need of all its strength.

Although there were three Assistant Secretaries of the Treasury, supposedly of equal rank, each of us receiving every month a check for $375, actually my post acquired somewhat more weight than the other two. This was attributable in part to the circumstance that between Mr. Gage and myself there had grown an affectionate attachment marked by complete trust. I had my own office but it adjoined Mr. Gage's office. He was a man who, rather than head of the Treasury, ought to have been a member of the Supreme Court; his legal training, his beautifully balanced judicial mind, had equipped him for greatness there. Most things that would have irked him became a part of my job; for instance, I dealt with all the newspaper correspondents. I do not mean to suggest that I usurped any slight part of his vast responsibility because he was very genuinely the head of the department, but I began to revel in the very great authority with which I was entrusted.

I who had never before had anybody working under my direction, found myself with myriads of subordinates; Mr. Gage had placed me in charge of personnel through the device of appointing a personnel committee of three and then making me the chairman of it. In the Treasury Department there were five or six thousand persons. That was in a time when the spoils system in politics was only beginning to be brought under control. All the employees, because there had been a change in administration, a change in the party in control of the government, trembled for their jobs before a host of old soldiers who crowded the corridors to besiege my office. I was the one who dealt with the job hunters' patrons, the senators and the other congressmen who came, some to implore, some to demand. With the nonsensical logic of a nightmare, civil Service limitations did not apply to Civil War veterans; legally any old soldier who had worn blue was eligible for, with few exceptions, any Government job. I learned a lot of things then.

I learned, for example, that with all my new power I had no freedom at all but to do the right thing. If, when you are given authority, you exercise it according to whim and without regard to duty you may be sure you will not long continue to possess authority. I found out whenever I did something merely because I wished to more than because it was the right thing to do, that I would surely arise to plague me afterward. The supposedly autocratic political boss, Senator Mark Hanna, seemed to understand that. Always he would say, "Mr.

Vanderlip, if it's right and you can I would like to have this thing done." He would be sincere with those qualifications, too. He was one of those who made me aware that behind the everlasting job solicitation of politicians the motive force, often quite as much as votes, is human sympathy, pity. I say again that black is never black.

Another lesson that was driven home again and again in those days when I was accustoming myself to authority was to beware of *ex-parte* impressions. Often during the job scramble of the first year I would have my sympathy worked on quite as if I had sat through a melodrama. Usually the effort would have been centered on making me believe that some professional old soldier had been discharged by the preceding administration just because he had been a defender of the Union, of the Stars and Stripes. Ah, it is always easy to believe when you listen only to one side of a case. I remember one old fellow particularly. After he had haunted the offices for a long time, supported in his plea for reinstatement by an influential politician, a place made for him, necessarily at the expense of some poor devil who lived thereafter only in the hope of similarly moving in with some future Democratic Administration. Well, after no great while it was reported to me that our professional old soldier was still military in his habits, after a fashion; that he was soldiering on the job.

"Why won't you work?" I asked him.

"Say," he chided me, "I worked hard enough to get this job."

Unhappily, he was not allowed to keep it. I took my own job too seriously.

It was one of the finest things that ever happened to advance my career that Mr. Gage gave me charge of the financial bureaus of the Treasury Department. I might have been given charge of the Customs or else had to focus my attention on the assorted functions of the miscellaneous bureaus that were only indirectly concerned with the big work of the Treasury; but as it happened, in handling the financial bureaus I got a tremendous dose of precisely the kind of experience I had hoped to have when I had accepted the offer to become private secretary to Mr. Gage.

Those rivulets of commerce I had been obliged to study in Scudder's investigating organization, and the business flow that I had observed as a financial reporter and editor now were revealed to me in the immensity of their currents. As a great river system at its mouth, blending itself with the tidal waters of the sea, reveals distinct colors in the convoluting mixture of fresh and sea water, so there would be disclosed to anyone who sat at my post in the Treasury Department another significant mixture. I could see the great swirling currents of two forces of the people; one of the power of their will to be a nation, their political power; the other of their will to work, of their economic power, their wealth. How should these forces that grow out of the people be

A JUNIOR CABINET OFFICER

blended so as to accomplish the greatest good for the greatest number? I did not know then; I do not know now, but I do believe that it is impossible to send the tidewaters of Government much farther in the direction of the stream's source without causing the people to thirst, to hunger and to die.

I met thousands of bankers, chiefly the heads of the National Banks that were issuing currency and receiving government deposits against the deposits of bonds made by them in the Treasury. With a reporter's best tool—the will to listen and to try to understand—I learned a great deal from them what other job might one have held that would have promoted contacts with all the country's important bankers, those of the small towns and cities as well as those of the metropolis? But I was also learning something of management. Some of the pride I felt at the time now warms into clarity a recollection of an incident with which was demonstrated my growing understanding of one of the essentials of management, the elimination and the avoidance of waste. The Treasury for two or three years had asked Congress for an appropriation to increase the vault space where the bonds deposited by National Banks were stored. The amount asked for was $50,000.

"Let's walk around and see that vault," said Mr. Gage.

Then we were taken into a large, a cavernous vault, where were serval thousand thin compartments, each one of which contained the deposit of Government bonds of some particular

National Bank. The compartments were like big pigeon-holes. The bonds, of a length of perhaps sixteen inches, were crowded into these small bins, upright.

"Why couldn't we put them flat?" I suggested. Only tradition was against the change. We could and we did put them flat, thereby doubling the capacity of the vault. So we did not ask for the $50,000 appropriation. When so many billions have been spent since then I perhaps out not to mention such a simple and microscopic defense of tax-payers' money except that this did something to me. A man's interest is apt to be enlisted for all time in any kind of activity, whether of sport or business, in which at his first try he is lucky enough to demonstrate capacity. That sort of experience works upon the ego, awakens an appetite for further gratification. Thereafter, I never ceased to try to become aware of flagrant waste in matters under my control.

I was also discovering through my exercise of authority what exciting fun it is to select the right man for the right job, finding something almost like adventure in estimating the capacities of an individual and measuring them against a particular post.

The Coast and Geodetic survey was one of the bureaus of the Treasury Department. The head of it had become old and we were looking for someone to replace him. There were a number of candidates, some of them so insistence may have been what aroused my interest in a man, professor in a university in St. Louis, who had been recommended but who himself never had made application for the position. We looked up his record, sent for him and were so delighted with his characteristics that he received the appointment. This was Henry S. Pritchett who, after a most successful career at the head of this bureau, later became president of the Massachusetts Institute of Technology and afterward of the Carnegie Foundation for the Advancement of Teaching. He also became and continues to be my closest friend.

In the Coast and Geodetic Survey there was a little sprout of an organization called Bureau of Standards. Previously its function had been chiefly to serve as the depository of the nation's standards of weights and measures; although some other things were done there, the bureau was a puny affair. We wanted a new head for it and I found myself thinking of one who had been a close friend of mine at the University of Illinois, a boy named Sam Stratton. He had become a physicist, and at the University of Chicago Professor Stratton had come to rank next to Michelson, the measurer of light. On my recommendation the place was offered to Sam with the idea that he could develop the bureau into larger purposes. He was a thorough scientist with a great deal of imagination and not narrow in any part of him. It is satisfying even so many years afterward to realize that I had a hand in bringing such a valuable servant into the employ of the government. That Bureau of Standards grew to its present vast important nourished chiefly in its growth by the intelligence of my old college friend. Afterward, he too became the head of the Massachusetts Institute of Technology, remaining there until his death a year or so ago.

Another selection of mine that made me proud was that of a man to head the Secret Service. When I had first become a reporter on the Tribune I had heard many legends of the detective prowess of John Wilkie, who by that time sat at the city desk; in the years of our association in the same editorial room I discovered for myself that there was a sound basis for the legends. So I told Mr. Gage about Wilkie and he was brought to Washington, appointed, and for some years thereafter successfully conducted the office. He had been but a few months the Chief of the Secret Service when there developed a national emergency that enormously expanded his responsibility; and mine, too.

RICHARD GREEN, CHIEF MESSENGER IN THE TREASURY DEPARTMENT

DR. P.N. BARNESBY AS A YOUNG MAN.

LYMAN J. GAGE, SECRETARY OF THE TREASURY, AND HIS THREE ASSISTANT SECRETARIES. LEFT TO RIGHT: GENERAL O. L. SPAULDING, WILLIAM B. HOWELL, FRANK A. VANDERLIP, AND MR. GAGE.

CHAPTER IX
THE SPANISH-AMERICAN WAR

IN his Wall Street office, separated by a floor from mine, my old friend and brother-in-law, Edward Walker Harden, keeps on his desk a curiously fashioned paper-weight. It is a talismanic reminder that he was not always a member of the New York Stock Exchange, a broker, a business executive and a director in many big corporations; but that once the world was glamorous and himself the young newspaper reporter fated to scoop all the newspapers of the earth with his story of a naval battle. It is a kind of talisman for me, too, because that paper-weight is a short and lovingly polished section of an oceanic telegraph-cable line, the one which was cut by American sailors at Manila Bay in 1898, and whenever I see it I hark back, in spite of myself, to those days when the United States went to war with Spain.

One day I the fall of 1897 I went aboard a revenue-cutter on the Potomac for an inspection trip that was also an opportunity to let my visiting newspaper friend, Harden, observe the small honors with which an ex-reporter, when raised to the dignity of an Assistant Secretary of a Government department, is received on a service vessel. Harden had succeeded me as financial editor of the *Tribune*. On this day of which I speak, we saw blue-prints of a new cutter, the *Hugh*

THE SPANISH-AMERICAN WAR

M'Culloch, then building, and which was to be sent in the spring to the China Coast.

"How would you like to make the trip?" I asked him, adding that I thought it could be arranged. There would be no cost to the Government, since he would pay for his food. Harden was enthusiastic, and after his return to Chicago we had some further correspondence, with the result that I fixed it for the *Hugh M'Culloch* to carry both Harden and our friend John McCutcheon, the cartoonist, at that time, of the Chicago *Record*. That was all I had to do with Harden's feat, but I still think that I would rather have made that scoop than to have gone charging in Roosevelt's Rough Rider boots at Las Guásimas.

Roosevelt, too, was an Assistant Secretary in the first McKinley administration of the Navy Department under Secretary John D. Long. In Washington that winter, when the war with Spain was being brewed by yellow journalists, Roosevelt was so belligerent as to constitute a show for the rest of us. Mr. Gage returned from a cabinet-meeting one day and told me how they had been entertained by the young Assistant Secretary of the Navy.

It was announced to the President during the cabinet-meeting, he said, that Roosevelt had arrived from the Navy Department with some information which had been requested. There was a mild gleam of mischief in the eyes of McKinley. "Has Roosevelt told any of you gentlemen what he thinks we ought to do as to the ships of Spain, which it is cabled, are now en route to their colonies off our coast?"

THE SPANISH-AMERICAN WAR

All said "no," and McKinley gave a signal for the admission of the fire-eater. Roosevelt gave the information which had been asked for and then McKinley asked him to repeat to the cabinet his idea as to the proper way of dealing with the Spanish ships which were then crossing the Atlantic toward the Antilles.

"I'm glad you asked me that question," Roosevelt said and became red with excitement. "I will tell you what I think we ought to do. We ought to send our warships to meet them on the high seas and sink every damned one of them."

Then McKinley, mild in tone, but strong in purpose, asked how such action could be reconciled with the comity of nations. "We are, as yet, at peave with Spain. War is possible, perhaps probable, but not yet certain."

Roosevelt's reply to that was, according to Mr. Gage, that war was inevitable and that in a fight the first blow was an immense advantage.

Mr. McKinley, when Roosevelt had gone, lifted his hands in a gesture of astonishment and asked his cabinet: "Did you ever hear anything like that since you were born?" Mr. Gage repeated the question to me and I had to confess that I never had heard anything like it.

Unquestionably Roosevelt was the mainspring of the Navy Department at that time and he had done a great deal to improve its efficiency; but in the chatter of Washington prior to the outbreak of war it seems to me that his goings-on were sometimes the excuse for laughter. If anything, he was underestimated because of the oversize of his ego; certainly he was irrepressible and completely at ease in any company on any occasion. Afterward, when he was Vice-President, at the White House one night he was standing beside the chair of the invalid Mrs. McKinley, chatting with her. A butler entered and in a low voice reported to her that dinner was served.

"Oh, what shall I do?" wailed Mrs. McKinley and looked rather helplessly across the big room to try to get Mr. McKinley's eye. Then, quite as though it were a country picnic, Roosevelt lifted his voice to shout:

"Mr. President!"

"What is it?" The answering question of Mr. McKinley was softly spoken.

"Dinner," boomed Roosevelt, "is ready."

Well, at any rate he solved Mrs. McKinley's problem. I suppose that willingness, indeed that joy in being looked at was a fundamental part of that which made him a leader.

My acquaintance with Roosevelt in Washington was not so close, but afterward when I had become a banker I had an extraordinary experience with him. He was going to make a speech in Kansas City and two or three days beforehand, to my utter surprise, he send to my office in Wall Street the manuscript of his proposed speech, with a request for me to go through it carefully and make any suggestions that occurred to me. I took a blue pencil and I went through it, almost in the manner of a copy-reader, and on the margins put notes about things I thought ought to be left out or

THE SPANISH-AMERICAN WAR

emphasized. He seemed to like what I had done because for a long time after that he continued to send me his speeches. He told me one time that Elihu Root speech for him. He frequently, but not always, followed my suggestions.

Mr. Gage was fond of quoting the adage: "The revenue of the state is the state." He had good excuse to quote it on April 21, 1898; war was declared. A short while before, with hardly a word of debate, Congress had appropriated $50,000,000 for the public defense; with the outbreak of war it showed courage by enacting a far-reaching tax bill so that the people began forthwith to pay something on account for their war. Grave possibilities of attack by the Spanish fleet on the cities of our Eastern seaboard created fears that were translated into swift activity; coast defenses were hastily strengthened, harbors mined, ships bought and the markets of the world searched for munitions of war. Money was being poured out in such extraordinary volume that provision was made for a $200,000,000 bond issue; that became my job—to handle the details of that loan flotation.

As a result of a fine piece of financial diplomacy by Mr. Gage, original coldness on the part of the bankers toward the loan was overcome. Congress, wishing this to be a popular loan on the theory that where the treasure is, there the heart is, had fixed in the law an unusual provision. This was that the allotment of bonds must be made in full to the smallest subscribers. Yet the nation dared not risk having the bonds offered and go begging. So what Mr. Gage did was to arrange that the bonds could be used by the National Banks as a basis for National Bank currency. At that time a bank could get in currency 90 percent of the face value of a Government bond which it deposited in the Treasury. The 4 percent of 1925 were selling in the market then well above par so as to yield 3¼ percent; the new bonds were to pay only 3 percent and were for a shorter term. But Mr. Gage was able to point out to the bankers that whereas to get $90,000 in banknotes a bank would have to deposit 1925 fours costing $117,000, an investment of only $100,000 in the war bonds would accomplish the same purpose. The result of Secretary Gage's suggestion was that on the morning of the day the subscription opened two syndicate bids were received;—one was from the National City Bank, Vermilye & Co., and the Central Trust Company, and the other from a syndicate headed by Mr. J. Pierpont Morgan. Each of these syndicates agreed to take all or any part of the issue not taken by the public. That guarantee put spirit into the loan from the first minute, but certain happenings on the other side of the world also helped enormously.

One 1898 May morning at 4:30 a watchman in the darkness on the second floor of the White House answered a telephone to be told by a voice coming over a wire from Chicago that he should summon President McKinley to the telephone. The watchman first refused to comply with this presumptuous demand, but that he soon changed his mind and went to rap on the President's bedroom door simply confirms my first judgment that Jim Keeley of the Chicago *Tribune* was great. What other newspaperman could have done that? Oh, there are plenty who would try, even today; but I do not think there were many

THE SPANISH-AMERICAN WAR

who in 1898 could have disturbed the daybreak slumber of President McKinley with a telephone call. My information is authentic because when Edward Walker Harden returned from the Orient President McKinley sent for him and said: "Perhaps you would like to know how I got the news you sent to your paper. I heard the watchman saying through the door, 'The Chicago *Tribune* is on the phone; they have the story of the Battle of Manila.' I got up. It was a nice warm morning and I went padding down the hall in my nightshirt and slippers. It was Mr. Keeley. He read your cablegram to me."

What Keeley had read to President McKinley was a forty-word bulletin from Edward Walker Harden, but those words had been clicked across the Pacific well in advance of any other information concerning the naval engagement in which the American fleet under Admiral Dewey had destroyed the Spanish fleet and silenced the harbor forts. As the Spanish cable to Hongkong had been cut after the Spanish Captain General refused to permit Admiral Dewey to use it, the world outside of Manila was completely unaware of the battle. Then the *Hugh M'Culloch* was picked to be the dispatch boat and before she left Dewey had talked with the three newspapermen who had seen his victory; Harden, McCutcheon and Joseph Stickney of the New York Herald. He had told them his dispatches must go first. Flag Lieutenant Brumby would carry Dewey's report to Hongkong. So the *Hugh M'Culloch*, carrying Brumby with Dewey's dispatches and likewise the three newspaper correspondents with their stories, steamed into Hongkong almost a week after the battle. As she approached the dock, Stickney was preparing to jump, so that Harden, much younger, jumped first; then all of them were in rickshaws, screaming "chop-chop" and Harden arrived first so that he was at the top of the cable-office stairs as Stickney reached the bottom.

Harden pushed a three-thousand-word dispatch through the receiving-window where a Chinaman quickly protested: "No can."

Then he told him to see the manager and Harden, refusing to take back his dispatch, went into the manager's office and there was Stickney.

"Am I first if I bring it here?" asked Harden.

"No, Mr. Stickney is."

"No, sir. I was at the top of the stairs when he was at the bottom and I brought my dispatch to the receiving-office where it belongs."

For me, that struggle in the cable office at Hongkong always has been the real battle of Manila Bay; there is suspense in it to a degree that there never was in the foregone conclusion of Dewey's smashing attack. My children, with the little Hardens, thrilled to it again and again, so that it is a family legend, but even if it were not I should lug it in here because in 1898 Harden's adventure made me know in every envious fiber that I was still a reporter in my blood and being.

Deciding that the cable-office manager and Stickney were too closely *en rapport* to insure him fair dealing, Harden wrote out two cables; one was addressed to the general manager of the telegraph company in London, the other to Harden's newspaper. In these he demanded the dismissal of the Hongkong manager after setting forth the circumstances of his arrival ahead of Stickney.

Stickney had gone away so as not to embarrass his ally; McCutcheon arrived, and discovering he was beyond question third in this race, filed his dispatches and left. So Harden and the manager continued to quarrel.

"I'll not send these messages," said the manager indicating the two which demanded his dismissal.

"Yes you will."

"They're not press messages."

"I'll pay for them," said Harden inexorably.

His determination, the vengeful gleam in his eyes, finally won the day for him. The manager conceded that Harden had been the first man across the doorsill.

"All right," said Harden and tore up the bloodthirsty demands for the job of the manager. "I want to file first a short dispatch, a bulletin."

From his pocket he pulled a trump card, a forty-word bulletin that he had composed on the ship secretly; it contained the essence of his news. Across the face of it he wrote "urgent." He had found out that conjure word by hanging around the cable office before sailing for Manila. The rate for a message marked "urgent" was $9.90 and Harden paid for his forty-word bulletin with gold; the regular cable rate was $3.30 and the press rate about $1.10; thanks to credentials, of course he could send his long dispatch collect. His rivals had not been aware of this special emergency cable service.

As he passed his urgent message over to the cable-office manager he said: "Now, this does not go ahead of the admiral's dispatches. I promised him."

"You need not tell me," said the manager, still miffed. "Government dispatches always take precedence."

Back in Manila Harden learned that he had scooped the earth and also scooped the admiral, and other naval officers assured him that the old man would set him ashore, and to be ashore in Manila then was the equivalent of being marooned. Scared stiff, Harden then discovered what had happened and asked for permission to come aboard the flagship to explain.

"Sit down," said the admiral. "I want to hear all about it."

Harden told him the whole story and then said: "And now I have found out how mine got ahead of yours."

"How?"

"So long as there was a single cable your dispatches kept ahead. But yours had been ordered repeated. When the dispatches reached an island in the Pacific where there were two cable lines, mine went on while yours were held up, pending an O.K. after the usual repeating. It was just luck."

"I have been making inquiries, too," said Dewey, "and I have told Brumby that he should have had newspaper experience." Harden's message had arrived five hours ahead of the dispatches from Dewey and since the Admiral's message was in code there was still another hour of delay while they were unpacked.

I remember sending a cable of congratulation to Harden, and also that I decided to try my hand at a letter to *World's Work*, to *McClures* and to the *Century*, announcing that I was writing this article and asking if they would be interested. All accepted it; the Century, I think, with a telegram. At that time, according to Mr. Dooley, the American people did not know but what the Philippines were a new brand of canned goods. As a matter of fact I knew very little myself, but counted heavily on the Congressional Library. There was amazingly little there, to my chagrin, but the article had to be written, and if, when it was published, there were fragments of it that were somewhat imaginative I am sorry. At any rate, when the Peace Commission met in Paris and drafted a treaty this was printed in a small Government pamphlet and so that the people would know what those things were, for which we were paying the Spanish government $20,000,000, my *Century* article was printed with it. As a matter of fact, it was probably with the same pen with which I wrote the article that I signed the five checks for $40,000,000 each, with which that payment was made to Spain. I have forgotten what my fee was from the magazine, but I have not forgotten that I wrote the article because I needed money and because I had every reason to believe that what lay ahead of me was a career in journalism. But I was still tremendously busy with the details of the $200,000,000 bond issue.

THE SPANISH-AMERICAN WAR

The load flotation became the most intensive clerical undertaking in which the government had ever engaged over a similar length of time. There was need for a headquarters and so there had been turned over to me the newly completed but still untenanted Post Office building of Pennsylvania Avenue. There I formed a staff of between six and seven hundred clerks, emergency workers and as such exempt from Civil Service; I had need of a great swarm of workers, truly. The action of congress in providing an issue of bonds of denominations as low as twenty dollars, in giving preference to individual bidders, and in providing that allotments should be made in an inverse order to the size of the subscriptions upon all individual offers created such myriads of small tasks as to make an amount of detail work unknown in the department's previous history. A provision for payment in five instalments, and the necessity for interest calculations on each partial payment, added vastly to the task.

The first move had been to have large posters printed and then these were distributed and hung in post-offices all over the land. The response to those appeals was simply staggering but it was not, however, due to unalloyed patriotism. As a matter of fact, we had to use the Secret Service, busy under Chief Wilkie rounding up Spanish spies, to uncover the schemes of those who realized that the owners of these new bonds would have a profit the minute they came into their possession. For instance, form Chicago a fake bid came in bearing all the names on the payrolls of the street railway lines, of hosts of conductors and cablemen. A number of shrewd traders devised similar schemes but all such applications were thrown out.

Actually, there was in the arrangements every element of popular success. The bonds were issued in a popular cause. They were issued at a time when money was easy and securities were high. They were issued at par; so that there was no calculation to discourage the most inexperienced investor. Any man with twenty dollars knew that he could invest it and get a twenty dollar security back. There was no commission, no premium, no restriction as to the character of the remittance. Subscribers were permitted to send their money in any form in which credits could be forwarded. There could not have been more perfect conditions for a successful popular loan.

Perhaps the chronology of my recollections is not accurate but in my memory, at least, the events of those days in July, 1898, were unfolded almost as if the whole affair had been something planned and written by Augustus Thomas, the playwright. I remember the time set for receiving the last of the subscriptions was three o'clock on an afternoon in July, and it had been ruled that, to be honored, subscriptions must be in by that time. Arrangements were made for a wagon to leave the post-office at the last possible moment in order to reach the department by three. It was a Treasury wagon and its horses came down Pennsylvania Avenue at a gallop. I seem to remember now that we could hear the horses clattering as a man in the office who had picked up a ringing telephone instrument suddenly began to shout. He climbed up on a desk and at the very moment the messenger ran in with the mail which closed the subscription the man on the desk repeated the news of victory in Cuba; Santiago had fallen. While most of the hundreds of clerks were cheering the announcement a few of us were checking the total of the subscription. The people had subscribed $1,400,000,000 to the war loan; $7 subscribed for every $1 that had been offered. That really was something to get excited about. It turned out that every subscriber asking for more than $4500 received nothing so that the distribution was very wide. The allotment was made to a total of 320,000 purchasers and of these 230,000 were persons who had asked for bonds in amounts ranging between $20 and $500.

LYMAN J. GAGE, CENTER, AND MR. VANDERLIP, SECOND FROM RIGHT, ON BOARD A REVENUE-CUTTER IN 1897.

WAR-BOND ACTIVITY IN THE TREASURY DEPARTMENT DURING THE SPANISH-AMERICAN WAR.

CHAPTER X

AN INVITATION FROM WALL STREET

WELL, with that news from Cuba the country's eyes were pretty well focused on such heroes as the Rough Riders and their new Colonel, Theordore Roosevelt; but someone had been watching Frank A. Vanderlip, too. On me, during my work in handling that $200,000,000 bond issue, there had been fixed, quite unknown to me, the sharp and piercing eyes of James Stillman, the head of the biggest New York bank, the biggest bank in the United States.

I only found that out one day when I had been in the Treasury Department for three years. I had begun to get suggestions and offers of jobs of one sort and another and whenever I did I would walk over the proposal with Mr. Gage. Most of them, we had agreed, were not especially worthwhile, but one day I told him of an offer that he could see was attractive and that unsealed his lips.

"Well, now," he said, "I'll tell you: I don't know whether it means anything or not but some months ago when I was in Mr. Stillman's office in the National City Bank in New York he asked me about you. I told him what I thought of you and he pointed to a desk in one corner of his room and said: 'When you are through with that young man I want him to sit over there.'"

Mr. Gage then explained that he had said nothing about it before because he was not through with me and then he went on to say, "I think now that you ought to write to Mr. Stillman and tell him if he has anything on his mind it is a good time to speak up."

Accordingly I wrote and promptly there came a handwritten note from Mr. Stillman asking me to come to New York and dine with him. I placed it before Mr. Gage to test its possibilities with his superior judgment of such things. His interpretation of the note was that Mr. Stillman intended to offer me a post, as a private secretary or, possibly, as an aide of that species which today is spoken of as "assistant to the president." My head was not swollen; I did not expect much when, on the appointed afternoon, I left for New York.

Mr. Stillman was living on Fortieth Street, just off Fifth Avenue, in an old-fashioned brownstone house. In spite of my position in the government I think some of my juices ran out of me at my knees as I mounted the steps to the stoop and rang the bell; there were stories about Stillman—his eccentricities, his domineering ways, his tremendous power. Well, I went to dinner and now that I am able to compare the experience with other meals eaten during seventy years, I still think it was the most trying dinner I ever lived through.

There were present his daughter Elsie, who became Mrs. Percy Rockefeller, a lady companion, Mr. Stillman and myself. Throughout the meal Mr. Stillman hardly spoke and I was obliged in spite of my distaste for small talk to carry on a conversation with the ladies, smothering as best I could my discomfort in

AN INVITATION FROM WALL STREET

the knowledge that Mr. Stillman was sitting there sizing me up. I did not enjoy a mouthful of the food served to me that night. When we rose from the table and went into another room I was introduced to another man, John Sterling, a lawyer and pretty nearly, I was to discover, the alter ego of James Stillman.

Sterling chatted with me about affairs in Washington for ten minutes or so; it was just ordinary talk-talk, without questioning, and obviously being for the purpose of giving Mr. Sterling an opportunity to size me up, did not relieve my embarrassment. Then Mr. Stillman, still almost ignoring me, said, "Mr. Sterling, I have a matter we want to talk over." So they withdrew leaving me to fuss with my tie, smooth my big brush of a black mustache, and to perspire deep in my mind. Presently they came back; Sterling said goodnight and vanished.

Now, up to that time my host had said just nothing at all, but then he started in philosophizing about New York banks, banking and bankers. I was to find out that he was much given to making personal estimates of men, which he could do with very great acumen; having just been put through his mill I should not have been surprised at that. He spoke hesitatingly; that is, over a particular word he would hang fire until under the pressure of embarrassment a listener would be tempted to supply a word, and that would be received by Mr. Stillman as if he were a graven image and, always, he would use another word when he resumed. So he talked with me for an hour or more, always about New York banking, and with the assistance of only one or two words from Vanderlip. Then, without preliminaries, he said to me, "when you are through with the Treasury, and I understand Mr. Gage wants you to stay there for another year, we want you to come into the City Bank as vice-president."

If he had suddenly struck at me with the fire-tongs, or if he had produced a telegram from McKinley offering to send me to the Court of St. James as Ambassador, I would not have been more surprised. I had fully expected after my strange evening to be given the chance to say "yes" to an offer of a position as private secretary. I would have said "yes," too; that I said to him that I would consider his offer of a vice-presidency of his bank is proof, I think, that I kept my emotions under control. Upon my return to Washington and after a decent interval during which I was several times congratulated by my jubilant friend Mr. Gage, I wrote to Mr. Stillman accepting his offer.

When one sits down at my age deliberately to produce memoirs, he is entitled to disregard time and space and by this license I choose to skip ahead to a time when Mr. Stillman was living in retirement in his house in Paris. My secretary, Edward Currier, who had a few years before, in 1909, been captain of the Harvard baseball team, was having luncheon with Mr. Stillman. As they finished Mr. Stillman set in motion his electrical piano-player and then retired into his bureau to play solitaire, a habit he shared with the elder Morgan. As he played his cards he unleashed his tongue and Currier, coffee cup in hand, standing like one enthralled, heard much that was astonishing to a young fellow not long out of college. Among other things that Mr. Stillman told him was that he had

AN INVITATION FROM WALL STREET

decided to bring me into the bank because of the manner in which I had handled the flotation of the Spanish-American War bonds, which was something he never had told me.

None but Mr. Gage knew of the arrangement I had made to go to the City Bank; it would have been fatal to the arrangement if any more had known about it. For one thing, there had developed a great public criticism of Mr. Gage and Mr. Stillman in connection with the purchase by National City Bank at auction of the Custom House in Wall Street. This was not so much because of the price, which was in excess by a quarter of a million dollars of the upset price fixed by Congress, but because of the shrewdness with which the bank avoided taxes on the property. Partial payment had been authorized by the bill that authorized the sale. Consequently, the bank paid the full price of the property, except for $50,000, and that little balance caused it to remain a piece of government land for a while longer, saving a tidy tax bill. It was quite legal, but the *New York World* endeavored to see it as a scandal; also to find something scandalous in the fact that the Treasury temporarily left on deposit in the City Bank the full purchase price, except for that $50,000, of $3,265,000.

I had never had the slightest thing to do with that transaction, but it was decided it would not look well for me to go directly from the Treasury of the bank; so I resigned as of March 4, 1901, when McKinley was inaugurated for the second time, with Roosevelt as Vice-President, and then I went abroad for a trip that lasted four months. The letters of introduction I carried were from the City Bank to the prominent bankers of Europe as well as the finance ministers of practically all the leading countries. It was the manner in which I was received in places of great power abroad which began to give me some glimmering of the new force with which I had become associated. I had experienced journalism. I had experienced Government. Now it was banking and I was really wide-eyed to see it as a great current in the ocean of the world's forces. None of that feeling came from money of my own. I had just about $2,000 when I reported for work at the National City Bank. I was shown to a desk on a platform where sat most of the executives of the bank; indeed, all of them except Mr. Stillman, who kept secluded.

    I sat there on the busy platform on the first floor and I did not have the faintest idea what to do; none offered to help me in the slightest with my problem. As a matter of fact, I became aware that the experts around me had a feeling that the newest face in their midst was that of an upstart.

CHAPTER XI
"STILLMAN'S MONEY TRAP"

"STILLMAN'S MONEY TRAP" was that Thomas W. Lawson called the enterprise with which I had become associated that summer of 1901. Until you understood it there really was something forbidding about the place, and when I had been there two weeks I had an experience that persuaded me I would not be there two weeks more.

The bank was housed in an old-fashioned building. From the street-level a steep flight of stone steps led up into the twilight of the main floor of the business where most of the employees to be seen were in cages. We officers had our places on the platform, a step higher than the rest of the floor. My flat desk, like the others about me, had a top as thick as it could be, but mine was a shining vacant expanse. I had succeeded nobody. No duties had been assigned to me. I was simply there and I still think that those were the most trying days that I have ever lived through. There were ten other officers on that platform and all of them were busy. They were technical experts of finance, but where I was concerned their noses were in the air.

I had been conscious from the beginning that Mr. Stillman's personality brooded over the entire establishment; by observation I became aware that it was fear of him that at times made the place become dreadfully quiet. On the infrequent occasions when his tread was recognized as he descended the stairs to the main floor a hush came over all the people working there. But the senior officers, all of us, saw him every afternoon at half past three in his office. In these meetings the business of the day was reviewed. I was quite the youngest man there; some of the others were old enough to have been my father; but it was the eldest of these, who had the ill fortune, on that afternoon I never have forgotten, to send Mr. Stillman into a passion. Over some single action the master of the bank broke into a rage that was, to me, amazing in its violence. There were no curses; oh, my no; never! But it was a long tirade of vigorous Anglo-Saxon in which the bank officer's intelligence was discussed in words of denigration. As Mr. Stillman stopped to organize more scathing statements I could hear the breathing of the object of his anger, that elderly man who sat next to me. I heard him breathe but he did not say a word; the outburst was received by him from beginning to end with humility, with entire quiet. We were all of us quiet. I rolled a pencil between my fingers and counted one by one each of its six sides. I was too uncomfortable to meet the eyes of any other human being in that room but I knew that if such tongue lashings were the regular course of affairs, when it became my turn we would have just one session of that sort. However, although I saw Mr. Stillman empty his wrath on other officers, on some of them again and again, what I feared, what I would not have tolerated, never came to pass. Between James Stillman and myself there never was exchanged an angry word. Indeed, that was the most astonishing thing of all.

From the beginning I was treated differently than any other person I the bank. Seemingly Mr. Stillman always had in his mind the intention to prepare me for an extraordinary position, but not from any direct word of his did I learn that this was the case. In later years I asked him several times what it had been that he saw in me, what he had intended to accomplish; but to such questions he never gave me any really satisfactory reply. At the start I think I was expected to know instinctively, just as the selected larva of a beehive becomes aware from its diet of royal jelly that it is being transformed.

When I returned from Europe I had been informed by Mr. Stillman that the Board of Directors would meet on the fifteenth of July and that he would want me in his office when the meeting began. After they had been in session a little while in the room adjoining, Mr. Stillman had appeared and had asked me to step into the board-room. Then he had made a mass introduction and indicated for me to sit in the chair beside him. That was the first board-meetings I had ever attended. These board-meeting were held at half past one every Tuesday, and the following Tuesday just before the meeting Mr. Stillman sent for me. Thereafter, he said, he wished me to attend all the board-meetings. That was mystifying to everyone. None of the old officers had ever been asked to sit with the Board of Directors.

I sympathize even now with the wonderment of those other officers of the bank at my exceptional treatment, and I can understand why they resented me as an interloper. Every morning we held a meeting there on the platform and in the beginning I merely listened, and not always with understanding, as the others talked. They talked shop in the argot of banking. As the habitués of the race-track or the campus or the gutter or the theater or the church all have their own private systems of speech, so bankers have their own slang and regard with some contempt whose who do not, in the words of the cartoonist H. T. Webster, speak their language. They were good-enough fellows for the most part. They were men who had grown up through the years in daily contact with the details of banking. As they discussed loans that had not been acted on or talked of any of the multifarious things that were of general interest to them, none ever paused to interpret his speech to me nor can I think now of any reason why they should have done so unless it might be that then they would have been kinder. As it was, I knew that even thought they were technical experts and possessed the experience of many active years, I knew more of the philosophy of banking than the while bunch of them. I had studied at the University of Chicago under eminent men. I had read and written and thought a great deal about our banking system. Well, what could I do?

"STILLMAN'S MONEY TRAP"

I knew a great number of bankers; the influential ones all over the country. As Assistant Secretary of the Treasury I had had charge of all the relationships between the Treasury and the National Banks. So I began to write letters to some of these acquaintances soliciting the accounts of their banks for the National City Bank. In comparison with the high-pressure drives for new business that developed in banking later, it is almost incomprehensible that until I came there the City Bank never had solicited an account. By doing so I had violated a taboo.

That I should have elected to do this is not surprising because, obviously, lending of the bank's money was as yet outside my province. The bank had experts, seemingly, who knew quite all there was to know about lending; but with respect to the other matter, the increasing of deposits, absolutely nothing was being done openly. To get a good account for the bank, Mr. Stillman would have risked his life, but he never would have stated his purpose in words. There would be dinners, there would be calls, there would be all manner of graceful attentions paid to the one controlling the money, but the convention was that no one could, with dignity, ask for an account. Wasn't that silly?

There were discussions of my unorthodox behavior at some of the morning meetings. I saw disapproving head-shakes as my work was considered. One of the vice-presidents said dogmatically that any business which came to the bank through the solicitation I was carrying on would be bad business. All of them were inclined to regard me as a fellow who simply did not know what was what in their craft. However, I persisted, and new accounts began to flow in. they were not only of excellent character but also some were of extraordinary size. Pretty soon in spite of the unusualness of the scheme, the National City Bank had a new-business department and I was it. I remember I got in the first year 365 new accounts, one for every day in the year. Before I had finished with the bank, deposits of $200,000,000 had been increased until they could be written in the form of an incredible sum of money —$1,000,000,000.

In that temple of finance of which Mr. Stillman was the high priest there were numerous tacit interdictions of which I became aware as I violated them. There were, for example, those magazine articles that I wrote to fulfil an obligation accepted before I came into the service of the bank. Just before sailing for Europe after leaving the Treasury I had agreed to write for *Scribner's* three articles under the title, "The American Commercial Invasion of Europe." However, during my travels there had been little time in which to think about that assignment. I did not even make any notes. Then, after my return, it was hot and the problem of adjusting myself to the banking atmosphere left me no time to concentrate on a writing job. Nevertheless, my promise galled my conscience so that at last I went to the editorial department of the magazine for the purpose of saying that I would have to renege; that I could not write the articles.

"STILLMAN'S MONEY TRAP"

I was greeted by the editor, Edward L. Burlingame, with great cordiality.

"We have just sent out about one hundred thousand circulars," he said, "to members of Chambers of Commerce all over the country announcing your articles."

For a moment I felt as if I had been tossed upon a swiftly turning merry-go-round but I managed to say with good grace, "That's fine." I could not let them down, of course; but even as I was agreeing to keep my word with them I knew that the compound of my reluctance was less a matter of the heat, of lack of organized notes and of pressure of other work, than it was a feeling that there was a hazard in the task. Without having formed the thought in words I had become aware that bank officers, especially officers of the great National City Bank, were not supposed to make public utterances. My awareness of that was an unuttered knowledge that I had absorbed from the atmosphere of the bank. Writing magazine articles just was not done.

I think now that I would have been skating on thin ice many times in those early days except for the fact that Mr. Stillman, with a profound belief that he possessed occult powers of perception, was persuaded I was a proper choice for the work he had in mind. Well, the articles were printed but nobody in the bank, lest of all Mr. Stillman, mentioned them to me. Yet I was conscious that I was being regarded by some of the others on the platform as having gone far off the reservation.

There had arrived in the United States about that time a most influential Japanese, Viscount Shibusawa, who was characterized in the press as the Morgan of Japan. Mr. Stillman, who wished to give a dinner in his honor, telephoned me quite early one morning while I was at breakfast to ask me to meet him and go to the Majestic Hotel to call on Shibusawa. Mr. Stillman was unwontedly impressed by the power, the sagacity, of this Oriental financier. I could sense that in his concern for his cravat as we waited after our cards had been sent up. Then we were ushered into the presence of Shibusawa and found him to be as roly-poly as a friendly, gilded statue of Buddha; in a richly made kimono of silk embroidered with golden threads, he sat with a fat leg tucked under him in an easy-chair. The fatty eyelids that he lifted to meet our gaze had been cast down as he read from an enormous scroll covered with the black brush-strokes of Japanese characters. The unread portion was still tightly rolled upon a polished stick but the yards of paper through which he already had tracked his way made a rustling pile upon the floor about his chair, and it was truly fascinating to find this big man of another world in the very act of absorbing information. Of course, at this interview I was just a small boy in attendance upon a quite big one, and I was flattered when the presentations had been made to have Shibusawa fix his attention upon me. What he had to say he spoke excitedly in Japanese. When this was translated I discovered that he was speaking of our meeting as a most happy coincidence. What he was reading, he explained, was something that had attracted his interest in Europe so that he had caused it to be translated. The Japanese characters on the scroll in his hands, he explained, were the translation of some articles about the American commercial invasions of Europe written by Frank A. Vanderlip.

Mr. Stillman extended his dinner invitation and then we left. One the way to the bank Mr. Stillman said not one word about Shibusawa's scroll, but a few days later Mr. Simonson, who was the last person in the bank who would have thought of doing such a thing, came to my desk to speak about my articles in *Scribner's*. He said the bank would like to republish them in a booklet if I did not object. Of course he had been instructed to do this by Mr. Stillman. Quite pleasantly I told him I had not the slightest objection; but that the copyright was held by *Scribner's* and that the bank would have to seek their permission. This was done; ten thousand copies were printed and distributed and then forty thousand more, and eventually the papers I had written were translated through the bank's initiative into seven languages including the Japanese. That incident was just one of the things by which Mr. Stillman became reconciled to the fact that I was deeply stained with printer's ink.

If Mr. Stillman began to see that there could be an advantage in my journalistic equipment, nevertheless I divined at times that he continued to be a little frightened by the newspaper background of this neophyte who had been admitted to the heart of the temple. Yet there was nothing he did not wish me to know and even at the beginning the deepest secrets of the institution were shared with me. Indeed, sometimes it seemed almost as if he were fearful that there would not be enough time to impart to me all that he felt I should know. From the first invitations to dine with him were extended on an average of once a week. Consequently after only a few weeks I ceased to be surprised when one of the numerous footmen would place before me in the Stillman dining-room a written menu. The awkwardness I had known the first time I had dined there was not experienced a second time because thereafter Mr. Stillman talked with me incessantly. He loved to talk about banks and men; especially men. But the conversations never were merely entertaining. He was instructing me, not in the principles of banking, but in the characters of the men with whom I should have to deal, and when he had studied a person his estimate was apt to be most astute.

Regularly on Sundays he would ask me to motor with him. He had one of the early automobiles, a German mechanism that would gasp and jump, and then, with surprising swiftness vibrate us through the horse-drawn traffic, the victorias, the brakes, the surreys, the phaetons and the miscellany of vehicles that rolled on Riverside Drive. We regarded it then as a daring expedition to start up the Hudson for the residence of William Rockefeller; sometimes we arrived, but whether we did or not Mr. Stillman all during our outing would instruct me. Often he would conclude a talk about some quite prominent business

"STILLMAN'S MONEY TRAP"

man by saying, "Never loan money to him." There came to be indexed in my mind many against whom I had been warned by Mr. Stillman. Down in Wall Street then these men appeared to be admirably solvent, and yet, in the course of time, I noticed that those of whom he had spoken warnings were not solvent. For my part I talked to him about the need for banking law reform. I had given a good deal of attention to this subject, theoretically. I believed that the whole system of National bank-notes was unsound, wrong; there were ideas in my head then that later on were expressed in the Federal Reserve Bank Act. So we talked and became friends and eventually the relationship between us was like that between a father and a son. Yet I could feel that the thing he loved most in the world was the Bank. He was devoted to the City Bank as a devout person is to his church. However, I myself became wholeheartedly enlisted in that service to which Mr. Stillman was dedicated: The Bank!

CHAPTER XII
THE MASTER OF THE CITY BANK

I REMEMBER dining one night with Mr. Stillman and Mr. Sterling. Now Mr. Sterling was just another piece of Mr. Stillman. Never were two men more closely in sympathy with each other. Counting upon that, or rather, presuming upon it, I spoke during our meal of some transaction in the bank. This seemed not improper in view of the fact that Mr. Sterling's firm, Shearman and Sterling, were the attorneys of the bank. However, Mr. Stillman's face altered as I spoke and I felt for a little as I fancy the last Mrs. Bluebeard did when her husband saw the tell-tale stain on the key to the forbidden room. The instant we were alone Mr. Stillman cautioned me. "Never," he said, "talk about the inside of the bank before anyone but its officers."

Keeping secret the affairs of the City Bank was a fetish with Mr. Stillman. He was so fearful that some unauthorized person might discover a source of information within the bank that sometimes, when he was abroad, cable messages from him would come to me in code through the office of John Sterling. That was his precaution against the chance that the bank's cable-operator had discovered the cipher key, and, reading the message, would understand that Zuckerat was J. P. Morgan, that Zoosperm was

Harriman, that Zigrino was George Baker, that Zurrusco was Sterling, Tumacar was William Rockefeller and Zwemkleed was I. whenever he was away from the bank Mr. Stillman kept close to him a small valise that contained his copy of our code. I had the only other copy in existence and when Mr. Stillman traveled not even his Swiss servant, Oscar, was permitted to carry the particular piece of baggage that contained the precious book.

In the earlier years when he was instructing me I learned things from Mr. Stillman, and about him, that made me forever completely tolerant of his idiosyncrasies. Within his skull was crammed the wisdom of the ages. I think I never have known a man with so great an ability to see far ahead. With the eyes and concern of a statesman he was looking always into the future, even beyond the unborn generation. The bank was not his; that was not at all the way he felt, not did I; the bank was the institution we served.

Caution was the thing he was trying to impress upon my character in all our talks and dealings. Because of the enormous financial responsibility he intended to impose upon me he taught me as carefully as one may suppose a parent mongoose teaches its young. These were his earnest precepts, that a man is never so rich he can afford to have an enemy; enemies must be placated; competition must never become so keen as to wound the dignity of a rival man or institution; and, above all, I was to avoid having too many banking eggs in one basket.

And then he could return to the subject of enemies; of one man concerning whom he cautioned me he said that in enmity he would be implacable, and that by mole-like ways that never would be traced to him he would accomplish revenge. Mr. Stillman never wearied of studying people and liked to check his estimates against those of others.

Many times I have heard Mr. Stillman say that when he looked at a man he saw that man's aura. He used the words in its Oriental, its Theosophish, meaning and not metaphorically; he was definitely mystical and believed that because of some sixth sense, and esoteric faculty developed in him and not in ordinary men, he could recognize truth from pretense merely by keeping his eyes upon the one who talked with him. Truly, though, if a man with a scheme to present, some overly enthusiastic promoter, did have the unusual luck of getting into Mr. Stillman's presence then this sixth sense seemed not to be a delusion. It was his method to keep silent while such a man talked. The man would finish his talk and Mr. Stillman would remain completely silent. It was not a lack of interest; simply there was no human response to the words. Disconcerted, the promoter would plunge again into his story and then more unwinking silence would start another round. I do not know that this was a trick consciously played by Mr. Stillman but repeatedly I have observed how effectively the weak points of a scheme were revealed under the test of embarrassed repetition.

THE MASTER OF THE CITY BANK

His eyes were brown, his mouth was masked by a mustache; he was rather thin man who dressed meticulously; occasionally he wore a pearl in the cravat that he had taken from among the hundred that hung in his closet, and on a finger of his right hand a large square-cut emerald. He had excellent taste and enjoyed himself most when he was shopping for presents for those who had his affection; he would select with exquisite care a frock for one of the ladies of his family or of mine. Be sure I did not understand him all at once, but when I did there had developed in me an affection for him so strong that anything I might say about him now would be sponsored only by the wish to reveal him in his greatness.

Few men understood him for he was really shy. He even preferred to come as unostentatiously as possible into the bank. In later years when he was in the United States it was his habit to ride downtown each morning on the subway, and then instead of proceeding down Wall Street to the front door, he would enter the alley-like Exchange Place so as to come in at the back door. On one of those mornings he was encountered in that back street by Charles H. Sabin.

"Ah, Mr. Stillman, back from Europe, eh?"

Mr. Stillman hesitated and impishly Sabin spoke again.

"You needn't commit yourself, Mr. Stillman," he said.

I myself had to know him a good many years before I fully understood that he imposed silence upon himself solely because of his feeling of responsibility for the bank. In the later years when I was carrying most of the responsibility and he felt himself to be in retirement it was amazing to me to find him on occasions warmly, humanly garrulous. One time we were going down together from Victoria Station on the boat-train to Dover. Oscar who was serving to us the contents of a luncheon hamper produced a Thermos bottle. As steaming coffee was poured from it Currier, my secretary, whispered in my ear, but I shamelessly betrayed him to the one he had referred to as "the old man."

"Mr. Stillman," I said, "Currier says you remind him of a Thermos bottle; that you are cold without and warm within." He smiled a quarter of an inch. Only a very few of us ever learned how warm and tender was the heart of James Stillman; he could be very hard to those who incurred his anger.

As I sat with the other officers around the big table on our platform during each morning meeting I began to note that among the letters that were read aloud frequently were some from banks wishing to buy Government bonds. I knew a great deal about Government bonds from the point of view of the Treasury. Every National Bank had to own a minimum amount of Government bonds according to a ratio fixed by the amount of the bank's capital. The requirements of each bank fluctuated so that there was a constant trade in Government bonds, and yet

THE MASTER OF THE CITY BANK

no bank had ever dealt in bonds with the public. The usual course at the National City Bank when an out-of-town correspondent wrote wanting to buy or sell was to transmit the order to the bond-house of Howard Fiske & Company. I began to wonder why we could not do that directly. There were profitable commissions in the business and I could see no reason why a banking institution could not with complete propriety take that profit for itself. So, I started trading in Government bonds and with the first trade I made I got into trouble.

An order had come through from an out-of-town bank for $10,000 of coupon bonds. I did not discriminate. I bought registered bonds and then when the error was revealed it was necessary to buy $10,000 of coupon bonds for the correspondent and have $10,000 of registers on hand; it seemed like a colossal blunder to me. Ten thousand dollars was what I was being paid for a year of work. However, all the trouble was in my own mind. I was not chided by Mr. Stillman; really it amounted to nothing.

Afterward, this undertaking of mine grew into a general bond business of vast proportions, was organized by me as the National City Company and earned as much as the bank itself.

When I was developing this Government bond business it was natural that I should then begin to see that there was also an opportunity for us to develop the general investment market. This, too, was a thing no National Bank had done in that period. It was a thing the private banking houses wished we would not engage in. Mr. Stillman was not critical of my intention but he was not enthusiastic. Yet even when some of the other big financial concerns through their masters began to protest he did not interfere. These men were his friends and once when he was telling me what they had been saying he chuckled and then explained that he had told them: "I can't control that young man." There was a tinge of pride in his voice when he said that. Largely I did what I believed was proper and helpful, using my own judgment, which was what he wished me to do for he wished me to grow.

How much I owe to my newspaper training! There is nothing in the world so helpful in forcing you to track your way through a forest of facts to a conclusion as the practice of writing what you believe you know. In my work of developing for the bank that business in Government bonds I found my excuse for writing. Some of the private bond-houses with which I had placed the bank in rivalry were at that time putting out monthly circulars giving descriptions of the wares they offered but containing nothing of general importance. Although no bank in all the world ever before had done anything of the sort, I began issuing on behalf of the National City Bank a four-page paper which I called *Government Bonds and Finance*.

I had an excuse, as I say, but actually the responsible factor was the split personality within me, the frustrated journalist who read in the poor circulars of the bond-houses a challenge to produce a good one. Mine was good. Because the issue of those bonds had been in my charge when I was a Government official only a short while before when I had been at the Treasury, there was no one in the county who possessed a better understanding of the subject. As Mr. Gage was still Secretary of the Treasury and my friend, I was easily able to keep myself well informed concerning changes of Government policy with respect to bond issues and retirements. These changes were occurring often because a surplus of finds was giving the Government an inviting opportunity to retire a lot of its bonds. I formed the habit of writing all that went into that circular, giving a discussion of Treasury policy, news of its actions and the influences affecting the Government bond-market. I did this for several years, until the burden of my duties increased too much to permit me to go on with it.

For a time all, or parts of it, were written by Milton E. Ailes who had succeeded me as Assistant Secretary of the Treasury, but who at this time was vice-president of the Riggs National Bank of Washington. We had arranged for him in connection with our bond business to act as our resident agent in Washington. In that way any National Bank in the country having some matter that required representation before the Comptroller of the Currency could, through us, be represented by Mr. Ailes. This, too, helped our bond business. Mr. Ailes was to become president of the Riggs National.

Eventually I brought George E. Roberts to the City Bank to take over the work of producing the circular. Mr. Gage had brought him from Iowa and made him Director of the Mint. Well, Mr. Roberts made of the circular the really splendid thing it became. My recollection is that the circulation of that publication attained a total of 200,000; depositors, alert business men, bankers, editors and students of economics were the readers. Mr. Roberts is still the editor, and for a great many years I have regarded him as the most lucid writer in the country on the subject of business economics. Through that publication I think that he has had profound effect on the nation by educating American business men.

But consider how disturbed in the deeper recesses of him mind Mr. Stillman must have been by the first issues of that circular. He had a real fear of publicity. He avoided reporters as carefully as he would have avoided lepers. There were among all the swarm that would have profited by interviews with him only two or three newspapermen with whom he would even pass the time of day; and now, thanks to me, the papers on their financial pages were quoting some of our information as if it came from the bank itself; and the bank, really, was James Stillman.

When I think of one of Mr. Stillman's characteristics I discover how much I like a story of George Eastman. He came home from Africa with pictures that he had made of big game animals. There was one trilling picture-record of a rhinoceros charging until its monstrous bulk shadowed the lens of the camera. When friends remonstrated with him for exposing himself to such dangers he explained it was his method to have just behind him, while he worked with his camera, a white man with a rifle. It was the duty of this man to stand in readiness to kill a charging animal before it could reach the camera and the cameraman. "But," protested one of Mr. Eastman's friends, "suppose the man's courage failed? What if he became excited and failed to shoot straight?" its Eastman's reply that I love. He said: "You have got to depend on your organization."

That was something it was difficult for Mr. Stillman to do, and makes all the more astonishing the attitude he came to have toward me. He had never worked with the staff as a unit. It was his practice to encourage the members to come to him to tell him things. Someone had bought a farm. Another had a new pair of carriage-horses. He responded to anything that touched the interests of the bank just as a horse twitches in response to the crawling on its hide of a tiny fly. Consequently there was some intrigue in the bank. I remember that one of the habitual intriguers had become adept in tale-bearing and tale-bearing, of course, is apt to become trouble-making. However, the significant fact that Mr. Stillman was informed about all that went on in the bank. He had a trick of interviewing a number of men on the staff without ever letting anyone of them know that he had talked to any other. He had a compartment mind; he would hear all these stories or opinions, and then in privacy, possibly in his bedroom, he would proceed with a synthesis and form an opinion. Generally his opinions were sound to the point of being prescient. In consequence of all this I am confident Mr. Stillman knew all about my sometimes unorthodox actions even when I did not myself tell him what I was doing. Those innovations must have horrified him, almost; my articles on European affairs, my publication issued under the bank's imprint, my frank solicitation of accounts. Yet I had to be content that he did not criticize me because even after my undertakings had demonstrated their value there was praise; no encouragement whatever. Mr. Stillman was a man who never praised. In later years he often confessed to me that his inability to give praise was a flaw in his character. I can smile now because I see so plainly against the years that in withholding his criticism that could be so violent, so awful, he was giving me the finest praise any man ever had from a superior.

JAMES STILLMAN AS PRESIDENT OF THE
NATIONAL CITY BANK

CHAPTER XIII
THE BANK'S YOUNGEST VICE-PRESIDENT

LOOKING at myself from Mr. Stillman's viewpoint I suppose it was thrilling for him to be training one as responsive as I. since I had no side-issues my whole mind, all my energies were devoted, every hour, to the City Bank. I did not play. I did not know how to play. I never have learned how to play. I would go abroad but always with a driving purpose to find out more about the currents of world commerce; all that I had previously learned was acquiring new significance. The truth is that for me this was all adventure and as I strive for some means of showing that this was so one of the most vivid of my memories comes into focus, brilliantly illuminated by cathedral candles.

In St. Petersburg at Eastertime in 1901 I was invited by the American Ambassador, Charlemagne Tower, to attend the service in St. Isaac's which would come to a climax as Saturday ceased at midnight and East Day began. We came into an almost darkened church with only a few candles to reveal to us that there were thousands of devout people massed in there, standing close herded on the floor and packed in the galleries. We were taken up into the chancel so that we were close enough to touch the bishop in his golden robe and the lesser dignitaries of the edifice as their procession entered under the protection of a swaying

THE BANK'S YOUNGEST VICE-PRESIDENT

golden cross that caught in its jewels the candle-lights and transformed them into a flashing beauty of ruby, emerald, sapphire and diamond. A chorus of bearded men was singing, one of the most moving songs I have ever heard though I understood not one of the words; only the feeling of sorrow and hope expressed in moody bass voices. There was constant movement; priests genuflected at the altar; thurifers swinging their censors were making wraiths of perfumed smoke; a golden chalice touched the chief priest's lips.

Then, at some signal, the vaulted darkness began to blaze with candle-lights; each person there lighted the candle of his neighbor and all the faces, the women's that were like rosy masks tightly framed in shawls, the men's dark with beard and shadowy eye-sockets, these faces ceased to have any trace of human coarseness and became, each one, as refined as an icon picture; and the gilded effulgence seemed to be that of myriads of haloes. These people had been fasting but on this night they held, every one, a small loaf of bread. Then a robed figure touched a candle-flame to a fuse-end dangling just off the floor beneath the place where echoes of the rich voices of the choir told the shape of an enormous dome. I saw the fuse-end as a sputtering galaxy of golden stars rise higher and higher into the darkness and then it began to travel horizontally. Once it seemed to go out and there was a gasp of concern from thousands of throats. That would have meant bad luck. I do not know if it was stage management, but the hidden light suddenly reappeared and the moan changed almost to a shout. One by one a great ring of candles took fire from the fuse and at that moment it became Easter Morning in St. Isaac's. Then all those people began to eat their bread, and I, who almost never went to church, began to feel the kinship of my work with that of the spiritual leaders of humanity.

Abundance in the fields will not place bread on our tables. The least understanding man in beginning to appreciate this fact nowadays, but there in St. Isaac's I was fully aware that prayers for bread in a world where there are so many crowded cities, would have to embrace not only agriculture but the functions of banking as well. It is by a series of steps in credit that grain in the shape of bread reaches the table of the most of humanity's two billions.

All statesmanship is simply an effort to answer that prayer for daily bread. In Moscow I met Sergius de Witte, as I met all the other finance ministers of Europe, and I found him and other alert to the fact that American exports had been expanding prodigiously; the value was expressed at the end of 1901 as $1,500,000,000; in six years we had sold abroad of goods and raw materials two billion dollars' worth more than we had bought. In many European cities the street-lamps and the street railways derived their energy form American dynamos. The shoes clattering on the pavements of European cities were American shoes. Increasingly, the sheep that ran to the far side of their English pastures at the sound of locomotive whistles had been frightened by mechanisms made in America. The flagstaff above Windsor Castle originally had been a fir tree in a Washington forest. The typewriters, the type-setting machines, the cash-registers and sewing-machines that were helping to speed up life on the Continent and elsewhere in the world were all importations from America and, in their sum, a matter of concern to the statesmen of Europe. The lack of balance in the trade was what troubled them. I was back in Europe again in the summer of 1902 and in October of that year I made my first speech as a vice-president of the City Bank. The result was a break in the stock-market.

I had gone to Wilmington, North Carolina, as the guest of the Chamber of Commerce and at a dinner I had made this speech. In it I had reported that the United States, in the opinion of keen foreign observers, had reached the high-water mark of its overflow of exports into the European industrial field. That speech had been carefully prepared and probably as a result of the swift market-reaction to it an article about me appeared in the *Saturday Evening Post* some time afterward and it was headed "The Voice of Wall Street." I was thrilled by that, of course, but I knew that the throat of the youngest vice-president of the City Bank was not exactly the place from which the Voice of Wall Street should emanate. Nevertheless, I began to be in demand as a public speaker and I conceived it to the part of my duty as a vice-president of the bank to speak whenever there was anything worth saying.

Unless I were to speak at intervals of my luck I should feel guilty, and it is as a part of that luck that I now tell about Miss Narcissa Cox. She was a friend of my sister Ruth, who had been a class or two ahead of her at the University of Chicago. In the winter of 1902-3 Miss Cox, a senior at the University, came to New York with her sister. They were on their way to Florida

THE BANK'S YOUNGEST VICE-PRESIDENT

but it was arranged that they visit my sister Ruth who was living with me that winter of 1902-3 in an apartment in 661 Madison Avenue that I was sharing with Lyman J. Gage. No longer was Mr. Gage a member of the Cabinet. I had been instrumental, in some degree, in the circumstances that had brought him to New York. I had known he was not happy in Roosevelt's Cabinet and Mr. Stillman, who had a high opinion of him, also had known it. So, one day, thanks to Mr. Stillman, I had gone to Washington to carry to Mr. Gage the information that if he chose he might become the president of the United States Trust Company in New York City. Shortly thereafter, Mr. Gage resigned as Secretary of the Treasury, came to New York and was elected president of the United States Trust Company. Then the two of us, glad to be together again, established ourselves in an apartment. It was there that Miss Narcissa Cox and her sister came to visit my sister.

All my adult life I had shouldered so much responsibility as to keep my mind closed to romance. However, I suppose I was ripe for it; I was thirty-eight. This Miss Cox, I thought, was an inexperienced school-girl, but when she went to Florida she was followed by the youngest vice-president of the National City Bank. I had never done anything like that before; I have never had any occasion to do it since. I had known her seven days when we became engaged; they were not, however, consecutive days. I still think I was the most surprised person by the change I had made in my life and certainly I was the most delighted. We were married in the spring and went abroad on our wedding trip.

THE BANK'S YOUNGEST VICE-PRESIDENT

Mr. Stillman's approval of my marriage went beyond the to-be-expected graceful gesture of an employer upon such an occasion. I would have understood his gratification better, I think, if I could have read his intention as I read it in a letter he sent me a few years later from his place in Pair, 19 Rue Rembrandt. He had just had a visit with the elder J. P. Morgan and what they discussed was the succession of command in the triumvirate of dominating financial structures in Wall Street. They had agreed that everything should be concentrated by Morgan on Henry Davison, by George F. Baker on another young man and by Stillman on me. We were, in short, the chosen successors of the three great men of Wall Street. Baker's man, after all, did not come into succession but Davison certainly became the leading active partner of J. P. Morgan and Company. He was the most lovable character in the whole of Wall Street, fair minded, extraordinarily capable, jovial, a real prince. A story that he told about himself, and which I love, was how as a quite inexperienced young man in a bank he managed to impress any visitor who approached the window of his cage. He would have in front of him staggering towers of figures running into the millions. Then with the speed of a lightning calculator, while the spectator gaped at his skill, he would run his eye up the columns and down and then without any hesitation would write the total. The total was invariably correct because always he had figured it out beforehand and had it in concealment under his thumb.

Certainly in the summer of 1904 I had excuse for believing that I was, if I may use an old newspaper shop expression, the fair-haired boy. Mr. Stillman turned over to me his house at Cornwall, above West Point on the west shore of the Hudson. It was a gentleman's estate complete to the last pin.

The house was the loveliest, I think, that I had ever been in. it was large and furnished in English style; the hangings were chintzes; the furniture was exquisitely simple and unutterably comfortable. There was a garden in which with complete contentment one, or rather two, might remain for hours and hours in a state of enchantment. There were boats at the dock on the river for our pleasure and in the stables, where each stall seemed to be the work of a fine cabinet-maker, there were handsome horses that gave me such thrills as I had not known since that day when first I had climbed on the back of my precious little pony Dutchman out on my father's farm in Illinois. There was a carriage and a team of matched trotters. There were three of us to go driving. The baby had been born who was to grow up to become Mrs. Julian Street, Jr. What did all that do to me? I had the feeling of being a kind of country squire. I seemed to be arriving somewhere. These things were more tangible even than the work that I did in a bank where I was a vice-president. Somehow I had the feeling that at last I belonged. That summer I went to town to work at my desk on Mondays and Tuesdays and on Thursdays and Fridays. I was taking my vacation one day a week. After all, I was forty and not likely to develop permanently into a loafer. However, I always had a thick bundle of papers with me when I came home on Tuesday and Friday evenings. I had the work habit incurably and I simply did not know how to play.

THE BANK'S YOUNGEST VICE-PRESIDENT

My responsibilities in the National City Bank in 1905 were such that I must have seemed to be working under tension. I had, within six months after I had joined the bank, left the platform and the other officers to seek a floor where my expanding staff could spread itself around me and freely grow. I sat at a desk where my varied activities were dramatized for all by the semi-circle of telephones and the panel of push-buttons placed within reach of my left hand; my right had had other things to do. Any man, no matter what his importance, walking into such a scene, was likely to seat himself, it at all, only on the edge of a chair and to begin a conference by saying, "I know how busy you are." I was busy, yes, but sometimes the visitors were men I did not wish to have feel hurried; on the contrary, when I made an appointment with a man I wanted him to feel wholly at his ease; to feel that we had time to discuss the matter in hand.

What I did to release the tension of my office conferences, and, if the truth must be told, on myself, was to acquire, deliberately, at the age of forty, the habit of smoking. Until then I never had used tobacco. My learning to smoke when I did was due to a sad circumstance. It happened that during my four years in Washington I had formed a warm friendship with a brilliant, friendly, always interesting, and somewhat bohemian theatrical man, Kirke LaShelle. We were about the same age and both of us had worked as newspapermen in Chicago. LaShelle had been successively printer, editor, dramatic critic, and theatrical manager. In partnership with Fred Hamlin he made himself independent by producing a play by Augustus Thomas, "Arizona." After that he had collaborated with Owen Wister in the dramatization of Wister's collection of tales called "the Virginian." He was something of a connoisseur of cigars, and whenever we had sat together for an evening I had admired and envied his relaxed approach to all the topics we considered. I watched, if I may say so, he smoke—by which I mean something quite different than what the same expression would have meant in connection with the hustling Vanderlip of that time. Then my friend LaShelle died, and his widow, quite unaware I did not smoke, gave to me the collection of cigars he had left behind.

After making some awkward experiments at home, I took a box of cigars into my office and placed them between my hand and the telephones. Ever since I have been smoking cigars and pipes at such a rate with such constancy, as to suggest that I have felt myself under some obligation to make up for the forty years when I did not know the sweet flavor of that contentment which hides itself in tobacco smoke.

The Vanderlip who began to smoke his inheritance of cigars in 1905 would have seemed an incredible being to that awkward stripling of the years 1885 who, as city editor of the Aurora *Evening Post*, had worn a celluloid collar. I may as well tell all, confessing here and now that I had worn, hooked at the front buttonholes of that collar, a "made" cravat. At birth in some factory it had been given an unalterable, a fixed knot, so that in its pretensions as something of my own devising it was a false as the shapes of the ladies of that period. However, as a banker of forty who was also among the vice-presidents of the City Bank, the favorite of James Stillman, I wore handsome cravats. They were the selections of his exquisite taste and were handed to me by the dozen each time he returned from a trip Europe. As for the rest of my costume, I think I was tailored just about the same as my associates in the Metropolitan Club and the Union League.

CHAPTER XIV
TAKING ROOT

I HAD been almost from the start of my life in New York a member of the Metropolitan Club. Mr. Stillman had put me up and while I was abroad he had cabled me that I had been elected to membership. The Metropolitan in those times was the up-town rallying place of the most important business men of New York; that was where they gave important dinners when the speeches were not intended to be reported I the newspapers. As for the Union League Club, I remember vividly a walk down Fifth Avenue in the company of Mr. Stillman, quite early in our association.

"You ought to join," he said, as we passed the Union League Club.

"Why," I exclaimed, "I understand there is such a long waiting-list that it would take an acceptable candidate six years to get in."

Significantly, Mr. Stillman turned and fixed his eyes upon me as he asked, "What of it?" That was not an expression of arrogance; he meant that I should be thinking always of permanence, building my life solidly, however slowly. As it turned out, I became a member of the Union League in the spring of 1903; afterward I was vice-president. The names of candidates for membership there are posted in a large book along with the names of the respective proposers and seconders. Any member who knows and approves a candidate may write his own name as an endorsement. The members of this Republican institution engaged with finance were quite numerous, and I remember that when Henry P. Davison had a candidate on whose behalf he solicited endorsements, the response was so great, because of the candidate's and proposer's popularity, that at last it was almost impossible to decipher under all the signatures the name of Albert Wiggin.

Al Wiggin, Charlie Sabin, Ben Strong, Harry Davison, these and numerous others found delight in each other's company at the clubs; they played poker or they journeyed into the country to play golf. I should have so greatly loved to have found myself playing with them, yet I could not. I think that has been one of the distinct drawbacks to my way of life. It was not because I had any opposition to card-playing, but that I had a low intellectual level when I was confronted with a pack of cards. They simply could not be made to have a meaning for me. Those others, the coming men in the street, were playing together, then and in succeeding years, and establishing a spirit of good-fellowship that gave their work so much the better flavor whenever they came in contact with one another. All life is ma matter of compensations and now that it is too late I am beginning to suspect that I swindled myself out of something quite precious by not playing more with my friends.

I never became a golfer, either, although I organized the Sleepy Hollow Country Club, directed the laying out of its links and was for years its president. Oh, I tried to play for a little while, but somehow the other matters bubbling in my mind were constantly, as a mirage, diverting my gaze from the little white ball at my feet. So, when I tried, I could not hit the damn thing and abandoned the effort with no proper realization that I was, also, abandoning one of the avenues to pleasant comradeship. As I did not drink at all, I was an involuntary wet blanket at the nineteenth hole, and the mention of that fact uncovers another of my disabilities: almost no one calls me "Frank."

If I saw that I simply had no talent for being a goodfellow, I must add that neither did I have the time; at least that was my belief then. The days were so completely full. If I brought out from town, for the night, some officer of the bank, a president of some corporation, or a distinguished foreign visitor, that was not a matter of comradeship so much as it was an extension of my job as banker. Nevertheless, I brought some one nearly every night, and at least a part of my reason was my pride in Beechwood. I had bought the place in 1905.

In town we had been living for several years in a house in Fifty-first Street, just west of Park Avenue. At the time I rented it I had been offered an option to buy during the life of the lease. I do not think I was an especially astute trader, but I had been taught that if you can pick up an option for nothing, you should take it. As it turned out, values in that neighborhood advanced. Our second baby, Charlotte, now Mrs. Norton Conway, had arrived in the world. So we were eager to have a country place and Mr. Stillman encouraged me, suggesting that I look along the Hudson, somewhere above Tarrytown. Later, I sold the option on the townhouse, getting for it enough money to reimburse me for all that I had spent as rent during the time we had lived there.

As a base of operations, a means of orienting ourselves, I rented a house in Briarcliff. Then, in Scarborough, I found a place I was disposed to buy, but while I negotiated some other buyer stepped in and closed a deal for it. Just across the way from this house that I had lost was a much more pretentious estate, a very old place, that sheltered a relative of the Vanderbilt family. Her children were grown and she felt that Beechwood was too big for her; seventy-five acres and an enormous house. If it was too big for a Vanderbilt I was quite certain it was too big for a Vanderlip.

"Buy it," said Mr. Stillman.

Suddenly, I realized I wanted it passionately; my hesitation had been largely because it seemed such a startling step for the boy I had been to own an estate on the Hudson. I valued Mr. Stillman's judgment more than that of any one in the world, so I bought Beechwood; that is I bought the house and twenty-three acres. Afterward from my neighbor, William Rockefeller, I bought enough land to make the place once more an estate of one hundred and twenty-five acres. I have a good deal of property around, but this seems an appropriate place to say I never have felt that things have belonged to me to the extent that I might do anything at all with them, stupidly or recklessly or selfishly.

Truthfully, I never had the keenness to make money that has dominated the actions of some men I have known. I have never been a market operator. I bought stocks, as time went by, but I never could trade in stocks; when I tried to I lost so I did not try often. Yet, all the time I was quite aware that stock appreciations were the means I should have to employ if I were to build up a large fortune. The simple fact of the matter is that the making of money was not my first objective. I wanted to have my family comfortable; I wanted security, oh, quite deep in my heart I yearned for security as do all men who love their families. What I really was interested in was running the bank. I was enthralled by the mechanism. I loved doing my job and I had very few side-issues. Nothing outside of the bank was half so exciting as the things that occurred within its walls. Possibly that was because the decisions we made there, the things we did, had repercussions reaching far out into the world. However, I never was pinched for money after I went with the City Bank.

Shortly after I went to the bank, at a time when I possessed about $2,000, savings accumulated out of my $4,500 salary in Washington, Mr. Stillman gave me a small interest in the United States Steel stock syndicate. My share brought me between $3,000 and $4,000. It was one of the few things to be handed to me in the whole of my business career. For almost everything else I had to work or else to risk something of my own.

Quite early in my career, when I was getting a salary of $10,000 a year, I reported to Mr. Stillman that I had received an offer of the presidency of a trust company in Chicago. I had no desire to take the offer, and I did not suggest to him that I was even considering it.

"You are getting twenty thousand a year; you should not be thinking of anything but the City Bank," said Mr. Stillman.

Well, doubling my salary was an effective way of dealing with what may have appeared to Mr. Stillman as a situation. He had no desire to be niggardly with me, yet he was opposed to paying salaries of too generous proportions to his subordinates. It was his theory that spending a large salary takes a good deal of a man's time and attention and that he is, accordingly, less useful. There is a good deal in that. I think it has become evident in recent years that some extraordinarily big salaries, especially those that were augmented by fantastic bonuses, did not invariably buy better work from the men who received them. I had been given another raise, to $25,000, by the time I bought Beechwood; also I had acquired a stock interest in the National City Bank. That was a fortunate investment.

My recollection is that I made the purchase in 1904 or 1905. As a meeting of the Board of Directors broke up one Tuesday afternoon I was called aside by Samuel Sloan. He was a very old man; a vice-president of the bank, a former president of the Delaware, Lackawanna & Western Railroad, and an influential person at the Farmers Loan & Trust Company. What he wished to reveal to me that day was that the Farmers Loan & Trust had to dispose of some National City Bank stock out of one of its trust funds. He told me of his faith in the stock as an investment, and he told me, also, that an officer of the National City Bank who had been singled out to sit with the directors, ought to be a stockholder.

"You would be wise, Vanderlip, to buy this block of stock," he said.

There were 260 shares and the price then, as I recall it, was $220 a share; eventually each of those units was to increase in value eight- or nine-fold. Opportunity does not always knock even once; sometimes she button-holes you, and whispers.

As I think backward, into that time when I was taking root at Beechwood, a whole pageant of my friends seems to move into position upon the lawn. Often Mr. Stillman would come to visit me, ostensibly to advise about a new garden or a change in the stables, but really to fill himself with pride in my new dignity as the proprietor of an estate. His was a pride as rich in affection as if I had been his son. How strange it is that I, who was early robbed by death of my own father, should have had from two men, first from Mr. Gage and then from Mr. Stillman, an affection that was so generously paternal.

Sometimes when I sat under a tree during a weekend, and worked, a friend stood beside my chair holding, for any who might have observed, to the pretense that we were master and servant; that was black-skinned Richard Green. It was for the sake of his dignity rather than mine that we had always to invent the excuse of a need of his services in the household to have him as a visitor. Another who came at intervals in those days was Woodrow Wilson, and with him the first Mrs. Wilson.

It was soon after my marriage that I met Woodrow Wilson. Mrs. Vanderlip, in the University of Chicago, had been a classmate of Margaret Axson, the sister of Mrs. Wilson and, possibly because she was there, we were invited down to Princeton for a weekend in the home of the president of the University. He told endless stories, superlatively well, and altogether was perfectly fascinating when rollicking in the midst of his family of daughters. I was utterly charmed by him.

In the succeeding years I saw Dr. Wilson frequently, at my home and at his, and more frequently at the meetings of the trustees of the Carnegie Foundation. Our friendship, then, made it difficult for me to understand his manner with me at a later time when each of us, I think, was trying to be of service to the country.

The Carnegie Foundation for the Advancement of Teaching was established in 1905. The idea had originated with my friend Henry Pritchett, who at the time was the president of Massachusetts Institute of Technology. After numerous talks with Mr. Carnegie, whom he had found sympathetic to his idea, he had felt he needed reinforcements. He introduced me to Mr. Carnegie, and the three of us talked over the plan. Then there came a day when, by appointment, I went up Fifth Avenue and into Mr. Carnegie's house.

"Well," said Mr. Carnegie, "I'll do it. How many millions do you want? Five? Ten?"

Quite quickly I said, "Ten." Then he sailed for Europe, leaving me to make the announcement of his gift. Eventually, Mr. Carnegie gave between thirty and forty millions to that Foundation which provides pensions for teachers in the form of free gifts and which also has come to do a great deal of educational research which is extremely valuable to the nation. Pritchett, from the beginning, was the president of the Foundation.

I was able to work as intensively as I did in those years only by managing myself quite carefully. By practiced design, as I dealt with a matter, I focused my whole attention upon it and then, when the thing was done, I dismissed it from my mind as you would erase chalk-writing from a blackboard. I had to do this because always there were a rapid succession of things waiting to demand a share of my attention. Consequently, the details of many bond and other large transactions seem to have left no impression upon my mind until I revive them, as ancient writings are brought to view by chemical treatments. I can awake my memory, magically, by turning through the yellowed pages of old financial newspapers of the time; however dull reading they might be for most persons, for me they are fascinating. Turning the pages that way I recall a piece of advice given to me by a private banker when I was starting the bond department. I was discussing with him some of the railroad bonds with which I was planning to stock our shelves.

"I have made a great deal of money in my life," he said, "by observing one rule: Never buy a security that the Goulds are connected with."

That man was still remembering Jay Gould as a bugaboo. He was a figure in Wall Street before my time, but the memory of his operations was responsible for a lot of the caution one encountered. It might even be true that some of Mr. Stillman's caution was a reflex of some transactions in which Gould had had a part.

CHAPTER XV
MEN BEHIND THE BANK

As Louis XIV was the State, so James Stillman was the National City Bank. Each Tuesday at the board-meeting I renewed my understanding of this fact. So unfailingly as to suggest that the habit was the outgrowth of superstition, rather than respect for time, those meetings began exactly at half-past one in the afternoon, not a half minute later. Always the previous meeting's minutes were read, and then there would be recited a list of those to whom the bank's money had been lent and the amount of each borrowing. This was pure ritual; when it was completed President Stillman would tell his directors what he wished them to know. The expression of a difference of opinion, indeed, any sort of debate, was unknown in that solemn gathering. Yet, for all their meek silence before Mr. Stillman, the directors were an extraordinarily powerful group of men. Excepting only a few, each was the ruler of something that had the riches, if not the shape, of a kingdom.

One of the powerful ones who listened carefully when Mr. Stillman talked at the board-meetings was Henry Clay Frick. This smallish, white-bearded, dapper man normally was delightful in his manners. Yet we who sat with him knew the legend of his fury against Andrew Carnegie, a quarrel that almost had involved them in blows. Consequently, there was excuse for Mr. Stillman to become disturbed one time when Frick was angry with Harriman. Frick, who owned a big block of Baltimore & Ohio railroad stock, was on one of the important Harriman boards, the Union Pacific, I think. This road likewise owned a heavy interest in the B. & O. A special meeting of his board was called by Harriman for the express purpose of getting authorization to sell part of the B. & O. holdings, but this purpose was not stated in the notice calling the meeting. Frick received notice of the meeting while he was at his country home at Pride's Crossing. Supposing the meeting had to do with some routine matter, he did not trouble to attend. However, when he discovered how closely his own interests had been touched by the meeting he became furiously angry at Harriman, and resigned from the Harriman board. On Harriman's part the failure to inform Frick of his intention may simply have been a piece of neglect, but you may be sure that James Stillman never would have been guilty of such neglect. One of the lessons he constantly strove to fix in my mind was that the richer you are the less you can afford to have an enemy. Anger, wherever encountered, was something to be placated. I think, too, that Mr. Stillman, from an appraisal of his own feelings, knew that the richest of men are as sensitive, really, as little boys. He was, himself, like that.

Only after years of association with him did I discover the key to this side of Mr. Stillman's character. It was in one of the last years of his life that he asked me to recall a trivial incident in connection with the opening of branches of the National City Bank in South America. I had hired to represent us down there a man who seemed peculiarly fitted for the preliminary work to be done, W. Morgan Shuster. He had been a member of the Philippines Commission and Secretary of Public Instruction in the Philippines, and after that had gone to Persia as the Treasurer General of that country. As it happened his connection with us did not last long, but while Mr. Shuster was at the bank in New York learning what would be expected of him, it was necessary to find some place in our crowded establishment where he could sit. Now all the years that Mr. Stillman lived abroad his office was kept as if he might arrive at any minute, but it was nevertheless an empty office. Well, I told Mr. Shuster to make himself comfortable at Mr. Stillman's unused desk, and there he sat for the little while of his stay in New York. I said nothing of this in any of my long and regular letters to Mr. Stillman because it seemed a totally unimportant thing. But someone among my subordinates wrote to him about it. A stranger was using his office! That hurt his feelings so much that even when he finally told me about it, the laugh with which he intended to make me feel that it was something out of the past was neither humorous nor free. The wound had gone all the deeper because of his affection for me. I shudder now to think how many times I may have hurt him, and I realize that his harshness with some of those he loved was because the unintentional hurts he received from them were sometimes intolerable. He was, really, as sensitive as a child during all those years that he was one of the most influential of Americans. To some extent, not to be measured, he adroitly managed even such giants as Morgan and Harriman.

Edward H. Harriman, chairman of the board of the Union Pacific Railroad, was not easily handled. He would have needed armies, yes, and navies, to have fulfilled all his dreams of power. A quite small man, carelessly dressed, and with a mustache as unkempt as if it had been worn by a Skye terrier, he clipped off his words forcefully, as if each one had substance. I recollect a night when the two of us, after dining, emerged from the home of Jacob Schiff into Fifth Avenue. It was near midnight, but Mr. Harriman, clutching my arm, said, "Don't you want to walk with me down as far as my house?"

We walked far beyond his house, and turning walked far beyond it in the opposite direction. How many times we walked back and forth I cannot say because I was completely absorbed in what I was hearing. We were in evening clothes and, because of his lack of stature, I had my taller head cocked far to one side to keep from missing any of his words. Consequently, I had to jam my silk hat nearly to my eyebrows to keep it from toppling. 'What Mr. Harriman was telling me was his version of his celebrated struggle with that other railroad Titan, James J. Hill, for control of the Northern Pacific Railroad. If only Jacob Schiff had carried out his order to buy another 50,000 shares of Northern Pacific, Mr. Harriman told me, he would have been victorious. Personally, I have always felt that Mr. Schiff had taken the proper, long-range view of the matter. Even in those times it was clear there was a limit to the economic power to which a single individual might aspire in the United States. Beyond that he would find himself curbed by an overwhelming public opposition.

That was something not so clear to Harriman as it was to Schiff.

Kuhn, Loeb & Company, a family as well as a partnership, was represented on the board of the National City Bank by Jacob Schiff. He was the head of the firm—and the head of the family. For his farsightedness, for his wisdom, and his rare capacity to understand the larger affairs of the earth, Mr. Stillman had great respect. Most of the younger partners of Kuhn, Loeb & Company were sons or sons-in-law of the elders of the firm, in keeping with old traditions. Schiff himself, four months after entering the firm in 1875, had married Therese, eldest daughter of Solomon Loeb. Twenty years later their young daughter became the bride of a new partner named Felix Warburg. A year later, in 1896, Otto Kahn, a young partner, became the husband of the elder daughter of Abraham Wolff. And they all prospered.

I never shall forget my astonishment the first time I was a guest at a dinner-party in the home of Jacob Schiff. Up and down the length of his table were gathered some of the most economically important people in New York. The table service was of gold plate, and behind the chairs of the guests were numerous men-servants. As a kind of period to this luxury, Mr. Schiff, at the conclusion of the meal, stood in his place and prayed to Jehovah. That prayer was as humble in its supplications as if it had come from the throat of the least materially blessed inhabitant of an East Side tenement; but it was also fervent with gratitude. However, even in such a family there were wide variations in interests. It must have been less than a year after I came into the City Bank, that Paul Warburg came from Germany to become a partner in Kuhn, Loeb & Company. He had come to take the place of James Loeb, who was retiring from active business. Mr. Loeb went abroad and there embarked on scholarly research out of which came his project to print in the original, and in English translation, every scrap of written intelligence that is left to us from the civilizations of Greece and Rome. Few students who make use of the Loeb Classical Library today realize that its existence is due to the fact that the study of the classics became the hobby of a Wall Street banker.

J. P. Morgan & Company were represented on the board after I became president, by Jack Morgan, but previously their representative was George, W. Perkins. Mr. Stillman had a hand in that.

One night at the Metropolitan Club, when Mr. Stillman was giving a dinner in honor of a visiting Russian banker, into his left ear the elder Morgan had rumbled: "Need some new blood in my firm. Who is a likely man?"

"Do you know Perkins? A vice-president of the New York Life Insurance Company." As Mr. Stillman related the incident to me, I gathered the impression that not much more was said; however, I suppose Mr. Morgan made further inquiries. At all events, Perkins came into the City Bank a few days later, and talked Mr. Stillman into making a generous contribution to a fund for the preservation of the natural beauties of the Palisades, those lovely cliffs along the Western littoral of the Hudson below Nyack.

"Have you asked Mr. Morgan to contribute?" inquired Mr. Stillman, slyly. "He is a very generous man, you know."

"But I don't know Mr. Morgan," said Perkins.

"Go over and talk to him," said Mr. Stillman.

"All right," said the unsuspecting Perkins. "I'll tell him you sent me."

The Morgan offices in that time were so arranged that the partners were all on the first floor in a series of small rooms, separated by glass partitions.

Mr. Perkins used all his persuasiveness in urging Mr. Morgan to help him save the Palisades for posterity, and at intervals he heard a grunt that told him nothing. But, when he had said his last word, Mr. Morgan swiveled around in his chair and pointed a finger at the adjoining room.

"I want you to sit in there," he said.

Perkins, probably somewhat chagrined by the abruptness of Mr. Morgan, rose to his feet. It was quite obvious from his movement that he supposed Mr. Morgan was asking him to wait in the adjoining, empty, glass-walled office while he attended to some pressing business in privacy.

"No," said Mr. Morgan loudly enough to abolish the error, "what I mean is, I want you to come in here as my partner. That's where you are to sit." That is all the preliminaries there were to the admission of George W. Perkins to partnership in J. P. Morgan & Company.

William Rockefeller, with a stock interest in the National City Bank that was, for a while, second only to that of Mr. Stillman, was an important figure in our councils. His face was handsome (gray-mustached), his manners velvety, his operations devious: gnawing at him was an obsession to capture a fortune as great as that of his brother John. During the first year of my service in the bank William's nephew, John D., Jr., had been on the board of the bank. Mr. Stillman's astonishing complaint against the young man was that he had a suspicious nature. Probably the younger Rockefeller had been cautioned by his father against voicing knowledge for just such reasons as prompted Mr. Stillman to be on his guard when the barber, Herr Bischoff, was around.

Herr Bischoff came every morning to Mr. Stillman's bedroom to shave him, and he came with that gleaming in his eyes that reveals excitement. Occasionally, while scraping his razor across the throat and down the cheeks of his rich patron, Herr Bischoff would be asking questions, such questions as even I hardly would have dared to ask Mr. Stillman. Then, in heavy, guttural sounds, Herr Bischoff would reveal what had been told to him that very morning in another nearby bedroom—that of Thomas Fortune Ryan, whom he also shaved. Would Mr. Stillman like to know what Mr. Ryan thought about copper? "Mr. Ryan tells me dot...." Of course, Mr. Stillman would listen, yet all the while he had the feeling that a dog that will fetch will carry.

One day, when there had been no time for the barber to shave Mr. Stillman at his home, Herr Bischoff came to his office, bringing his shabby black satchel from which he produced a mug on which was inscribed in gilt the name Stillman; he enveloped Mr. Stillman in a white cloth, tucking it with brisk gentleness into his collar. Then he lathered him, and began his usual effort to get some valuable information.

Just as Herr Bischoff had finished his ministrations, and was repacking his tools into his satchel, Mr. Stillman, seemingly oblivious of his presence, summoned his secretary and dictated a crisp memorandum. It was an instruction to buy at the market several thousand shares of Consolidated Gas. Consolidated Gas! Who possibly could know more about its prospects than Mr. Stillman and the Rockefellers? Eyes bulging, Herr Bischoff departed" and if he fulfilled the hope of Mr. Stillman he went straight to the office of Thomas Fortune Ryan. However, the instant the barber had vanished, Mr. Stillman again summoned his secretary, and countermanded the order. If there was a sequel I never learned of it, but I do know that the barber's delicacy with a razor made him so important to Mr. Stillman that when the bank moved into its new building there was provided in the basement a shop for Herr Bischoff.

The really surprising thing to me is that it should be so reasonable to suppose that when that hook was baited with a bit of misleading information, Thomas Fortune Ryan in actuality really may have been tempted by it. He was a mystery, always; no one ever knew exactly what he was doing. His interests spread far over the earth. In the development of mines in

Africa he took for a partner Leopold, the King of the Belgians.

For all the wealth and power of Harriman, Schiff, Frick and the others whose names lent prestige to Mr. Stillman's bank directorate, after Mr. Stillman, the one man whose good opinion of me counted most heavily was John Sterling, the lawyer. Mentally those two were as Siamese twins; they never went to bed in complete comfort unless they had said goodnight to each other over the telephone.

Largely for Mr. Stillman's piece of mind, I think, when he was out of the country I saw Mr. Sterling daily. Usually, I went to his offices where, when he emerged from a mysterious little den of a room, he would sit with me at an absurdly small table in a plainly furnished, almost shabby conference-room. Even Mr. Stillman, so he told me, never was ushered into the tiny room where this oracle worked out the answers to the problems presented to him. Once, in later years, Currier, my secretary, came back to the bank in great glee: Mr. Sterling had permitted him to cross the threshold into the private office. But that visit merely served to spoil a good mystery because all that Currier could see was a plain table, a small filing-cabinet and a hat-tree. The fact of the matter is that the vital tools of John Sterling were all locked up in his skull and soul. Ridden by phobias, as he undoubtedly was, his strength was in his rich understanding, and in his utter devotion to any one so fortunate as to be his client.

A small man, rosy-cheeked, his clothing suggested that he was about to attend a costume-ball as Mr.

Pickwick, or, maybe, as Daniel Webster. He was subject to gout and if at his home I found him with his foot fat with bandages, and supported by a stool, he was certain to be fairly peppery. But his one facial feature that always pops up in my memory was seen when he opened his mouth; a peculiarly bloodless, white tongue.

Soon after he had built a house on Fifth Avenue, a bachelor establishment where his companion was a lifelong friend named Bloss (by his familiars called Blossy), I was invited there to a big dinner-party. Except for myself, I discovered, all the guests were elderly ladies and gentlemen so that in their quavery-voiced company I felt as if I had stepped through a door two generations into the past. Their manners, their fashions, and the subjects of their conversation were all of a vanished New York in which John Sterling had been something other than a gouty old man. When I think back on it I realize that it might have been a fascinating piece of research to have tried to identify among those old ladies the one whose decision had turned Sterling into a bachelor. Certainly he never had been a bold lover; he was too timid, indeed, the most timid man I have ever known.

Death was what he feared! For his security the windows and doors of that house of his were protected with steel bars like those of a jail. I cannot begin to list all the precautions that he had built into the dwelling. He was also afraid of water. Much of his important law business came from English clients who were constantly pressing him to come to London. Nothing could have induced him to go, because his fear of drowning had the intensity of a phobia. Although he would go North every June to fish for salmon, when all his cronies were out on the stream in boats, Mr. Sterling would be doing as well as he could casting from a bridge.

Now, because he was a rich man and a bachelor, Mr. Sterling might have indulged himself with any sort of hobby; he might have played with a racing stable, or have become a patron of the arts, or an angel of the theater. What he actually did, to the exclusion of almost all other interests outside of his work for corporations, was to devote himself to the affairs of an old ladies' home up in Rye. A woman friend and client, dying, had made him trustee of a $3,000,000 fund to establish and maintain this philanthropy. Mr. Sterling got the notion fixed in his mind that it was an obligation of his trusteeship to build the home and install a suitable collection of old ladies, without invading the original fund; and he succeeded.

It was not difficult for him to make money even though he never seemed to want anything for himself, and never rendered a bill for personal service. Of course, he could at times quite legitimately profit by his knowledge of corporative affairs in which he was engaged and the friendship of the men who controlled them. He knew when a security was good and he knew when one was likely to be better. That was how it happened that at his death he was able to leave to Yale, his alma mater, something like $18,000,000 in securities which appreciated so swiftly that after eighteen millions had been spent, Yale had intact at the current quotations during the boom the original amount of the bequest. It was his possession of this sort of skill as an investor which leads me to say that it would have been cheaper all around if Mr. Sterling paying their bills as they came due. Instead, he ran that home in Rye, supervising every detail. Early and late he was to be found at his offices, except on Saturday when he went, unfailingly, to Rye. He settled the quarrels sometimes, on a Monday morning, he would be entirely distracted between his twinges of gout and feelings of frustration over trying to smooth the lives of so much querulous temperament as was sheltered at Rye.

Eventually, to the pleasurable surprise of Mr. Stillman, I was revealed to have the confidence of Mr. Sterling to such a degree that he made me a trustee of the old ladies' home. He never displayed any desire to have me inspect the place. However, once a year he read to his trustees the most detailed report of operations that could be imagined; when he had finished we would know everything, even how many chairs had been recanted.

Mr. Sterling liked to play poker, but no game ever held his attention as did that Rye philanthropy. Although I did not play cards at all, occasionally I went to the Metropolitan Club to sit with the group of his poker cronies. Everything considered, the stakes were moderate. That is fixed in my mind by one of Mr. Sterling's stories about Jim Hill. Sterling, Hill and some others were playing out West one time, when a stranger insisted on homing into their game, and with a gesture distasteful to the gentlemen who were playing, slapped down on their table $100. After an interval of painful silence, Mr. Hill growled through his beard to the banker of the game, "Give the man," he said, "a white chip."

Cyrus H. McCormick was another of the interesting human beings who sat at that long table in our boardroom. He did not attend the meetings with the regularity of the others, because his home was in Chicago, but when he did come one would be conscious of his presence. He was always so carefully dressed that I think I never saw him without realizing how handsomely he filled the role of big business man. He was tall, carried himself well, and on his upper lip wore an abundance of carefully groomed, gray mustache.

The chubby, rubicund, Teutonic countenance of Henry O. Havemeyer, the president of the American Sugar Refining Company, masked the soul of a man subject to wild fits of temper. I have been told that when he got into a rage he would shut himself up in a room and playa violin until he succeeded in quieting his emotional storm. Although Havemeyer remained on our board until the troublesome year of 1907, I never saw him lose control of his temper, but at 117 Wall Street, where the American Sugar Refining Company had its offices, he did have, as part of his office equipment, a violin.

Well, those were the sort of rich men I had to persuade when, in 1906, I undertook to lead the bank into an adventure, with some of its funds, that was an entirely new thing in American banking. Mr. Stillman was away at the time and I, who had been only five years in the bank, recited to the board the details of a project that, I was sure, would make money for the bank.

MEN BEHIND THE BANK

Photograph by Brown Brothers

WILLIAM ROCKEFELLER

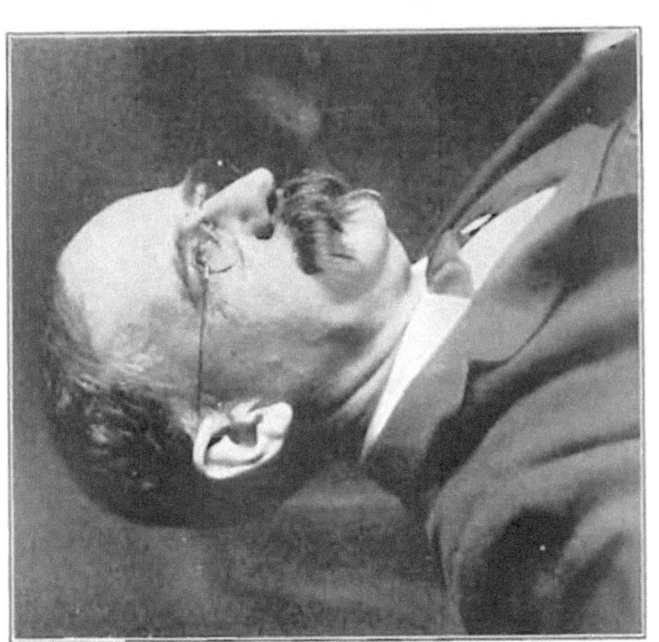

Photograph by Brown Brothers

E. H. HARRIMAN

MEN BEHIND THE BANK

Photograph by Brown Brothers
JACOB SCHIFF

Photograph by Brown Brothers
H. C. FRICK

CHAPTER XVI
A FOREIGN INVESTMENT

A BOLIVIAN gentleman, small, dressed as for a wedding, with a gray mustache and exquisite manners, had come to see me at the bank and renew an acquaintance that had begun in Washington. He was the dean of the diplomatic corps, the Bolivian minister, Señor Calderon.

The important thing he wished to tell me was that the Government of Bolivia, as a result of what was known as the Acre dispute, had received from Brazil an indemnity of $12,000,000. His Government wished to employ this windfall to help finance the building of a railroad from their scat of Government, La Paz, straight south across the 12,000-foot-high plateau to join the end of a railroad that descended the mountains and traversed Chile to one of its Pacific ports, Antofagasta. That Antofagasta railroad was owned by British interests. Well, the President of Bolivia at that time was quite as high-grade a man as Minister Calderon. He was General Montes. All of the Bolivians with whom I had to deal, directly or indirectly, inspired confidence, and as I found eventually, fully merited it.

The result of many conferences was that we united with Speyer & Company, and made a contract to build a railroad estimated to cost $27,000,000; we to take first-mortgage bonds to the amount of $15,000,000;

the Government to take second-mortgage bonds of $12,000,000; we to have all the handling of the bonds and, through a subsidiary construction company, to build the railroad at cost, plus 10 percent. The Bolivian Government's $12,000,000 was to be transferred immediately from London to New York as a deposit—half with the National City Bank and half with Speyer & Company.

That was the proposition our Board of Directors heard from my lips, and I can tell you that my eyes were fixed on Mr. Harriman as I revealed that the railroad was to be built across a bare plateau that was 12,000 feet above sea level. Indeed, La Paz itself lies in a deep bowl, and its location is indicated for travelers on the plateau by a lighthouse. With practically no changes, the board approved the enterprise.

So far as the bank was concerned, we got immediately a deposit of $6,000,000 that could not be withdrawn and was subject to the working out of the railroad-building enterprise; also the bank had placed itself in a position to market, and receive commissions on, the sale of $7,500,000 worth of bonds. The interest, but not the principal, was guaranteed by the Bolivian Government for twenty years.

Well, we formed the construction company, and at the head of it I put Philip W. Henry, an engineer of wide experience. He is my brother-in-law, having married my wife's sister.

Henry selected F. C. Hitchcock to go to South America as the field engineer in charge of the construction. Later J. P. Hallinan became the manager down there; now he is chief engineer of the Rapid Transit Commission in Detroit. Hitchcock later built the great Moffett tunnel in Colorado.

Our first plan was to bring ship-loads of Sikhs from India, on the theory that better than any other breed of humanity they would be able to work at the high altitude. The Bolivian Government objected to this plan, arranging instead to supply our construction company with native labor. What they did was to use soldiers to conscript Indians. At intervals the impressed swarms were released and their places were taken by another round-up of conscripts. We shipped redwood ties south from the Pacific Coast; we sent southward many ship-loads of American steel rails. Oh, there were obvious advantages in sending American capital afield.

I thought it was grand business at the time, and two years later it proved to have been in every way profitable. We had completed the first one hundred and twenty-five miles of the railroad when the British interests that owned the line from Antofagasta began negotiations to buy the line. The Bolivia Government was agreeable and so we sold the enterprise to them. My recollection is that the bank got out with something like $1,000,000 of profit. We never sold any of the bonds to the public; all that had accrued were turned over to the British company. They never were floated in this country.

Now there was not a dollar of graft spent in that entire business. Furthermore, none was asked for and there were no commissions that had to be paid to any one's son-in-law. The Bolivians with whom we dealt were as high principled as any gentlemen I have ever known. There never developed any single thing that could have been criticized in any way. Yet, today, I would say it was an improper banking transaction. As it happened, the holders of the bonds received their interest for twenty years, during the period guaranteed by the Government; after that there was a default. The business of the road was not so good as had been anticipated. My objection to such a use of a bank's funds today would be the fruit of a much wider experience; the reason I would advance against it being that the bank had to agree to buy the bonds over a series of years, creating a continuing obligation, extending too far into the unknown, that is to say, into the future.

About the time of the conclusion of that first South American project, I had been thrilled to my marrow by a conversation with Mr. Stillman. He had asked me to come to his house for dinner. That was not in the least unusual, but when we were alone he informed me that he had determined to live in Paris; that he was going to retire to the chairmanship of the City Bank.

"You," he said, "are to succeed me as president."

This was in December, 1906. Mr. Stillman planned to effect the change at the annual meeting in the following month. Night after night we met at his home to lay out a program. Just before the annual meeting, however, he confided to me that there was considerable opposition to his retirement. The other officers were shocked by his intention. I remember that he reported to me, and he was amused, that G. S. Whitson, the eldest of the vice-presidents, had behaved almost as if he were going to suffer a stroke of apoplexy.

"On the whole," said Mr. Stillman, "it may be wise for us to wait. Let's do this in June. In the meantime I am going abroad and I am holding you responsible for everything."

Unwisely, this was kept as just a little secret between Mr. Stillman and me; it would have been much better for me if he had announced that, while he was away, I was the boss. Well, who would not be willing to wait from January until June? Before June came, though, something quite unforeseen occurred.

Shivers began to run through the nation's financial mechanism. These were the first tremors of an economic earthquake. Before I got through with the experiences of that year I had begun to know some of the terror that always had made the master of the City Bank preach his creed of caution. I think my graying hair became white in that panic year of 1907.

CHAPTER XVII
1907

THE specters that haunt a banker when his world goes mad are terrible. I can tell you because I remember 1907.

A "run" is always appropriate material for the nightmare of a banker. Just fancy yourself as a banker—and discovering outside your plate glass facade an ever-lengthening column of men and women, all having bankbooks and checks clutched in their hands. Fancy those who would be best known to you, the ones with the biggest balances, pushing to the head of the line—there to bargain excitedly with the depositors holding the places nearest the wickets of the paying tellers. Even that won't give you a hint of what a banker's dread is like unless you heighten the effect with a swarm of hoarse-throated newsboys, each with his cry pitched to a hysterical scream; and then give the hideous concert an overtone of sound from the scuffling feet of a mob.

Although the depositors never gathered as a mob outside our bank, I knew the flavor of terror just from contemplating the possibility. We had the biggest and strongest bank in the country, but obviously we could not hope to be in a position, ever, to pay their cash to all of our depositors if they should demand it simultaneously. Bigness does not save an elephant staked on an ant-hill. Bigness will not save a bank if a run endures long enough. In that year, 1907, the size of the National City Bank was regarded as phenomenal in America, and more than impressive in London, Paris, Berlin and St. Petersburg. We had in our own vaults as our lawful reserves more than $40,000,000—and three-quarters of that sum was in gold. On our books were sums representing millions due us from other banks; we had paper that represented nearly $120,000,000 of loans and discounts; we had many other millions in the form of Government bonds; every day we held possession of pieces of paper representing millions of dollars which were expressed on our books as "exchanges for clearing house." In August, 1907, we were a fabulous organism.

Our total resources were:

$231,455,057.07

But, of course, our liabilities were:

$231,455,057.07

If it was a big, strong beast, it was a gentle one, and I was one of its mahouts, charged with responsibility for its well-being, its continued existence, its further growth. You can bet I worried as the nation became infected with fear-madness.

The Roosevelt in the White House at that time was Theodore, and his policies and behavior were thoroughly obnoxious to the orthodox financial group. They called him a demagogue, and he, for his part, threatened dire things. Once he threatened to take over the coal-mines as a way to settle a strike. He said he would use the Army to do it. As a matter of fact, most of the things that Theodore Roosevelt wanted to do were good for the country; but some of his schemes were dangerous.

However, his antagonism to railroads and railroad financiers was intense; that antagonism extended to practically all of the very large corporations. Even without his enmity, the railroads would have been having a hard time. Their facilities were unequal to the task of moving the freight on the first continent "ever to have a single nation spread clear across it. James J. Hill had shocked the country by declaring that twelve and a half billion dollars would have to be spent within ten years if the railroads were to be put in shape to do the work that was demanded of them. Industries quite generally found themselves in unsatisfactory position, and so were dismissing many of their employees. At the same time all of the unemployed were finding themselves in competition for such jobs as there were, with myriads of immigrants. In the ten months ending in October, 1,150,000 strangers had reached our shores, and all had come to seek their fortunes in America. In the very month that the panic began, 111,000 immigrants were landed. In view of what was happening, that one fact represented a ghastly piece of bad management on the part of the Government. But this was not all: the copper industry had received a severe shock—a drop in the price of copper. In six months copper had declined from twenty-six cents to twelve cents a pound. Amalgamated Copper cut its

1907

dividend in half, and certain speculators in the stocks of copper companies found themselves in a financial vise.

The Knickerbocker Trust Company had been financing some of those copper speculations. It had improperly loaned some of its money to Charles W. Morse; something for which John T. Barney, the president, was held responsible later. This, of course, was a hidden weakness in the structure. What started a fatal run on the Knickerbocker Trust was an entirely different matter.

In our individualistic banking system of that time, the trust companies, operating under too-tolerant state laws, were engaged in some unsound banking practices. These created an annoying element of unfair competition for the more strictly controlled National Banks. In that period none of the rapidly growing trust companies was a member of the Clearing House Association. Some of the stronger trust companies made shift to use the facilities of the clearing house by having special arrangements with one or another of the banks which were members. In such a case, a bank would send a trust company's daily accumulation of checks for collection to the clearing house, just as if those checks were a part of the bank's own business. This parasitical device, akin to the habitual borrowing by an improvident neighbor of one's lawn-mower, finally tried the patience of the National Bank of Commerce, which had been performing this service for the Knickerbocker Trust Company. In a curt announcement, the public read that the National Bank of Commerce had declined any longer to clear the checks of the Knickerbocker. The depositors of the Knickerbocker believed they read in this statement something of deeper significance. They began to pour into the trust company, determined to withdraw their deposits. The Knickerbocker did not have much cash. Trust companies were not required to keep cash reserves against their deposits at a ratio at all comparable with that required of the National Banks in the central reserve cities, New York, Chicago and St. Louis, which had to have in their vaults, always, cash equal to 25 percent of their demand deposits. Lacking cash, the Knickerbocker quickly had to close its doors.

Immediately, an already timorous public grew suspicious of most of the other trust companies, and lines of depositors began to form in front of their doors. Extra editions of the newspapers, falling prices registered in the stock-market, wild rumors, these things contributed force to the wave of emotion that engulfed the banking system.

Almost every caller was someone needing to be soothed. One acquaintance who came to my desk was a man with black eyebrows so mobile from excitement they seemed likely, any moment, to scamper up his forehead and vanish into his hair. He was Julian Street, the young author, and he was clutching in a trousers' pocket something unprecedented in the pockets of all other authors I had ever known. Street had fifty yellow $1,000 bills.

1907

He explained possession credibly; the money was part of his wife's inheritance and, after an adventure, he had just retrieved it from one of the trust companies.

On that first morning of the panic Street had taken fright as had everyone else; you could catch the infection of terror over the telephone from the tone of a voice. A short while before a considerable part of his wife's fortune had been turned into cash. Pending reinvestment, it was on deposit with one of the trust companies; but even the strongest trust companies had become suspect. As he came downtown everywhere Street saw men and women dashing about in the manner of ants when their hill is trod on. He determined to get the money and bring it to me.

When he presented his certificate of deposit at the trust company he was invited into a conference with a vice-president. This man attempted to reason with Street; he said the company was as strong as the country itself and that it was foolish for Mr. Street to incur the risk of robbery or loss by some other means. But Street was firm, and so another official added his arguments and when he could not change the client's mind, the president himself joined the group. For nearly three hours those men argued and cajoled. Probably their pride was involved, but all that they said simply frightened Street more, until he was the personification of the 1907 panic.

1907

"The country is in terrible shape," he said, "if you three men can spend hours making such a to-do about an account of this size."

"But for your own good, Mr. Street..."

"Cash!" roared Street. "I want the cash. Read what it says on this certificate: payment on demand. I demand the cash."

"Not so loud, please, Mr. Street, because we are simply trying to keep you from a foolish action. What can you do with the money?"

"None of your business. I want that cash."

"Well, if you insist, let us give you a certified check."

"Cash," repeated Street shrilly, "or I go out and give the story to the newspapers."

They surrendered then and gave him his bundle of thousand-dollar bills. As I received that welcome money from him and gave my hurried assurance it would be quite safe in the City Bank, neither of us had a clairvoyant hint of a future in which his son and my daughter would marry and make us grandfather-partners in a completely adorable little girl; indeed, two adorable little girls.

Madness, of course, is the word for the sudden, unreasonable, overpowering fright that communicates itself through all the human herd at such a time as that to which I refer. From too much usage, the word "panic" has ceased to have its proper cutting-edge as a tool for the mind. It has degenerated into a mere time symbol in our vocabularies, a sort of asterisk, marking the calendar of our memory opposite such years as 1873, 1893, and 1907. Yet, a banking panic, such as occurred in 1907, is actually akin to that which happens when a leaking ship's company is mastered by fear, instead of a stern captain, and rushes for the small boats, forgetful of all obligations except the brutish one of self-preservation. This swift contagion comes, when it does, as quickly as you can say the word: "panic!"

Oh, but we had a stern captain in 1907; it was during those days of strain that I discovered for myself what an admirable intelligence gleamed through the fierce eyes of J. Pierpont Morgan. He was our captain; he was literally the nation's captain. His leadership was something that was taken for granted when the banking mechanism was floundering in difficulties. The most important men responded to his call, eagerly, and usually were quick to do his bidding. Mr. Morgan could be savage when he was out of patience, and, when he was crossed, unrelenting.

One of the first moves that Mr. Morgan made, in an effort to quell the panic, was to summon the presidents of all the trust companies. Astonishingly enough, they never before had been brought together.

Well, Mr. Morgan, with his back to the fireplace, watched those men as they gathered in response to his call. In sharp contrast to the linkage of the bank presidents, through their Clearing House

Association, and in other connections, was the complete lack of organization among the trust companies. In an angry undertone, Mr. Morgan complained to Mr. Stillman that on this morning he had actually had to introduce to one another the presidents of some of the biggest trust companies. As was true of all bankers, Mr. Morgan had been going without sleep—hurrying from meeting to meeting; at the Morgan offices, at his home, at the Waldorf, or in one or another of the banks. His nerves were raw that morning. He was using every fiber of his intelligence to encompass the problem of a nation. Moreover, he had, I think, a sound banker's contempt for the slovenly banking operations of some of those who were then gathering at his bidding.

Old Governor Morton moved about clasping and unclasping inky-veined hands under the tails of his Prince Albert. As was his custom, he was wearing on his egg-bald skull a wig, one of a series of three that he owned, graded as to length of hair, and which he wore in succession. That old man—he was 83 in 1907—had been Minister to France, he had been Vice-President of the United States when Benjamin Harrison was President, he had been Governor of New York; for eight years he had been the president of the Morton Trust Company. Presently he planted himself before Mr. Morgan, mouth partially opened as if he were carefully trying to select words for an important utterance.

"John," he said at last, "how old are you?"

Mr. Morgan's scowl would have blighted an oak. "Too old to waste my time talking to you," he growled as he strode away.

That particular morning Mr. Morgan had time only to urge upon the trust company presidents a need for united action. Hastily the New York Clearing House Association amended its by-laws so as to permit the admission of any trust company which agreed to keep a 15 percent cash reserve. But it was clear to all of us, I think, that the big weakness was in the lack of coordination in the banking system as a whole. This banking panic was rooted in imperfect banking law. New York was the final reservoir of the reserves of the country's banks, but just when the reserves were most needed—in a panic—was the time when each individual bank drew into itself all of its resources that could be made liquid. I remember that one important bank out in Indiana issued a statement in which it boasted that it had 67 percent of its deposits in cash; some of that cash had been pulled out of New York, and in every town and village some such pull was making itself felt in the big institutions in Wall Street. All of the big New York banks had been forced to dig deeply into their reserves—far below the legal limit. This was caused by the rapid withdrawal of cash by out-of-town correspondents.

Those withdrawals were the good excuse for the quick decision of the New York Clearing House to issue Clearing House Certificates. I should perhaps explain here that the function of a clearing house is to simplify the exchange between members of all checks drawn on one another during the previous day's business. Instead of each bank sending swarms of messengers chasing all over the city to collect cash, there is this one big settlement. Each morning a representative of every member-bank goes to the clearing house, carrying all the checks that have been deposited with it that are drawn on any other member. All checks are totaled and any member's debit balance must be paid in cash the same day. Well, in the 1907 panic, the solvent New York banks that found themselves unable to meet these obligations with cash were enabled to do so with Clearing House Certificates. These were issued against deposits in the clearing house of certain assets. A special committee of the organization was appointed to pass on the collateral. It included A. H. Wiggin, Gates W. McGarrah, president then of the Mechanics National Bank, Henry P. Davison, a vice-president of the First National Bank, Walter E. Frew, vice-president of the Corn Exchange, and James G. Cannon, vice-president of the Fourth National Bank. The certificates only circulated as between banks, bore 6 percent interest and were secured by collateral in the proportion of four dollars of assets to three dollars of certificates. The strong banks disliked to make use of such a device, but there was no other way. Clearing houses in other cities quickly adopted the same device. The price of money was fluctuating wildly.

I remember a man coming to my desk in the bank and saying that he wanted to make a deposit. He

1907

wanted my personal assurance that if he made the deposit he could draw it out in currency whenever he wanted to.

"Is your deposit cash?"

"No. Checks on other banks; all members of the New York Clearing House Association."

"I'm sorry. I cannot give you any such assurance."

Probably he wanted then to make me feel badly. I know he succeeded. What he did was to take from his pocket, with a grand flourish, checks aggregating $400,000. When he was quite sure that my eyes had conveyed to my brain their handsome total, he restored the checks to his pocket, and stalked out of the bank. I have no doubt that in some other bank, eager for the account, he was given a promise that no bank was in a position to fulfil. A new $400,000 account was a devilish temptation.

I remember that I was personally under the necessity of raising $200,000 during the panic. Call money was so high that expressed on a yearly basis it reached 186 percent. Most banks were charging all that they could get if they would lend at all. At the City Bank we never charged a customer more than 6 percent. I should add that the bank did receive more than 6 percent through its participation in the money pools. However, I did not feel free to borrow from the City Bank. I had arranged to buy a block of stock in a Seattle bank, which was to increase its stock. The date of issue came right in the midst of the panic. I had obligated myself not only because I thought it was going to be a good investment, but because it would establish a helpful relationship for the City Bank. Mr. Stillman for years had been creating such ties through his personal fortune. I explained this situation to Mr. Stillman, and he, vent with me to the Farmers' Loan & Trust, where he spoke to the president, Edwin S. Marston.

"Vanderlip," he said, "wants to borrow some money on this Seattle bank stock, and it is all right."

Mr. Stillman's word was very nearly law in the Farmers' Loan & Trust. Nevertheless, I did not quite draw a deep breath until Marston, after a decent interval, had nodded his head. As it turned out, that was one of the only two bank loans that I have made in the whole course of my life, which seems to me to be remarkable in view of my career.

Those weeks in October and November were a period of swift education for most bankers, and I was certainly an eager student. I was learning that the banking reforms which I had long been preaching would have to be expressed in the form of some sort of a central banking organization. We would have to invent a wholesale banking mechanism that would relieve our economic system from the intolerable strains to which periodically it was being subjected. I was learning also that banking is not a field for weaklings. If I was strong, I had need of all my strength and my own physical reserves were being drawn upon in the same way that we were having to take assets out of the bank's vaults. I ate when I

1907

could, and slept, if at all, in the home of Mr. Stillman; at this time he had a house in Seventy-second Street.

In response to some prescient warning of the trouble to come, Mr. Stillman had returned to the United States before the panic began in earnest. Be sure that I welcomed him. If any man possessed power to look into the future, that man was Mr. Stillman. His mind was ceaselessly trying to fit together the things that he knew, so as to give him a better understanding of what was coming. It was not precisely like having a crystal ball to have access to Mr. Stillman's intelligence, but it was, I think, the next thing to it. Often the proposal that Mr. Stillman uttered quietly was the thing that Mr. Morgan executed; but Mr. Stillman was above the struggle, rather than in it.

One of the early features of the panic had been the discrediting of individuals who had come to occupy important positions in the banking structure. Among them were Charles W. Morse, Edward R. Thomas, and Orlando F. Thomas. These men who had acquired important banking interests by daring operations were forced to retire from all banking positions. Public opinion was aroused against Morse in particular, and his resignations created vacancies on the boards of a number of banks. In some cases entire boards of directors were forced out of office. There was, as a result, just that much more work to be done by those experienced bankers in whom confidence continued.

1907

I remember one incident in a small, private room of one of the up-town banks. It was quite late at night. Seven or eight of us who represented the strongest institutions in the city had gathered to determine if we would be justified in using some of the doubly-precious cash of our banks to enable a weaker one to open its doors on the following morning. Mr. Morgan had come to this meeting.

Mr. Morgan's utterances usually came with a force that suggested his words wen; literally fired from the remarkable, cannon-like cigars that he smoked habitually. He was a connoisseur of wines and in tobacco, too, his taste was aware of equally subtle gradations. He smoked only the tobacco of certain favored crop years. It was Havana tobacco, but it was rolled in shapes never sold in any cigar store. Morgan cigars had the form of a Hercules club, bulging thickly at the outer end, and they were absolutely poisonous for all but the most experienced smokers. I know I smoked myself giddy the first time I lighted one that he had thrust into my hand. Thereafter, until I had become inured to strong tobacco, I would always put his gift cigars in my pocket, and so keep my mind free for the calm consideration of whatever financial matter we might be under the necessity of discussing. On this night to which I refer, Mr. Morgan was listening as a report was made on the contents of the portfolio of the bank we were considering. That astonishing brain of his would take into itself a welter of facts and then, after consideration, he would speak, and we who listened would know that we were hearing wisdom. Suddenly

I saw that the hand holding his cigar had relaxed on the table; his head had sunk forward until his chin was cushioned on his cravat. His breathing had become audible. The weary old man had fallen asleep.

Someone there, with a touch on the arm, silenced the one who was talking; another reached forward and lifted from the relaxed fingers, as one might take a rattle from a baby, the big cigar that was scorching the varnish of the table. Then we sat quietly, saying nothing whatever. One who went for a drink of water walked on tiptoes. The only sound that could be heard was the breathing of Mr. Morgan. It seems to me now that it was a long while before he awakened. When he did consciousness returned abruptly; in a second he was wide awake and our conference was resumed with no reference being made to Mr. Morgan's nap.

We were not always so gentle in those harsh days. I recall as if it were an act in a melodrama a day in November, when a group of us gathered for a meeting in a private office in the Trust Company of America Building. We were the directors of the Norfolk & Southern Railway. The road was in difficulties, as were most railroad corporations. The problem could be expressed always in one way: cash. We were there to go through the legal formalities necessary to authorize the issuance of a mortgage for $25,000,000. The share-holders had given their approval.

1907

Among those present was Oakleigh Thorne, president of the Trust Company of America. He was as restless as a cat detained from its basket of mewing kittens; downstairs were many things demanding his attention. Who could say what bad news there might be coughing out of the stock-ticker? At any minute that menacing line of depositors might begin again to extend itself into the street to grow monstrously until it would be giving off a wave of hysteria, having repercussions all over the country.

As the lawyer lifted papers from his bag in preparation for the reading of the mortgage, there was a little talk of the latest gossip out of the Knickerbocker Trust Company mess. Most of us there knew, and had an affection for, John T. Barney who had been its president. Some were inclined to blame Charles W. Morse or F. Augustus Heintze for Barney's difficulties. Then the lawyer began his *pro forma* reading.

While he was in the midst of its dull phrases a telephone bell rang and, as Oakleigh Thorne answered it, the lawyer stopped reading.

"Barney has committed suicide," said Thorne. "Shot himself with a pistol."

No one commented. The lawyer went on reading. That was not callousness. We simply had no time to express our feelings. At that moment the battle was on; we were in it.

CHAPTER XVIII
THE NEW PRESIDENT OF THE CITY BANK

AFTER a financial panic the process of convalescence is never swift. As with any other accident the thing happens explosively, but the recovery is tedious, except as it is interrupted by further alarms. Late in November, 1907, Mr. Stillman was convinced that the worst was over. However, he cautioned me to be prepared for a relapse-possibly more than one. He reminded me that after the two previous panics dull business had oppressed the nation for periods of from two to four years. This time, he was persuaded, normal conditions would be restored with less hesitation. I wished to know why he thought so. He said that among the things that argued for his point of view were the general development of the country, an increase in railroad earnings, the improved skill in the operation of industrial enterprises, and the accumulations of riches in the nation. Events proved that he was perfectly right.

As the harbinger of returning prosperity Mr. Stillman himself was the most significant sign: Early in 1908 he sailed for Europe. For discerning people his departure should have been as rich with meaning as that olive branch seen in the bill of the dove that

THE NEW PRESIDENT OF THE CITY BANK

returned to Noah's ark. James Stillman was content with the state of the country; yet, I did not have to be told that it was not a propitious time to announce his retirement. He left me in charge, but he did not tell the other vice-presidents that I was to be held responsible for what they might do. What it boiled down to was that Mr. Stillman regarded me as the *de facto* president, but my associates in the bank did not so regard me. It was a situation not too comfortable, especially as I knew that one of those other officers (a man no longer living) was rather eager to get me into hot water. I was annoyed as I became aware of some of the things he had done slyly, of unfriendly letters sent abroad, but he had no real power to harm me, except as I might become tempted to forget my real job and turn my attention to him. I never did, and so what might have been a cause of vicissitude was rendered innocuous.

Never for a minute was I bored. There were thrills every hour in what I was doing. Sometimes now when I find myself regretting that I did not play as other men, I laugh at myself because, without knowing it, all those working years I was playing constantly. Actually, I suppose, I got more excitement out of my work than most men would get out of a bear-hunt. The simple truth is that I loved what I was doing as I loved the people with whom I found myself in contact. There may be a more fascinating set of men than those with whom I mingled in Wall Street, but I cannot imagine what they would be like. Even before I can form the letters of his name, I can see in front of me the alert and intelligent face of Benjamin Strong. Our friendship was something that began to grow in the days of the panic.

It was on an occasion when we were trying to help the Trust Company of America out of its precarious condition. We needed to examine its assets to see whether the banking pool could afford to lend it funds. I furnished a man from the City Bank, and another, a vice-president, was sent from the Bankers' Trust Company; that was Ben Strong. So, the first time I saw him he was exercising a highly competent skill. He displayed an admirable, an uncanny ability in estimating the value of the paper in that trust company's portfolio. Strong and two other men put in a day and a night—all night—appraising those assets, and at dawn furnished a total which was the amount of money that we would be justified in putting into the institution before nine o'clock in the morning. At nine it would either have to suspend or, with counters piled with currency, open its doors to a rush of frightened depositors. Strong did not make a single mistake in that work. I decided right away that he was a man for the City Bank. I made him an offer, but he could not leave the Bankers' Trust.

Henry Davison and Paul Warburg were others who had my deep respect after the panic. These two and Ben Strong and I were among the few men who, at that time, were fully persuaded that the remedy for the weakness in our banking system was the creation of some sort of a central institution to hold the reserves of the country. Only when such a common reservoir existed, we were convinced, would it be possible to use the reserves effectively.

We were entirely right because, if the Federal Reserve System had been in existence in 1907, the thing that brought about the financial paralysis, the mad scramble for individual reserves, would not have occurred; there would have been no panic in 1907. However, even when the madness was over, and when their lesson should have been well learned, many of the oldest, the most distinguished and respected bankers of the country, were still opposed to banking law reforms. They understood the old, the haphazard system. Consequently, they were disposed to reprove younger men, who wanted to change, by reminding them that the existing national banking system had served the nation through the years of expansion after the 'sixties; it should not, they insisted, become the plaything of tinkerers or theorists. Their minds were as little engaged by the obvious as are those of their successors by the weaknesses of the gold standard. Nevertheless, Paul Warburg continued to write lucidly about the central banks of Europe. Ben Strong was equally zealous in his advocacy of change, and I wrote articles, delivered speeches and argued with every banker with whom I came in contact. The minds of legislators were somewhat quicker to grasp, to see, that there was a problem, but, for lack of banking experience, such minds were not likely to develop a blueprint of a workable machine. It was going to be a big job.

THE NEW PRESIDENT OF THE CITY BANK

Reform, no matter how urgently required, was not primarily my job. My job was running the City Bank. It was an institution to be proud of in 1908; mightily proud. That others who were alive in that time would agree with me is shown by the fact that the deposits had increased during the months when most institutions were shriveling, somewhat, from the effects of a widespread disposition to hoard against a possibly worse panic. Also, some who had been hoarding money had faith, when they brought their buried treasure to light once more, only in the nation's biggest bank. The simple fact that we were far and away the biggest was prestige enough to satisfy the most timid soul with riches in his hands.

I was steering the bank, rather than running it. I do not think my associate vice-presidents ever felt that I lacked conservatism in the quality of the business I was getting or preparing to get; rather, they felt that there was a lack of conservatism in my methods of going after the business. I was constantly after the younger officers, urging upon them the desirability of traveling more, of getting acquainted with people who were in a position to give business to the bank; also, when they returned from a bit of traveling I wanted to know about results. I had developed the bond business until this still swiftly growing phase of the City Bank's work was beyond dispute a thing responsible for a large share of the bank's profits. Even if it was not old-fashioned banking, old-fashioned John Sterling was giving me daily doses of encouragement. Moreover, he was in constant communication with Mr. Stillman who was sometimes in Paris, sometimes in London and sometimes in Rome. I wrote a long letter to Mr. Stillman every Saturday; occasionally oftener. I remained at Beechwood on Saturdays and devoted long hours to each letter.

Some years after I had become president, and while I was visiting Mr. Stillman at his house in 19 Rue Rembrandt, Paris, he confided to my secretary, Ned Currier, the reason why he was living in "exile." "When I made Mr. Vanderlip president of the bank," he told Currier, "I realized that if I did not get out of the way, Mr. Schiff, Mr. Morgan, Mr. Harriman, Mr. Baker and others would not go to Mr. Vanderlip, but would come to me as they always had done, and the only way I could avoid this, and make Mr. Vanderlip a real president, was to move abroad for the greater part of the time." He was living in that splendid house he had bought in the rue Rembrandt, one that was filled with art treasures, and hung with ancient tapestries. That was where he received the letter I wrote to him at the end of the first week in May, 1908. I refer to the letter now only because it seems typical of the many I wrote. I had just returned after a week in his company. "....deposits," I reported to him, " [have] continued to grow rapidly while loans remained about stationary. Today we had the largest amount of cash in the vault we have ever had in the existence of the bank and a reserve of 43 percent."

That would make him content for a few minutes, I knew, but no more than a few, because Mr. Stillman was never an optimist. He was always uncomfortable

THE NEW PRESIDENT OF THE CITY BANK

about the future. No matter how good a thing was he would caution me, "Don't take too much of it."

I read again in a pink, typewritten copy of my letter to him: "I saw Mr.—Tuesday morning at his house and came downtown with him. He was in good humor and said he was entirely satisfied with the decision as I reported it." My memory fills in that blank with the name of Mr. Morgan, whose humors were important. Mr. Stillman had been horrified to receive typewritten letters from me; the interposition of a stenographer was too disturbing for his comfort. He had told me that if I must dictate such confidential matters that I should say "blank" to my secretary when I came to an important name and that I should say "blank" when I had occasion to mention a sum of money. It was his notion that I might fill in these blanks in my own handwriting. Well, I did write in such names as Morgan, Baker, Taft or Bryan; I wrote in all the sums; but I declare that never once did I say "blank" to my secretary. I could not have had one around me that I did not fully trust. For Mr. Stillman's peace of mind, I simply instructed my secretary, in transcribing notes, to leave appropriate blank spaces. Afterward Mr. Stillman and I used a private code; that one in which his son, Jimmy, was Zulanmen, and Sterling was Zurrusco, and Harriman was Zoosperm.

In December, 1908, I had a letter from Paris which told me:

The object of this is to urge upon you the necessity of keeping the operating expenses of the bank down, and not to increase salaries at this time. With poor business, small earnings (for those of the bond department are now only equalizing the lean years it has had) and low interest rates, no increases are warranted.

In fact in all other lines of business wages and operating expenses have been reduced. Those who are really worthy of more pay must wait until general earnings are better, if they are not willing to they are not of the right stuff and had better go. The tendency always of moving into larger and more commodious quarters, whether in a corporation or family is inevitably towards, if not extravagance, the incurring of greater expenses. It has been my great fear, as I think I have told you, concerning the new building.

The way this is handled is going to be one of the tests of the Executive Officers' management.

We moved into our new building late in December. McKim, Mead & White were the architects. It really was breath-takingly lovely, a palatial colonnaded structure of commerce such as Mr. Stillman had wished it to be; my desire had been for a tall office building. In fact, I had caused plans to be drawn for a very high building covering the whole block. Of course, it would have been most advantageous if that had been done. Later, the bank had to rent office space in various places in the financial district. However, I was as proud as Mr. Stillman of our new building.

I had become infected by that time with some of the spirit, the atmosphere of London banking offices. So, I arranged to have tea served in the afternoon. But I did not like tea myself; nobody else seemed to, and the reporters thought it was funny—so that idea

THE NEW PRESIDENT OF THE CITY BANK

did not flourish. Nevertheless, there is a great deal to be said for British practices. English bank directors pay much more attention to the operations of a bank than is the case with a board of directors in America. English directors are apt to be at their bank for luncheon.

In a London bank the luncheon will be on a sideboard so that you may pick out what you wish to eat. There will be fine old silver with a proper polish on it; appreciative eyes will detect in that silver a delicate blue that comes with age. The hall-marks, for those who can read them, will reveal that this silver may have been used by hungry men who interrupted their eating to complain against the rebel, Washington. We began serving luncheon in the City Bank, and, of course, a great many banks have that sort of thing nowadays. But, we were proud because we were one of the first. There were other nice British influences about us. Personally, I was addicted to the London *Times*. I have been reading it for thirty-three years. I think I read more columns in it than I do in any single American newspaper. That is rather a curious confession for one who once gave all his energy, mental and physical, to the Chicago *Tribune*. I have read the London *Times* because I have always found in it better and more succinct accounts of foreign affairs. I have read it for its editorials, written by men who have mastered their subjects, for the proceedings of Parliament—of which I have read pages and pages, as compared with the thousands of pages of the proceedings of Congress that I have not read. The *Times* knows how to report a speech. We do not report speeches. We compel a speaker to write something in advance, and we pick out from that any paragraphs that are a little sensational. Whenever an Englishman does any thinking, he writes a letter to the *Times*. Distinctly, when I have finished reading a copy of the *Times*, I have the feeling that I have been in contact with true British thought.

I do admire them; especially their bankers. Sir Edward Holden, who for years was at the head of the Midland Bank, was quite a good friend of mine. Always when I was in London, and I was frequently, I would see him; he would visit me when he was in America. There were others, too. I remember going into the office of Walter Leaf, a distinguished London banker, and finding him during what might have been supposed to be the busiest hour of his day, pecking away at a typewriter rather slowly. He was making, quite for his own amusement, a translation of some ancient Greek writing. I thought of James Loeb, then, and of the love of the classics that had impelled him to retire from a partnership in Kuhn, Loeb & Company. Really, there is a great deal of significance to that. Sadly enough, it is our national characteristic to devote ourselves entirely to work, in the erroneous belief that someday we shall do what we wish to do. The time to do that is now.

Lord Revelstoke of Baring Brothers was another London banker who had my high regard. Mr. Stillman admired him; he was interested in Mr. Stillman. Lord Revelstoke always entertained me at his house in London, and frequently in the company were the governors of the Bank of England. I recollect my first meeting with him. It was sometime before 1907.

I had conceived the idea that it would be a good thing for large American banks to carry in their portfolios a certain amount of British consols and so, in any period of strain, to be in a position to borrow money in London against consols. No matter what happened in America we would, I felt, be able to offer the finest collateral that there was in the money world. I had talked over the idea with Mr. Stillman. It had appealed to him. He had not known much about consols, so I went to London to study the consol market.

What the English did was to consolidate their loans into one type of obligation and this was the thing called a consol; it was the premier security, an obligation of the British Government. Next to gold itself, a consol was the safest thing into which one might transmute a fortune. Surprisingly enough, there was no such thing as a piece of paper called a consol; when you bought them your name was registered at the Bank of England, opposite the amount you owned. Well, I arranged to have consols registered in the name of the City Bank, and then I sold to other hanks our certificates, thus permitting these others to share in the arrangement. We sold a good many millions of those certificates, but consols declined a little, and we found that we had lost a little money through an investment in the world's supreme security. However, that was how I met Lord Revelstoke.

Well, we had moved into the new building late in December, and about three weeks afterward, on January 12, 1909, I was elected president. Mr. Stillman, who was in Paris, became the chairman of the board. My new salary was $50,000. I was forty-five years old. And in six moves from overalls I had become the head of the country's biggest bank.

Of course I am proud that I was able to do that, but I have never ceased to wonder whether I was able to do it because I was Vanderlip, or because I was an American. However, in those days I had other matters to worry about. As it happened, there was brewing a scheme to create in New York a consolidation of banks that would rob the National City Bank of its enviable first position. If I was any good at all I had to block that, even if J. Pierpont Morgan was behind it; and he was.

THE NEW PRESIDENT OF THE CITY BANK

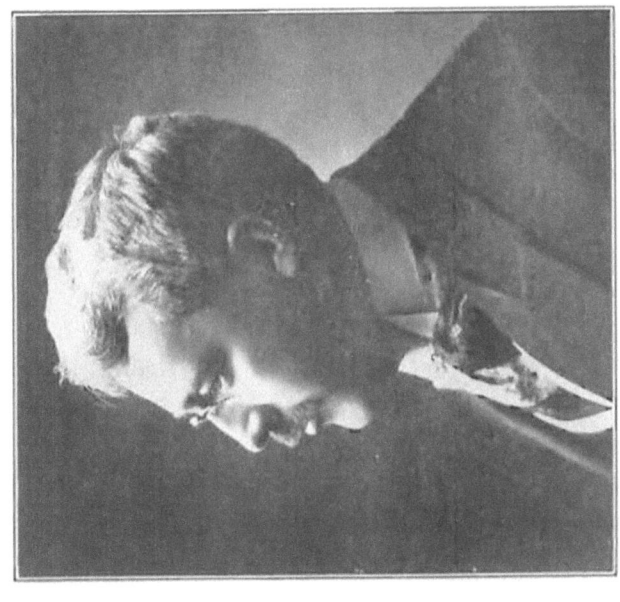

FRANK A. VANDERLIP SOON AFTER HE WENT INTO THE NATIONAL CITY BANK.

FRANK A. VANDERLIP AFTER HE BECAME PRESIDENT OF THE NATIONAL CITY BANK.

CHAPTER XIX
THE ELDER MORGAN AS AN ALLY

FOR a number of years, between the City Bank, the First National, and J. P. Morgan & Company, there was an agreement that on any issue of securities originated by any of the three, the originating house was to have 50 percent, and each of the other two was to have 25 percent. There were other arrangements that reflected the existing balance in the money power in Wall Street. Personally, I attached a great deal of importance to the fact that the City Bank was the biggest bank in the country. Mr. Stillman attached even more, I think, to a state of good-will among the big houses. He was constantly urging upon me the importance of keeping on pleasant and cooperative relations with all the important interests. He would remind me, over and over, that this meant a great deal for the nation in the development he felt was bound to occur in the succeeding years. I, too, believed in cooperation, but a situation began to develop that threatened our place as the nation's first bank. Those responsible, I felt, were partners in J. P. Morgan & Company.

The Bank of Commerce was really the troublesome factor. After the insurance investigations that brought to the forefront of American life the vigorous, acute and persistent Charles Evans Hughes, there had been an unmeasured shift of banking power. Harriman, as it happened, had bought control of the Equitable Life, which in turn owned control of the Bank of Commerce. All during 1910, the Bank of Commerce was a cloud on my horizon. At intervals I would hear of new plans for dealing with that rival bank, owned by the insurance company; each scheme was designed to make it more important in New York. In February, I recall, I had a conference at the Morgan offices with Mr. Morgan, Jr., and Harry Davison. We talked behind closed doors in a back room.

They were fearful, they told me, that the Bank of Commerce would become a derelict in the financial sea unless the house of Morgan took command of it. Their plan was for Mr. J. P. Morgan, Sr., to retire from the board of the Bank of Commerce; then a finance committee was to be formed, consisting of Mr. Morgan, Jr., Davison, Paul Morton, Mr. Peabody of the Mutual, Woodbury Langdon, Mr. Snyder of the Bank of Commerce and Jacob H. Schiff. I sniffed at that as suspiciously as a wild horse inhaling strong odors on a prairie wind.

I said the plan appeared to me a very radical step; that I thought it settled forever any question of consolidation of the City Bank and the Commerce; that if there was any reason for discussing such a consolidation as that, it ought to be discussed promptly, before this other action was taken. I told them the Bank of Commerce was directly competitive with the City Bank in every way and that putting J. P. Morgan and Company behind it could not but dissipate the value of their connections with the City Bank.

THE ELDER MORGAN AS AN ALLY

What I urged upon them was that Mr. Stillman ought to have time to consider any deal involving the Bank of Commerce.

Davison and Jack Morgan told me plainly that delay was impossible; action had to be taken at the meeting of the Bank of Commerce Board on the following day. Then I went uptown and saw Mr. Morgan, Sr., in his library. I told him that I regarded the action proposed as of the very greatest importance to the City Bank.

"Mr. Morgan," I said, "I feel it is my duty to say in the strongest way I can that this matter should be held up until you can discuss it with Mr. Stillman."

"Impossible," he said. "Mr. Stillman will approve this entirely. My loyalty to the City Bank is as great as my loyalty to the firm of J. P. Morgan and Company."

"This step with the Bank of Commerce is one not easily retraced. It is much simpler to wait until Mr. Stillman has given his approbation."

"You should trust me to do what is right," said Mr. Morgan. "I would cut off my right hand before I would injure you or Mr. Stillman. You can count on that absolutely. But there are endless complications; the difficulties we are having with the Insurance Commissioner, the attitude of Schiff, the hostility of Ryan to our plan, make it quite unwise to wait."

"I regret," I said, "that I was not given more notice of the intention. The Bank of Commerce stands squarely face to face with us in competition. If Morgan and Company get behind the Bank of Commerce your pride will be staked on making the Bank of Commerce bigger and bigger."

He repeated what his san had said to me, that I ought not to feel concerned about the Bank of Commerce becoming larger than the City Bank. I told him, as pleasantly as I could with the force I felt the situation called far, that its position as the biggest bank was of the utmost importance to the City Bank.

My cables to Mr. Stillman must have alarmed him because I found it necessary to assure him with further cable messages that the interviews I had had, while firm, were entirely pleasant. I told him, further, that it was a possible thing far Morgan and Company to put the Bank of Commerce ahead of the City Bank in deposits any time they chose; they could do it with the deposits of trust companies they controlled and with railroad accounts.

The matter dragged along then, without serious developments, until there were only forty-eight hours left of the old year, but what I learned then made me feel that 1911 would be anything but Happy New Year for me unless I went speedily into action. The new plan was a proposal by Mr. Jack Morgan and Henry Davison. Their suggestion was that a pool be formed to purchase the Equitable Life Assurance Society's holdings of the Bank of Commerce stock. President Snyder was to resign from the Commerce and the bank was to be merged with the Chase Bank into an institution that beyond question would overshadow the City Bank. I began to swell with something very much like rage. We were to be included in the pool, along with Morgan and Company, the First National Bank and Kuhn, Loeb & Company. Why Kuhn, Loeb & Company? They were too strong and had not heretofore been included in our banking group. My indignation increased.

I remember now how vigorously I crushed my hat on my head and started forth. So deeply did I breathe on that cold day as I strode along Wall Street to the Morgan offices that I am sure that any who observed me must have thought there was a lot of smoke blended with the frosty breaths that snorted from my nostrils. Happily, I had the good sense to cool off as I began the interviews. We had recognized the Morgan House as the head of the investment field and I had been supposing that Mr. Morgan recognized the National City as the greatest bank. Second place for us? You can be sure I was made indignant by the proposal.

Harry Davison and Mr. Jack Morgan sat down with me. I told them that, without indicating for the moment any opinion in regard to the fundamental proposition, I was curious to know what led them to include Kuhn, Loeb in the matter. They quoted Mr. Baker as believing it was necessary. They said they wanted to have me talk with Mr. Morgan, Sr., and with Mr. Baker, and as I wanted to play for time I cut this interview short. They desired a further talk in an hour.

In the meantime, I saw William Rockefeller and Mr. Sterling. Both seemed to feel there was no use attempting to combat the issue; that the best thing for us to do was to acquiesce as cheerfully as possible. The important thing, they felt, was to play for a third of the purchase. The way to get a third was to keep Kuhn, Loeb out of the transaction. They had no objections to Kuhn, Loeb, but they did want a third of

THE ELDER MORGAN AS AN ALLY

the purchase for the City Bank. I returned then for an interview with Mr. Morgan, Sr., Mr. Baker, Mr. Jack Morgan and Mr. Davison. In my own mind there was no agreement whatever with the view of William Rockefeller that there was nothing left to do but acquiesce.

The interview started off fortunately.

"I am ready to put my arms around you, "began the elder Mr. Morgan, "for the stand you are taking about Kuhn, Loeb." He clearly did not want in this matter to make partners of them. Mr. Baker at once coincided with Mr. Morgan's view, saying that on further reflection he had concluded the thing ought to be done without Kuhn, Loeb. The others then coincided very heartily and there was, as I wrote to Mr. Stillman, "enthusiastic shelving of the Kuhn, Loeb part of the program."

But I had only begun.

"I am still in an unhappy frame of mind," I said, addressing myself to Mr. Morgan, Sr. "I feel that the City Bank by every right is entitled to keep its first position. Any plan evolved by itself, or its friends, that would make an institution larger than the City Bank—well, that would be unfortunate."

Breathing forth a blast of blue cigar-smoke, Mr. Morgan said: "Absolutely I agree with you!"

Never did a voice so gruff sound as sweet to me. I knew in that moment the full flavor of victory. Mr. Morgan was on my side! I grew to love him then and there. He was a great gentleman. What he thought was fair as between friends was the course you could know he would follow. Nevertheless, he was in his own soul, in his ego, a king; royalty. There were royal prerogatives and he knew how to exercise them. I do not mean to suggest that he surrendered; it simply happened that when he found that something in which he had acquiesced was displeasing to friends, he changed his mind and did it heartily.

It was left to Davison, J. P. Morgan, Jr., and myself to work out the details. In my letter reporting these happenings to Mr. Stillman I said, with complete accuracy, "Conditions were never more harmonious than they are at this moment between this institution, and Morgan's and the First National." In the end the merger did not occur at all and I became a member of the directorate of the Bank of Commerce and of its executive committee.

Photograph by Brown Brothers

J. P. MORGAN

CHAPTER XX

AN ADVENTURE WITH E. H. HARRIMAN

THE things that happen in a lifetime are apt to come crowding back into the memory with as little heed to order as cows herding up at a pasture-gate. Sometimes, though, the events have actually occurred that way. April 8, 1909, I wrote to Mr. Stillman, in Paris, "I have been so occupied for a few days with domestic affairs that I was unable to write you my usual weekly letter."

At Beechwood on a night near the end of March that year I was summoned to the telephone. It was a long-distance call from Chicago. In that time a voice relayed over such long stretches of wire would be faint, then loud, then faint again. By the tiniest thread of sound I learned that my mother was dying. She had developed pneumonia suddenly. Today, I might fly to Chicago in five hours, even less; then, the fastest way was by train.

I talked on the telephone with the president of the New York Central, William C. Brown. I told him the trouble I was in and he went into action. Within an hour an engine, a couple of empty coaches and a private Pullman car came roaring up the Hudson Valley, pausing at the Scarborough station just long enough for me to step aboard, alone. My wife could not go; she was required by the imminence of a new life in our family, to remain at home.

AN ADVENTURE WITH E. H. HARRIMAN

As I stepped down on the platform at Englewood and saw the concern in the blue eyes of my old friend and brother-in-law, Ed Harden, I knew I was too late. My mother had been dead for half an hour. Twenty-four hours later my grandmother, who was eighty-five, was told of the death of her daughter and herself died of shock. There was one funeral service. Soon afterward, when I had returned to Beechwood, I was holding in my arms a new bit of life, my youngest daughter, Virginia, who has become a Barnard graduate and efficiently attends me as a secretary.

Traveling was a part of my job because I never was the sort of banker to chain myself to a desk in a bank. I went to Europe often and, as a railroad director, I traveled thousands and thousands of miles every year under conditions designed to give me the feel of America. I had become a director of the Union Pacific; of all the roads of the Harriman system; also of the Hawley system, the Chesapeake & Ohio, the Missouri, Kansas & Texas, and some minor roads. I remember that at first when I had been invited to serve on the boards of some lesser railroads, and was rather eager for these fresh distinctions, Mr. Stillman had said, "No, don't accept. Wait. You will be offered seats of the best type." He was so right that, eventually, I found myself serving as director in about forty big corporations. Indeed, I think I overdid it, in spite of the fact that seats on such boards permitted me to be informed about things that never would have been revealed to me by the newspapers, or the other ordinary channels of information. The railroad directorates were especially valuable for the information one received at their board-meetings. I kept, through those relationships, a sensitive touch with business in different parts of the country. A group of men such as Harriman would have about him on a tour of his system, exchanged a lot of information. I knew what kinds of freight were moving, and what kinds were not moving. I even was informed as to the temper of the people in various parts of the country. And that reminds me of something!

Because I was a railroad director, when I traveled in those days I traveled habitually in a private car. I remember a particular trip of the directors of the C. & O. The scene was somewhere in West Virginia. I had become accustomed to the feel of a silk hat on my head, but I rather like to fancy that I had not forgotten what overalls were like. At any rate, our train had paused as we sat at dinner, as exposed in our plate-glass elegance as if we had been seated in the show-window of a department store. Outside of our car a group began to cluster on the slope of the hillside that rose steeply above us. They could look down upon us as we fed, quite as though they were looking into a bear-pit. The men of the group were in overalls; the few women wore sun-bonnets. We could hear them talking as the waiter placed the thick steak on the table. It was in a perfectly pleasant way that one of those spectators commented to some new-comer: "See how those sons of witches eat!" Of course, I may have misunderstood him.

I wanted in those days to see the inside of any bank with which I was doing business. I wanted to talk with men, not merely to exchange written communications. So, as I rode on those trips of inspection, I was something other than a railroad director. I was a banker, yes; and I was an American, but most of all I was a human being, seeing myself in the person of every small boy who might be observed standing ankle-deep in barnyard muck watching our incredible passage.

No single individual ever sees all of the United States. At best the most traveled person sees only sample areas of its vastness and the aviator who spans the continent in a day sees less of it than a man who attends a push-cart in some slum street-market. Mine, however, were journeys to be enjoyed as a rule, because of that peculiar comfort that one has in a private Pullman car. As a rule I slept in a real room with a real bed, and had about me familiar things so that the car would take on the snug feel of home. But what a home! As though the change had been accomplished by a wizard, each morning would bring to me and my companions a freshly exciting scene, with important personages arriving as visitors for breakfast; but at luncheon-time the world outside would be completely altered, and there would be other guests of consequence, and then dinner would be a quite separate adventure, even, perhaps, in another climate. The intelligences one encountered made those trips colorful and worthwhile. Out of a host of those who clamor for recognition, I find myself fixing my mind on Epes Randolph.

Mr. Randolph was a grand man, one who was peculiarly lovable. I am sure you might find a thousand men who would be as fully aware as I of his endearing qualities; but there was much more to him.

After developing tuberculosis he had moved to Arizona, in order to stay alive, but out there, despite his affliction, he went ahead with his work. It was he who built the Southern Pacific Railway of Mexico. It was no ordinary work; rather it was one to rate with the more heroic railroad-building jobs that helped to fix our part of the continent into a single nation. It was as though every mile of steel that was laid below the Rio Grande projected years into the past. He told me a story about it one time.

Camp-followers had accumulated in such numbers as to be troublesome. Every payday was followed by wanton revelry; among the gamblers, thieves and panders were some truculent gun-fighters. These people became so obstreperous that something had to be done. Randolph sent to the governor of the Mexican state a request for permission to arm a sufficient number of his engineers and foremen to keep order. Back came a letter as courteously phrased as if it had been written by a noble Spanish diplomat. The governor suggested that there were ways possibly better than the one proposed by Señor Randolph; it would be impolitic to arm men from the other side of the Rio Grande in order to keep order among Mexicans. The governor promised to come in person and look over the situation. He came, *muy hombre*, a half-pound of silver spur clinking at the heel of each fancifully stitched boot, and swept from his coal-black hair a sombrero wide as his shoulders. Strapped at his waist were two pearl-handled, hog-leg guns. He was of that great breed of men of Northwest Mexico, of Sonora, that have ruled all Mexico since the rise of Calles.

"Now, Sir," he said politely, "if you will please point out the people who have been giving you trouble, I will myself take care of the shooting."

That was a little strong for Randolph, and he found himself imploring the governor to use less sanguinary methods; which to the governor seemed almost like ingratitude. Epes Randolph was the kind of man who could make realities of the dreams of Harriman.

Another who greatly helped to give substance to Harriman's visions was Julius Kruttschnitt. Harriman had in Julius Kruttschnitt precisely the kind of a chief-of-staff he should have had. Harriman was rich in vision, in imagination; there was in him something of the quality which a poet brings to his work. But Kruttschnitt had absolutely no imagination. His implements were facts; he was a living index of all railroad facts. Kruttschnitt himself told me a story one time that illuminates his character somewhat. From a quite inconsequential beginning in railroad work he had risen to the post of division superintendent on a railroad that crossed Kansas.

In due course, the president of the railroad was reported as ready to make an inspection trip over the line. Young Kruttschnitt never had met this great personage who held in his hands the fate of all who worked for the railroad. He determined to be letter-perfect in his knowledge of his own division. He boned up on every possible statistic, until he knew the precise number of tie plates, rails, spikes, shovels, hand-cars, and every other piece of physical property for which he was responsible.

At last, early one frosty morning, the special train arrived at the station where he waited. The president, from his private car, stepped down to the platform and to young Kruttschnitt propounded a dismaying question; it was the only one he was not prepared to answer.

"What," asked the president, "is the temperature?"

Kruttschnitt, when I met him, had become a ruddy-faced man of great bulk and slow movements. He had become the catechist of a host of divisional superintendents. Kruttschnitt was the one who kept Harriman's railroads in tune. He was not a man to let enthusiasm run away with his judgment and that was something that made him the perfect complement of E. H. Harriman.

Harriman had the philosophy, the methods of an Oriental monarch. He was not easy on his subordinates. He did as he pleased, ruthlessly seizing every advantage that he saw, regardless of the rules that govern ordinary men. I recollect a time when Robert Scott Lovett was just about heartbroken by a thing that Harriman did. Judge Lovett had learned about a certain matter in the strictest confidence. It was important to his honor that that confidence not be violated, particularly from any quarter where violation of it would be harmful. Judge Lovett, who was general counsel of the Harriman roads, also felt obliged to tell Mr. Harriman what he knew. In doing so, he impressed upon him the confidential character of what he had told him. Mr. Harriman immediately made use of the information.

Judge Lovett, when he found this out, felt so dishonored by the occurrence that for a while he felt he must resign. He was, literally, grief-stricken and miserable.

"I don't see how you could have done such a thing to me," he chided Harriman in his bewilderment.

"I understand these things so much better than you do," retorted Harriman, in a tone such as he might have used to a small boy. He told Judge Lovett that with his old-fashioned sense of honor he could not hope to understand the higher levels of thought with which the Harriman intelligence was concerned. Then, with great emphasis, he said: "Of course, I can't respect a confidence that ties my hands in a matter of momentous consequence to the operations in which I am engaged. I must be the judge of what is right-in these things."

Well, I was not willing to let Mr. Harriman be the judge of right and wrong for me. There were times during his life, when I was sitting on the boards of his roads, when I opposed underwriting fees because I felt they were too high. As a director I believed my obligation of trusteeship ran to the stockholders, and not to Mr. Harriman. I have in mind recollections of occasions when it was pointed out to me, in a hurt tone, that the City Bank was sharing in those underwriting profits that I thought were too fat. I hope I do not sound mealy-mouthed now, because, actually I am trying to throw light upon something that was built into my character. Words that were spoken solemnly to me through the bearded lips of my father when I was small seem to have filled little reservoirs of emotion that have controlled many of my decisions.

Now it should be said that when a company is run by a strong, dominant executive, his Board of Directors usually is glad to vote for anything he wishes. Quite often, I suspect, directors have voted without troubling themselves to inquire as to the purpose behind some move they authorized. Indeed, I recollect an illuminating story Mr. Stillman once told me concerning the board of the New York Central, under the autocratic direction of Commodore Vanderbilt.

There had been a leak of some information to the public and Mr. Vanderbilt was greatly irked by it. It was information that never had reached the board. One director suggested, with something of a stutter, that the best way to stop further leakage was to elect the culprit to a place on the board; then he would not know anything worth leaking. Well, Harriman did not always take his directors into his confidence, either.

There came a day when Harriman was departing for Europe. The executive committee had a regular meeting scheduled for that day, but as Mr. Harriman's ship was to sail at noon, we were asked to meet at his house and then, in the afternoon, to finish the routine matters without his presence. Accordingly we gathered at his home, transacted some business of no great importance, and, after bidding him bon voyage, went down-town. Otto Kahn of Kuhn, Loeb & Company, remained behind so that he could go with Mr. Harriman to his ship. Mr. Kahn came from the ship to our meeting and reported that there was an important matter requiring our attention, something that Mr. Harriman had forgotten to mention.

The Union Pacific, Mr. Harriman had concluded, ought to sell something quite valuable which it owned j a large amount of Wells Fargo & Company stock. The reason relayed to the board by Mr. Kahn, from Mr. Harriman, was that competing railroads objected to the operation over their lines of an express company owned by a competitor railroad. We were told this was particularly true of the Chicago, Milwaukee & St. Paul Railway. Mr. Harriman, we were assured, desired the directors to authorize the sale of the express company stock. He wanted the thing done as soon as possible.

The matter had come before us with what I felt to be disturbing suddenness. I wanted to know how so much stock could be sold without loss. It was listed on the exchange, but because it was so closely held transactions in it rarely occurred. In spite of the fact that opposition to Mr. Harriman was akin to lèse majesté, I asked for more time to consider the proposal. So the matter was laid over.

Privately, then, I addressed some inquiries to friends on the board of the Chicago, Milwaukee & St. Paul Railway, and when I was told no objections of any kind had been raised, and that, further, there was no basis for objection, my view was strengthened that the proposed sale was extraordinary. My opposition became unyielding. One other director sided with me, and so the sale did not occur. Again and again it was brought up for consideration, but we stood fast.

Because of his power to shift railroad deposits, and for other obvious reasons, Mr. Harriman was an important figure in the eyes of Mr. Stillman, Mr. Sterling, and William Rockefeller. Any crotchet of Harriman was something that might, I knew, have unpleasant repercussions. I was entirely aware of this on a day when a friend came into the bank to inform me that Harriman had sailed from Europe for New York, after declaring that he was coming home for just one reason—to get my scalp.

Harriman came home, but on the surface there never was any unpleasantness between us. Eventually, at a price $4,500,000 higher than could have been obtained at the time it first was proposed to sell the Wells Fargo stock, the sale was made. I regard Harriman as a man of great ability who rendered service to the country, however selfishly he went about it. He built up his properties and extended them, usually with wisdom. When he fought he fought as statesmen fight, with all the forces at his command. The most important of those forces was money.

As early as 1907 I had found myself in hearty accord with Woodrow Wilson about this matter of the social value of publicity for the affairs of big corporations. He had stated publicly at that time that he thought the aggressive pursuit of trusts was due to the fact that the people were kept in ignorance of the affairs of the trusts. He had said further, and I still agree with him, that corporation lawyers injured the interests of their clients by counseling secrecy. Dr. Wilson at that time advocated the drafting of a statute that would compel officers of corporations to file for public inspection complete reports of directors' meetings. Well, there are some of us who have been on many boards who would say such reports might not reveal much. None of the big men of Wall Street could tolerate the thought of publicity when I arrived there. If they were suspicious of reporters, they were equally suspicious of men who would talk with reporters. Baker, Morgan, Stillman, habitually avoided journalists; it was an honorable but mistaken part of their creed. If I might be permitted to give a single piece of advice to my countrymen it would be to insist, as a national policy, on being given a better understanding of the affairs of business; after awhile, I think, "insiders" would include approximately all thrifty persons.

A great corporation carrying on a public service is not a private thing; it affects too many lives. From my earliest days as a reporter, when I had to cozen my way into stockholders' meetings by buying a single share of stock, I have felt that corporate secrecy generally was wrong. I thought then, and I think now, that corporation wealth would be better administered from the viewpoints of small stockholders, labor, and the public, if the affairs of corporations had a great deal more publicity. My views on this subject were considered radical by some of my close associates when I was president of the National City Bank. I remember when there was a discussion by the New York Clearing House of a proposal to create a special authority to be vested in a clearing house examiner. The idea behind that suggestion was that if a bank was not being run properly the clearing house members ought to know about it. I favored that; Mr. Stillman was horrified.

Everything in his character cried out against a proposal to admit somebody representing all the other banks into the affairs of the City Bank. I did not feel that there was anything then that might not be looked at; Mr. Stillman felt that advantage could be taken of us by some rival or some speculator if all our affairs were subjected to outside scrutiny. I felt that there was a greater risk for us in blinding ourselves to improper dealings in some other bank. It has been my experience that honest business men greatly outnumber dishonest business men. I have found that, usually, business is fairly conducted. It is because I am so sure of this that I think that publicity rather than a ceaseless flood of new laws is what we need. Publicity would sharply curb the grasping fellows.

AN ADVENTURE WITH E. H. HARRIMAN

MARVIN HUGHITT AND JULIUS KRUTTSCHNITT

CHAPTER XXI
A CONCLAVE ON JEKYL ISLAND

DESPITE my views about the value to society of greater publicity for the affairs of corporations, there was an occasion, near the close of 1910, when I was as secretive, indeed, as furtive as any conspirator. None of us who participated felt that we were conspirators; on the contrary we felt we were engaged in a patriotic work. We were trying to plan a mechanism that would correct the weaknesses of our banking system as revealed under the strains and pressures of the panic of 1907. I do not feel it is any exaggeration to speak of our secret expedition to Jekyl Island as the occasion of the actual conception of what eventually became the Federal Reserve System.

Congress, after 1907, had realized that something had to be done to strengthen our banking system. To provide itself with a better understanding of the problem, there had been appointed a joint commission of twenty-five members of both houses, under the chairmanship of Senator Aldrich, who was on the whole the best informed and the most dominant man in Congress on financial measures. This group had gone to Europe, had interviewed bankers and the heads of the central banks, and then, after a pleasant summer, they had returned to the

A CONCLAVE ON JEKYL ISLAND

United States without any definite idea of what they ought to do. Senator Aldrich did not know what they ought to do, either, although he really had been working hard for two years.

For me the beginning of the adventure, I should think, was a letter that came from Mr. Stillman in Paris. He said he had just had a long conference with Senator Nelson Aldrich (Zivil in our code) who was very keen to get to work on banking and currency revision. Aldrich, Mr. Stillman reported, regretted that Henry Davison of J. P. Morgan and Company and I had been unable to join him in Europe during the summer; he felt that over there we might have had plenty of time for our discussions, and been free from interruptions. In a moment of entire candor he would have said: "free from reporters." Mr. Stillman said he had told Mr. Aldrich that freedom from interruptions was essential, but that it could be accomplished by getting Davison and me down to his estate in Rhode Island without any one's knowing of it. That was Mr. Aldrich's plan as he left Paris. Mr. Stillman wrote me that I should make everything else subservient to giving my whole time and thought to a thorough consideration of the subject. He said Aldrich was persuaded that he could accomplish more by getting out of the Senate, so as to put the work of revision on a non-partisan basis. Mr. Stillman expressed to me his fear that after revision the banks might not be so well off. He wrote that from that time on Davison and I ought to follow the matter very closely, and keep in touch with Aldrich. Aldrich, I was informed, believed in some sort of centralization, but not in the establishment of a central bank such as France had. Mr. Stillman also reported to me that in his talk with Senator Aldrich he himself had not expressed any views, except as he had impressed on the senator his belief in the necessity of not being too much influenced by "our Wall Street point of view."

But would the electorate have believed that? I question their ability to do so. Just to give you a faint idea: Senator Aldrich was the father-in-law of John D. Rockefeller, Jr., and himself a very rich man. Once I had written to Woodrow Wilson at Princeton, inviting him to speak at a dinner. Wishing to impress him with the importance of the occasion, I had mentioned that Senator Aldrich also had been invited to speak. My friend Dr. Wilson had astonished me by replying that he could not bring himself to speak on the same platform with Senator Aldrich. He did come and make a speech, however, after I had reported that Mr. Aldrich's health would prevent him from appearing. Now then, fancy what sort of headlines might have appeared over a story that Aldrich was conferring about new money legislation with a Morgan partner and the president of the biggest bank.

On October 28, 1910, I wrote to Mr. Stillman in Paris: "Senator Aldrich met with what came very near being a severe, if not fatal automobile accident. You probably have seen the report of it in the papers. He was pretty well bruised, having cuts on each side of his face. He is very much better now, but the accident has naturally postponed the conference that was in mind. He will be about in a few days and Mrs. John D., Jr., tells me that they do not think there will be any serious effect from the accident."

As the time for the assembling of Congress drew near, Senator Aldrich became increasingly concerned about the report he must write on behalf of the joint monetary commission; likewise, there ought to be, he knew, a bill to present to the new Congress and none had been drafted. This was how it happened that a group of us went with him to the Jekyl Island Club on the coast of Georgia.

Since it would be fatal to Senator Aldrich's plan to have it known that he was calling on anybody from Wall Street to help him in preparing his report and bill, precautions were taken that would have delighted the heart of James Stillman. Those who had been asked to go were Henry Davison, Paul Warburg, Ben Strong, and myself. From Washington came A. Piatt Andrew, who was then an Assistant Secretary of the Treasury, and who now is a member of Congress from Massachusetts. We were told to leave our last names behind us. We were told, further, that we should avoid dining together on the night of our departure. We were instructed to come one at a time and as unobtrusively as possible to the railroad terminal on the New Jersey littoral of the Hudson, where Senator Aldrich's private car would be in readiness, attached to the rear end of a train for the South.

When I came to that car the blinds were down and only slender threads of amber light showed the shape of the windows. Once aboard the private car we began to observe the taboo that had been fixed on last names. We addressed each other as "Ben," "Paul," "Nelson," "Abe" (it is Abram Piatt Andrew). Davison and I adopted even deeper disguises, abandoning our own first names. On the theory that we were always right, he became Wilbur and I became Orville, after those two aviation pioneers, the Wright brothers. Incidentally, for years afterward Davison and I continued the practice, in communications, and when we were together.

The servants and the train crew may have known the identities of one or two of us, but they did not know all, and it was the names of all printed together that would have made our mysterious journey significant in Washington, in Wall Street, even in London. Discovery, we knew, simply must not happen, or else all our time and effort would be wasted. If it were to be exposed publicly that our particular group had gotten together and written a banking bill, that bill would have no chance whatever of passage by Congress. Yet, who was there in Congress who might have drafted a sound piece of legislation dealing with the purely banking problem with which we were concerned? Indeed, there were surprisingly few bankers, besides those of us who had been called together, who had given the special matters under consideration any thorough study whatever. Most bankers were reluctant to accept any change; George Baker was.

A CONCLAVE ON JEKYL ISLAND

We proceeded, in the rear room of that private car, to get to work as soon as the train was moving. That first discussion of the banking structure and of what ought to be done about it produced scraps of ideas as formless as the contents of a rag-bag. Everyone had some little piece of a project to throw on the table for discussion and every one's pet scheme encountered some other fellow's objection. We had traveled a good many miles without making much progress, when I told my companions of a piece of advice, as to the proper way to conduct a conference, that had been given me by Frank Trumbull, a dear friend of mine who was then the chairman of the board of the Chesapeake & Ohio Railway.

"What we ought to do first," I said, "is to set down those things about which we are agreed; then, one by one, we can take up those things about which we seem to disagree."

From then on we made swift progress. I was appointed amanuensis and in my paleolithic shorthand recorded those proposals which we all were ready to echo as we heard them; of course we knew that what we simply had to have was a more elastic currency through a bank that would hold the reserves of all banks.

We were taken by boat from the mainland to Jekyl Island and for a week or ten days were completely secluded, without any contact by telephone or telegraph with the outside. We had disappeared from the world onto a deserted island. There were plenty of colored servants but they had no idea who Ben and Paul and Nelson were; even Vanderlip, or Davison, or Andrew, would have meant less than nothing to them. There we worked in a club-house built for people with a taste for luxury. The live-oak trees wear fantastic beards of Spanish moss on Jekyl Island; in November brown leaves make its forests utterly charming. Without our ever stopping to hunt, deer, turkey and quail appeared on the table; there were pans of oysters not an hour old when they were scalloped; there were country hams with that incomparable flavor that is given to them in the South. We were working so hard that we ate enormously. We worked morning, noon and night.

We put in the most intense period of work that I have ever had. Sometimes Davison and Strong would be up at day-break to get a horseback ride, or a swim before breakfast, but right after breakfast the six of us would gather around the table and resume where our discussion had ended the previous midnight. We stuck to the plan of putting down on paper what we agreed upon; there was no back-tracking, no wrangling. Harry Davison was a splendid person to prevent wrangles in any company. Warburg, the best equipped man there in an academic sense, was so intense and apparently felt a little antagonism toward Aldrich, so that some of our moments of strain might have developed into real hindrance had it not been for Davison. Always he could be counted on to crack a joke just at the right moment to ease a strain. No telephones rang, none could bother us to ask for an opinion of the market, there were no directors' meetings, no interruptions whatever. Thanksgiving occurred during that week and we ate wild turkey with oyster stuffing and went right back to work. We gave, each of us, every bit of our mental energy to the job and I enjoyed that period as I never have enjoyed anything else. I lived during those days on Jekyl Island at the highest pitch of intellectual awareness that I have ever experienced. It was entirely thrilling.

As we dealt with questions I recorded our agreements in that shorthand I had first practiced with chalk on the tail stock of my lathe back in Aurora. If it was to be a central bank, how was it to be owned, by the banks, by the government, or jointly? When we had fixed upon bank ownership and joint control, we took up the political problem of whether it should be a number of institutions, or only one. Should the rate of interest be the same for the whole nation or should it be higher in a community that was expanding too fast and lower in another that was lagging? Should it restrict its services to banks? What open-market operations should be engaged in? Those were the sort of questions we dealt with, and finally, at the end of our week we had whipped into shape a bill that we felt, pridefully, should be presented to Congress. As I recall it, Warburg had some objections, but we were in substantial agreement on the measure we had created. We returned to the North as secretly as we had gone South. It was agreed that Senator Aldrich would present the bill we had drafted to the Senate. It became known to the country as the Aldrich Plan. Aldrich and Andrew left us at Washington, and

Warburg, Davison, Strong, and I returned to New York.

Congress was about to meet; but on a Saturday we got word in New York that Senator Aldrich was ill, too ill to write an appropriate document to accompany his plan. Ben Strong and I went on to Washington and together we prepared that report. If what we had done then had been made known publicly, the effort would have been denounced as a piece of Wall Street chicanery, which it certainly was not. Aldrich never was a man to be a mere servant of the so-called money-interests. He was a conscientious, public-spirited man. He had called on the four of us who had Wall Street addresses because he knew that we had for years been studying aspects of the problem with which it was his public duty to deal.

As is now well known, the bill we drafted did not get through Congress. Aldrich retired from the Senate, and then a Democratic majority came down to Washington along with Woodrow Wilson who had defeated President Taft. The platform on which he was elected contained a statement expressing the opposition of the Democratic Party to the Aldrich Plan or a central bank. There was a good deal of discussion about that. It was contended that originally the platform committee had agreed upon the statement: "We are opposed to the Aldrich Plan for a central bank."

Now, although the Aldrich Federal Reserve plan was defeated when it bore the name of Aldrich, nevertheless its essential points were all contained in the plan that finally was adopted. It provided an organization to hold the reserves of all member banks and arranged that they would always be ready to relieve a member-bank under pressure by rediscounting loans that it held. The law as enacted provided for twelve banks instead of the one which the Aldrich plan would have created; but the intent of the law was to coordinate the twelve through the Federal Reserve Board in Washington, so that in effect they would operate as a Central Bank. There can be no question about it: Aldrich undoubtedly laid the essential, fundamental lines which finally took the form of the Federal Reserve Law.

CHAPTER XXII
MILLIONAIRE

ALL the experiences with which my personality has been drenched, since I was born, have been working changes in me. A small boy is changed when for the first time he straddles a pony and thinks, "this exciting creature is mine." As a lad, in August I would drop watermelons over the fence into the hog-lot, and as the green spheres burst into vermilion lumps that pigs devoured, I was changed by what I then felt. The wretchedness of looking down into an open grave at the coffin of my father changed me. The feel against my flesh of grease-stained, gritty overalls, and the smells of a machine-shop—red-hot iron, cinders, new wood, tobacco juice—all those things put substance to my ego. Hours of newspaper reporting, the feel of my first dress-shirt bosom, a Government carriage at my disposal, awkwardness at parties, becoming a rich man's protégé, entering a bank; all the things that are indexed in seventy years of life have worked chemical changes in that which is labeled Frank Vanderlip. Naturally, then, I am disposed to admit that I was changed when I discovered that I had become a millionaire.

A million and a half dollars became mine almost with the swiftness with which it might have happened to Aladdin. I had come from Washington in 1901 possessing barely $2,000. In nine years I never had spent all my income, and I had made some beyond my salary as a bank officer. Then I had scented a rich opportunity in a Texas land deal. There was a deposit of sulphur on the property. I made a substantial commitment of one or two hundred thousand dollars, as I recall it. I went into the venture with E. P. Swenson. He had large land interests in Texas and also commanded an active organization down there which could be relied on to develop the property on a sound basis. The speculation proved highly profitable for all who went into it. What we developed is called the Freeport-Texas Sulphur Company. A million and a half! I assure you that for me it was more than an entry in my account-book. It was a throbbing emotion.

Upon each of the six occasions when I was freshly aware that I was the father of a new personality, I grew excited; but I managed to do a day's work. I was forty-six when I had this experience of becoming a millionaire, so my appetites were under control. I did not indulge in a champagne celebration; that was not my way. I felt a sensation of pride, of well-being, of confidence in my ability henceforth to look after those for whose lives I was especially charged with responsibility. From boyhood I had been driven, always, by the haunting knowledge that I had dependents. Security for them was the thing I had been trying to buy with all my efforts. Now that I believed I had achieved that goal I felt, if the word is permitted, swell.

I never bought a yacht, I never bought a stable of race-horses, I never, so to speak, kicked up my own heels. Let me see, Narcissa was born in 1904,

Charlotte Delight in 1905, Frank Arthur, Jr., in 1907, Virginia Jocelyn in 1909. With plenty of money I could create a school for them! Education was what I had yearned for always and they should have it right at their front door. Kelvin Cox came along in 1912, and John Mann Vanderlip in 1916, and none of the six ever had to go off the premises to get into the Scarborough School. Eventually there was a school with 300 pupils and all told I contributed to it about half a million dollars. That, I confess, was luxury. Wherever I was, in Europe, on the ocean, on trains at night, I could feel comfortable in the knowledge that my children would all be there waiting for me when I should return to play with them. But the truth is that by the time I really could play with them, most of them had gone right ahead and grown up.

On hot days, after a train ride from the city, from the Scarborough station I would walk, invariably, up the steep hill—not a short climb—to the lower fringe of the wide lawn. After further hill-climbing when I was in front of the house, beneath a tree as big as Charter Oak, I would be met by a man who used to be a London omnibus-driver. For sixteen years after 1910 Saunders was our butler, and something more; to the children he was "Saundie," the to-be-wheedled keeper of the latch-keys. When he met me on those days he would have for me in a tall and frosty glass, a fluid white and crinkly as lamb's wool. He called it a "Ramos Fizz" and he would assure me that for taking the curse off a stuffy day it was the finest drink that could be concocted. The juice of half a lime, I believe, was put in a glass with two teaspoons of powdered sugar and two ounces of cream. The glass was loaded with ice and squirted full of vichy. If there was concealed in, it a jigger of gin, that was entirely the fault of Saunders; I swear I never said gin to him in all the years of our association.

Whenever Mr. Stillman was in the country for a visit Beechwood was a likely place to look for him. He had kindly acted as my agent in the purchase of some old paintings, and he could enjoy the beauty of my Van Dyke as he could not relish his own. He told me one time that when he looked at his own paintings, in spite of anything he might do, he could see in plain figures on the canvas the annual interest figured upon the cost of the picture. Of course, he smiled when he said that but I am quite sure it, was not entirely a whimsical invention.

We had in Mr. Stillman a most sensitive guest. Our car and chauffeur, Eddie Mahon, were at the disposal of Mr. Stillman. For a month one time Eddie knew what it feels like to grow rich; Mr. Stillman was tipping him with a lavish hand; ten, twenty, fifty dollars at a time, until he could not contain in his lungs all the air he wished to breathe. Then, probably through some household slip, Eddie received instructions to make an all-day trip somewhere to pick up some visiting member of the family. When he returned he discovered, to his intense chagrin, that because he had been deprived of the car Mr. Stillman's feelings had been hurt. Thereafter, when Mr. Stillman wished to go anywhere, even for a journey of less than a mile, he would telephone to the home of his daughter, Mrs. Percy Rockefeller, and ask for a car to be sent to him. For Eddie it was an earthquake in Eldorado.

Perhaps that is why, in later years, he has enjoyed telling on the Rockefeller chauffeur. It seems that one day as Mr. Stillman stepped from his daughter's car at the station he chided the chauffeur, saying:

"You did not brush the car-cushions last night."

"Oh, yes sir, I did sir."

"No you didn't," contradicted Mr. Stillman. "See here!" From the soft crevice between the seat and the side of the car he drew out a green bill. "I had put a present in there for you," he explained. But what shocked the servants for miles around, as the gossip traveled in our part of the world, was the fact that Mr. Stillman then tucked the recovered bill back into the Stillman trousers.

Once I had Mr. Stillman and William Rockefeller come to Beechwood for luncheon on a Sunday so that they could meet my highly entertaining houseguest, Dr. Woodrow Wilson, of Princeton. The conversation was guided by me into a discussion of national affairs because I was proud of my friend Wilson. I did not get a reaction from William Rockefeller, but Mr. Stillman, by what he heard, was profoundly disturbed. He held me by the sleeve as he said, close to my ear, "He is not a great man."

During the long acquaintance that began in 1903, Wilson and I had many fine, stimulating talks. In our conversations he never challenged my viewpoint on the ground that I was a banker; on the contrary, I had the feeling he was quite willing to learn from me about the banking and currency problems. There were practical matters involved which could be dealt with only by banking minds. However, Mr. Wilson ceased to be a trustee of the Carnegie Foundation when he left Princeton to become Governor of New Jersey, and so we saw less of each other; as he moved to the front in politics we had no contacts that I recall.

After he had been nominated for the presidency, we were on the same train one time when I was coming North from Florida. George Harvey came back to my private car which was at the rear end of the train. "I want to bring Wilson back here so you can talk over banking legislation," said Harvey, vibrant with enthusiasm.

"All right," I said, "I'll be glad to."

Harvey left my car and went forward; he never came back.

During the 1912 campaign, William Gibbs McAdoo came to me a number of times to discuss one thing or another on behalf of Mr. Wilson. Chiefly, as I recall it, what was wanted was advice on banking and currency statements to be made by Mr. Wilson from the platform. These conversations had a sub-rosa quality that, in view of my previous relations with Mr. Wilson, annoyed me. I told Mr. McAdoo I was unwilling to talk to Mr. Wilson through the kitchen-door.

Very soon afterward I got an invitation from Mr. Wilson to meet him at McAdoo's house in Hastings-Upon-Hudson, not far from Scarborough. We had a long talk together, alone, and quite in the warm tone of our old friendship. He gave me renewed assurances of his splendid feeling for me and of his belief in my understanding of the currency problem and kindred matters.

"But you don't understand politics," he said. "It does not make any difference what I think ought to be done; I've first got to be elected in order to do these things."

He repeatedly assured me of the confidence he had in me but I have believed since that he was just smoothing my hair with one hand and keeping me at arm's length with the other. Now I, myself, did not feel that it was a crime to be the president of the National City Bank, but Mr. Wilson felt that it would be a political crime if he were caught talking with me.

I don't like that; it seems to me to reflect a significant weakness in our type of civilization that the specialist—whether biologist or banker—is so often because of mass prejudice shut out of those conferences in which laws are made dealing with his specialty. Mr. Wilson, of course, was a man subject to violent prejudices and swift suspicions. When these were aroused what happened was akin to that which occurs in the revolution-torn countries to the south of us when cavalry raiders ride into town. Then there is a great banging as merchants pull down steel curtains to cover the front of their shop windows. In the case of Mr. Wilson the steel curtains were in his mind.

While Congress was shaping up what became the Federal Reserve Act, Harry Davison, Ben Strong and I were called to Washington to offer testimony regarding the proposed legislation. When we arrived in Washington, my friend, Milton Ailes, told us the hotels were all full and he had secured rooms for us at the Army and Navy Club. That seems unimportant but it turned out to have some significance. On the stationery of the Club I wrote a note to Mr. Wilson and sent it, by my secretary, Ned Currier, to the White House. President Wilson refused to see us. I had a note from him in which he said, "A conference such as you suggest would be of no advantage to any of us, or to the ends that Congress is now seeking to serve."

Just why Mr. Wilson felt this way was long a puzzle to me, but later I learned that it was an illustration of his suspicious turn of mind. He had been having a great row with Senator O'Gorman. None of us was aware of that further than what we had possibly gleaned from newspaper headlines. We had no interest in it. Senator O'Gorman, however, was living at the Army and Navy Club and when Mr. Wilson received a note from me written on Army and Navy Club stationery, he jumped to the conclusion that we were in cahoots with Senator O'Gorman. At least, that is what I was later told by one of his closest advisers who had learned that Mr. Wilson thought he sniffed some kind of a Wall Street trap in the fact that the four of us happened to be at the Club.

CHAPTER XXIII
RECRUITING FOR THE CITY BANK

I WAS always on the lookout for men for the City Bank's service. Whether I was in other banks, in the homes of friends, or encountering people on steamships or trains I felt that I was, after a fashion, Fortune's adjutant for some people.

An offer from the City Bank was something calculated to tempt most men. I am reminded now that when I reported to Mr. Stillman in 1914 about an offer I had made to a first-rate bank executive of Boston, I said: "The City Bank can have almost anybody it wants." That was true; the big problem was to find out whom we really wanted. Eventually in that hunt for qualified men it became almost a habit to offer a man $25,000 to start; a better salary depended on what he might show in the way of effort and intelligence.

About the first man I brought into the bank was John Gardin. I had known him in Chicago when I was a reporter and he was manager of the foreign exchange department of Lyman Gage's bank, the First National. He was made a vice-president in 1909 when I became president. The next one I brought into the bank had been my assistant when I was financial editor of the *Tribune*; John H. McEldowney. Between this sound thinking, faithful Scotchman and myself there was a strong bond of sympathy. Our backgrounds were alike except that when I had been a shop apprentice he had been' a country school-teacher. When he came to the City Bank he knew nothing of practical banking, but he quickly caught the idea of banking and he won Mr. Stillman's confidence as completely as he had always had mine. In five years he became a vice-president, but he wore himself out in the bank's service and in 1911, after Mr. Stillman had sought Europe over trying to find doctors who might mend his leaky heart, he died.

I brought Sam McRoberts from Chicago where he had been the treasurer of Armour & Company. I brought Joseph Talbert who had been for eleven years with the Commercial National Bank of Chicago, and I think I have never met a man with a more expert knowledge of commercial banking, by which I mean all those self-liquidating transactions which are so vital to a thriving nation. These men, like myself before them, and like James Perkins in 1914, came into the bank's service as vice-presidents.

Jim Perkins was an Albany banker when my attention was first directed to him. After I had completed an arrangement with Perkins I spoke about him to two in the bank who at once became almost delirious with joy. Jimmy Stillman, who was a vice-president himself, had been a classmate of Perkins at Harvard. Perkins (he stands inches above six feet and has extraordinary wrists and heavy forearms) had been a crew man and he was a hero to my secretary, Currier. Currier had been captain of the Harvard baseball team of 1909. Concerning Perkins I wrote to Mr. Stillman, on June 5, 1914, a prophecy that "his selection will be one of the best things I have ever been able to do for the bank." Twenty years after, when James Perkins has become the chairman of the board of the City Bank, I take pride in seeing my judgment so well confirmed. I know no man in the business world with sounder character or finer moral qualities.

I had some really astonishing luck with young fellows. Quite often it is possible to mark a boy and say, "this one has the stuff in him." Charlie Rich had it; his story begins, for me, on that day in 1893 when he walked into the office of Ed Harden on the grounds of the World's Columbian Exposition in Chicago. Harden was the reporter in charge of the *Tribune's* bureau. This lad had been peddling a bundle of newspapers carried under his arm but he said he had come to apply for the job of office-boy; Harden's office-boy, he explained, was quitting. That was news to Harden but when it was confirmed this applicant, Charlie Rich, was hired. I do not mean to suggest that he was a Ragged Dick; on the contrary he was not even shabby and he was certainly handsome; dark as a gypsy. After the fair closed we got him a job with the Illinois Trust Company and later on, because of his brightness, I brought him to Washington. When Mr. Gage resigned as head of the Treasury Department I brought Rich to New York. That boy became a vice-president of the City Bank, but more than that, he became a person in whom J. P. Morgan saw rare qualities. Twice Rich was invited over there and if he had gone he certainly would have become a partner. Once Jacob Schiff tried to induce him to come with Kuhn, Loeb & Company.

RECRUITING FOR THE CITY BANK

A scene comes into focus now: it was 1914 and Rich had stepped into the new Morgan bank building. J. P. Morgan, Jr., by then the head of the firm, was just about to leave as Rich offered his congratulations on the completion of the building. Mr. Morgan put the crook of his walking-stick around the neck of Charlie Rich.

"Of course I'm glad to be in this new building," he said, "but I would have been much more glad if something of interest to us both had happened before we came in." Rich had refused all those outside offers because of his loyalty to me. Afterward, to my lasting disappointment, his health broke down. Toward him I felt as Mr. Gage and Mr. Stillman, in turn, had felt toward me.

It was always exciting to me to realize that the green eye-shade of any one of the hundreds of young fellows in the bank might mask the face of a James Stillman of the future. Any messenger or office-boy who came into my presence was as interesting in his potentialities as a lottery-ticket. One day a document I called for could not be produced from the files. Well, I roared about it. A gangling boy of about fifteen or sixteen heard my roars. The next morning he came to place the desired document on my desk.

"Where did you find this?"

"In the file. Wrong index."

"When did you find it?"

"Oh, about day-light." He had been at it all night.

His name, he told me, was Bill Morrison and naturally I had my eyes on him from that day forward. He became chief trader for the National City Company, one of its most intensely occupied employees, buying and selling bonds. As long as the City Company lasted you might have seen him using a battery of fifteen or twenty telephones to make his trades. He was a find! Today he is a vice-president of the East River Savings Bank.

Early in my association with the bank I needed a typist. I telephoned the Remington Typewriter Company and Tommy Thompson, the young man they sent, thereafter took earnest hold of every bit of work that was tossed his way. He had charge, finally, of the Government bond department; a $250,000,000 business.

Scores who had been messengers, office-boys, or clerks were rising in the organization as we began the year 1914. The six hundred who worked there then worked hard, but they were not fear-ridden in the presence of the boss. I was the boss and they addressed me, a great many of them, affectionately. They called me Mr. Van. And I was proud. I was the coach and they were the team. Mr. Stillman, writing to me, frequently used another figure of speech. He would tell me that the bank was our mother. I was prepared then for years of growth, but not in my wildest dream did I have any vision of the fantastic expansion that was coming.

CHAPTER XXIV
WALL STREET ADJUSTS ITSELF TO WAR

ON an afternoon late in July, 1914, before there had, been any declaration of war, James Stillman stepped out of my office and stopped beside the desk of Ned Currier, my secretary, whom he liked. There was a pencil in his hand and through the open door I saw that he was shaking it vigorously in front of Currier's face as he exclaimed passionately, "The Germans cannot violate my beautiful France."

In the previous month, just before sailing for New York, Mr. Stillman had written me from Paris to say that banks were refusing credit and forcing merchants to pay up their notes. Money was closer than it had been since the Franco-Prussian War. He had been told by reliable parties that pearl necklaces of any considerable value could be purchased for cash at 60 percent of what they formerly had brought. Such things were as significant to him as a falling barometer to an experienced mariner, yet he continued to hope for peace.

Later on this July afternoon as we rode in my automobile from the city along the Hudson toward Scarborough, Mr. Stillman was clearly laboring under strain. He was to remain with me overnight. At Tarrytown he turned abruptly to Currier.

"I can't stand this suspense any longer. Would you mind returning to New York?"

"Certainly not, sir," said Currier.

"I want you to take my keys and go back to the bank. Get from my desk a little, red Morocco leather code-book that I use for communicating with Lord Revelstoke of Baring Brothers. Cable him, signing my code name. Ask if there will be war."

Currier could not get a train from Tarrytown before seven and would not reach the bank until about nine at night. By that time it would be 2:00 A.M. in London. There could not be any reply until morning. Nevertheless, Currier was characteristically cheerful and willing as he turned his back on his dinner.

The next morning at the bank there arrived a cable message from London. It was from Lord Revelstoke and when it had been decoded Mr. Stillman read aloud to me: "War is inevitable."

Germany and Austria started war against Serbia on Tuesday; by Friday, although actual war remained localized along the Serbian front, it was obvious the situation of all nations was wholly critical. On the advice of bankers it was decided to close the New York Stock Exchange. There had begun at New York a heavy export of gold; to get that gold European owners were selling out their American securities and as always when sellers greatly outnumber buyers, prices were dropping. A fearful strain existed in every part of the financial mechanism.

As in 1907 the foremost problem was how to create an extraordinary amount of sound currency. Some of us began to think at once that arrangements should be made for the issuance of Clearing House Certificates; but from Washington came word that William Gibbs McAdoo, the Secretary of the Treasury, desired that we should avoid doing this. He was confident such a step would be unnecessary because of the greater elasticity given to our currency by the passage of the Aldrich-Vreeland Act. This untried measure was a forerunner of the Federal Reserve legislation. Under the provisions of the Aldrich-Vreeland Act National Banks were permitted, during an emergency, to take out National bank-notes, temporarily, against the deposit of self-liquidating commercial paper; that is, notes given to banks by people engaged in commerce. Mr. McAdoo asked for a conference, in Washington, with representatives of the Clearing House Association. Accordingly, on Friday night two men departed for the capital to talk with him. One was Francis L. Hine, the president of the First National Bank (Baker's institution), who was president of the Clearing House Association; the other was William Woodward, president of the Hanover National Bank, and who was acting chairman of the important Clearing House Committee in place of Albert H. Wiggin, who as it happened was in Europe at this time. I was a member of the committee.

Saturday brought to us the shocking news that the Central Powers had declared war on Russia. During the preceding night I had come to the conclusion that the Government was too optimistic in its view of what could be accomplished under the Aldrich-Vreeland Act. SO, I arranged to meet at the Clearing House Association with the members of the Clearing House

Committee who were in New York; three, of course, were absent, Woodward, Hine and Wiggin. I pressed on the others my view that because of limiting conditions the Treasury could not practically distribute all of the emergency currency it was being contended was ready for shipment from Washington to New York. A bank, I knew, could get these National banknotes only in proportion to the total amount of commercial loans which it might have, and would use it only as it individually thought desirable.

My associates on the committee had been informed there would be more than $150,000,000 of this emergency currency available on Monday morning. I was persuaded there would be considerably less. So, I determined to get some firsthand information from one who had long been my eyes and ears in Washington; that was Milton E. Ailes, then a vice-president of the Riggs National Bank.

I should explain now that Ailes was my devoted friend and operated for the City Bank in Washington a rather special service. He kept me posted and, furthermore, he wrote for our monthly circular all the data of legislation and Treasury Department orders which might be of interest to our correspondents and bond customers. Beyond these duties he performed important duties at the Treasury Department for our correspondents; arranging for the withdrawal of bonds from deposit and the retirement of bank-notes and similar matters. If the service was extraordinary this was because Ailes was an extraordinary person.

Born in Sidney, Ohio, and reared there by a school teacher father, Ailes had gone to Washington during the Cleveland administration to become a Treasury messenger. When I came there he was the secretary to an Assistant Secretary. I was prejudiced at first—he was a Bryan Democrat; but he was full of homely and humorous Lincolnesque stories of his boyhood; he was capable and he was utterly loyal. Before long he became my secretary and when I left the department to come to the City Bank, Mr. Gage arranged for him to be made my successor as Assistant Secretary. Milton Ailes knew the Treasury Department as the average man knows the inside of his hat.

From the clearing house I called Currier and directed him to talk with Ailes over the private telephone-wire that linked the National City Bank with the Riggs National in Washington. I told Currier to ask Ailes to find out precisely how much of the emergency currency was available for each New York bank. I specified that I wanted the information bank by bank; not merely a round sum. Late in the afternoon I got word from Ailes; the information was dismaying.

Instead of more than $150,000,000 as we bad been led to believe, there was no more than $98,000,000 of emergency currency available for New York banks, and there was no certainty each bank would use the full amount available for it. For some banks in a position to use much there was little; for others that would make use of little there was excess.

"But how could McAdoo be mistaken?" asked my associates on the Clearing House Committee.

I could only tell them at the moment how sure I was that we could rely on the figures sent by Milton Ailes. The fact was that he had gone directly to the custodian of the emergency currency; wisely, he had avoided the Comptroller of the Currency because that was the blustering John Skelton Williams who bore for Ailes a jealous grudge. That grew out of something with which I was concerned.

Before he had been named Comptroller, Williams had been a banker in Richmond, Virginia. He was also a director of the Seaboard Airline Railroad. A group of us had bought control of this road and began to feel that Mr. Williams, who held over as a fellow-director, was a most cantankerous man. At board-meetings we would spend our time listening to Williams. When we returned to our offices he would deluge us with mail. He got to be so very trying that when the annual meeting approached I simply said I could not sit on the board with him. I am sorry to have forgotten the name of the inspired observer who first pointed out that John Skelton Williams could strut sitting down. However, Williams retired from the Seaboard directorate and in his place Milton Ailes was elected. Thereafter, Williams mistakenly believed he had been displaced simply because I wished to oblige my friend Ailes. Naturally, then, one of his great objectives when he became Comptroller was to use his authority to revenge himself on Ailes and, if possible, on me.

The Riggs Bank had been handling real estate mortgages and he got after the bank on that account. At the City Bank I maintained a card-index showing the principal figures of the statements of all the National Banks. From one of those cards I could tell how a particular bank's loans were going, how its deposits were running; I could get the whole picture at a glance. This information was made public by law; it was in no way private. We simply had happened to have enough enterprise to go and get it; but Comptroller Williams raised a most awful roar about the privileges that the City Bank had been accorded. In his eagerness to get something more compromising he was constantly alert. I know that his bank examiners surreptitiously carried papers out of the City Bank; bank examiners have no right to remove papers, but, prodded by Williams, their boss, they acted as his spies and we had some pretty tough times. Once, I remember, I wrote a letter to him that was filled with all the scorn I felt for him and it contained a good deal of defiance. Currier read it aloud to me with appropriate histrionics. Then he said:

"Now that we have gotten that off your mind, let us tear up the letter and drop it into the waste-basket." That was what we did and it was the right thing to do; my job was to run the City Bank; not to carry on a vendetta.

In the light of the figures compiled for me by Ailes it was perfectly clear we should have to issue Clearing House Certificates on Monday morning. In order to do that it was necessary to call a meeting of representatives of all member-banks; we called the meeting and fixed the time for 9:30, Monday.

On Sunday the German Army began marching into Belgium.

On the morning of that Sunday I went to an informal meeting at the Metropolitan Club. Among those present were J. P. Morgan, Jr., Harry Davison,

Charlie Sabin, Gates McGarrah, James N. Wallace, and numerous other bankers.

J. Pierpont Morgan, Sr., had been dead for more than a year. Mr. Stillman, shy always, remained at his house in Seventy-second Street and at intervals Currier talked with him over the telephone.

Morgan and Davison sat quietly, close to a window, looking out into Fifth Avenue. From time to time a fresh bulletin was read aloud apprising us of some development overseas. We were waiting, all of us, for the return from Washington of Frank Hine and Will Woodward.

They came; and when our action of the day before, the decision to issue Clearing House Certificates, was reported to them they were about as angry as two gentlemen could be. In good faith they had pledged their word to McAdoo that no Clearing House Certificates would be issued, and it was small comfort to them to be told McAdoo was basing his judgment on erroneous information. The result of our discussion was that we determined to ask McAdoo to come to New York and bring Williams with him. As I was serving as chairman of the meeting I directed Currier to telephone the invitation. He reported back in a little while that the two officials would leave Washington on the Congressional Limited. Currier met them and brought them in my car to the Vanderbilt Hotel about nine o'clock Sunday night.

Aside from these two Government officials and the bankers, the only other persons allowed to be within earshot of the proceedings on that carefully guarded floor were Currier and my chief stenographer, Errol Horner.

Well, we had a fine row. Mr. McAdoo, whose forcefulness I have always admired, was at first courteous in his insistence that there was no need to issue Clearing House Certificates, but John Skelton Williams entered the discussion with a challenging manner that was hard to endure.

"Just how much emergency currency is practically available, Mr. Williams?" I asked him.

His answer came like a roll of drums, "One hundred and fifty-four million dollars, sir."

"Well," I said, "your information does not coincide with the figures on the list that I have received from our correspondent-bank in Washington. The amount yesterday afternoon was ninety-eight millions. The amount which will practically be used is far less."

Both McAdoo and Williams were made explosively indignant by the bare suggestion that I presumed to be better posted than themselves about the business of the Treasury Department. As our argument grew intense this fact, in Williams' eyes, took on vastly more significance than it deserved.

I read off the amount of currency which was available for each bank. Every time I spoke an amount and named a bank, somewhere around the room an informed head nodded confirmation. My figures were irrefutable. Mr. McAdoo was chagrined and Mr. Williams was enraged. The Comptroller made it apparent that he felt there was some impropriety in the fact that I was better informed than he was; my contention was that the only impropriety was that a responsible official had been so poorly informed about a matter of such vital concern to the nation.

Well, Clearing House Certificates were issued and they were needed. Without them we should have been in a fine mess; probably some banks would have been in serious difficulties. Secretary McAdoo accepted our point of view; but Comptroller Williams was chiefly concerned because a private citizen, a banker if you please, had walked into the Treasury Department and gathered some information. When he returned to Washington he summoned Ailes. What Ailes told him I have forgotten, but the young people of today have a proper phrase to deal with such an empty situation. They simply ask, "So what?"

"Gold is trumps," James Stillman cautioned me as he sailed for Europe in September, 1914. He was never more right. London very much wanted about $98,000,000 due on a New York City bond issue; it was wanted in gold. Everything in America that was owned in Europe seemed to be for sale as the war began. Those who sold wanted gold. That was the most cogent of the reasons for keeping the New York Stock Exchange closed month after month. There simply was not enough gold to buy back all our bonds and stocks that were owned abroad and if the attempt to do so had not been effectively hampered it would have been as apparent in 1914 as it is in 1934 that the gold standard is something that ceases to work when everybody is suddenly eager to possess gold. With the Stock Exchange closed and stock and bond trading reduced to a small volume of illicit transactions, we managed to ride the storm.

Even if there had been no war we would have had a tough time in 1914; indeed, the war saved the Wilson Administration from the blame for a serious domestic situation. Along with other factors, the Democratic tariff had increased unemployment to an alarming degree; millions were out of work and the number was increasing. However, it was soon apparent to most business men that the war was going to create a fabulous market for American goods, for American labor and for American capital. I had been made chairman of a committee that raised a pool of $100,000,000 in gold to ship abroad to preserve American credit. Just as soon as it was known overseas that we had that gold and would ship it on demand, the demand eased. None of that $100,000,000 of gold was exported. What began to come over then were orders for goods and requests for credits.

Immense numbers of horses were being bought by late September. The British Government had placed an order with the Studebakers for $550,000 worth of farm-wagons. I had learned of a $1,000,000 credit that was to be expended for nitroglycerin. These were but the first drops splashing down ahead of a rainstorm of orders. Those people overseas quickly ceased to want us to ship them gold; they wanted something much more vital to them. They wanted to hire the productive energy of the most effectively industrialized nation that has ever existed; they wanted to buy all the food that we would sell them; they wanted everything that was required to keep them alive and to kill their enemies. And they wanted everything quickly. The one French word I never can forget is *vite*.

Banking is an essential function in the existence of a society in which masses of individuals have removed themselves, or are born away from the soil. The average man, I think, looks upon bankers as a group apart from the herd and, in the main, leeches. Yet that average man's breakfast really reaches him only because it has been constantly attended by banking processes. Somebody has to furnish credit to buy the wheat from the farmer; there has to be credit first to build and then to operate the railroad that carries the wheat to an elevator and then to a miller; and the miller has to have credit while transforming the wheat into flour and then a baker has to have credit while he changes the flour into bread. These self-liquidating processes of commerce are the unseen forces by which chains of people are induced, in their proper turns, to cooperate in society, to serve others far removed from their presence. What is true in peace is true in war. The soldier generally gets his breakfast as a result of banking processes and it is by those same processes that guns and ammunition are started on their way to a battlefield.

In Washington, President Wilson was striving to impose upon all citizens an obligation to be neutral, not only in action but in mind. For a time the City Bank undertook to be neutral. From London, at a time when the French Government had abandoned Paris in the belief it could not long be defended against the Germans, Mr. Stillman wrote to me counseling neutrality; it was a time to keep the bank "snug." Well,

Mr. Stillman was not neutral in his heart; nor was I. Besides, how could a big New York bank remain neutral?

We had accounts then with the biggest banks of all the belligerent nations. In Germany we had been having dealings with the Reichsbank, the Deutsche Bank and the Darmstadter Bank. Those accounts were closed out by wireless. It was significant of the close watch the Allies were keeping on all channels of communication that within a few days a representative of the French Government thanked me very prettily for the action we had taken. By that time we were in the thick of negotiations designed to provide a big credit for the French Government. That undertaking nearly caused a row between the City Bank and Morgan & Company.

Within a week after France and Germany went to war the French Government had sounded Morgan, Harjes & Company in Paris on the possibility of making arrangements through J. P. Morgan & Company for a credit of $100,000,000 in New York. I knew that Henry P. Davison, quite soon after the war began, had gone to Washington and discussed this proposal with William Jennings Bryan. What came of that was a telegram from Bryan to J. P. Morgan & Company in which he declared: "In the judgment of this Government loans by American bankers to any foreign nation which is at war are inconsistent with the true spirit of neutrality."

The proposition was then brought to the door-step of the City Bank by Maurice Leon, a New York lawyer of French birth. As a result of our talks I met

Ambassador Jules Jusserand in Washington on October 5, 1914. Sam McRoberts was with me. Four days later I wrote to Jusserand outlining the conditions on which it would be possible for the French Government to sell $10,000,000 of one-year Treasury warrants on a 6 percent basis, the money to remain on deposit here until spent; all of this subject to the approval of the United States Government.

M. Jusserand, beyond question, was dissatisfied at that time with the way Morgan & Company had dealt with their application for a loan. Nevertheless, this was a situation calling for diplomacy of that kind which had enabled the City Bank and Morgan & Company to get along peaceably for so many years. I suppose that both McRoberts and I had a suspicion they might not like the idea of having the City Bank hunting business on their international preserve. At any rate, intending to tell them tactfully of the deal we were about to close, McRoberts, because of my absence on account of illness, went down to see them. To his distress he found the partners dour almost to the point of sullenness.

Apparently, through some of their extraordinary sources of information, they had learned all about our negotiations and to say that they were indignant is understatement.

Harry Davison explained that they felt the City Bank had usurped their position with the French Government; that we had exercised what was definitely understood among us to be a prerogative of Morgan & Company. Jack Morgan spoke as forcefully as ever his father had done when the elder Morgan was aroused. It was not a pleasant situation.

McRoberts was distressed and did all he could to soothe our friends. He pleaded that we had understood we were free to proceed for the simple reason that Morgan & Company seemingly had determined not to go ahead. As a matter of fact we had been under the impression that the Morgan partners, with the French Government on the run, had not been displeased with the Bryan ruling that a loan to a belligerent nation would not be consistent with neutrality. However, Mr. Morgan and Mr. Davison made it more than clear to Mr. McRoberts that they were angry with us.

On that same morning Charlie Rich went to the Morgans' on some errand and made a point of mentioning the French negotiations to Thomas Lamont.

"I have not been active in it," said Rich, "but I wanted to ask if you had any suggestions about the matter?"

"Let me get Mr. Morgan," said Lamont.

J. P. Morgan, Jr., emerged angry. "If the City Bank won't play the game with us," he said, "we'll disregard them in our operations-much as we'd regret the end of an old friendship."

"Look," said Rich, "the friendship and cooperation of this house means more to us at the City Bank on the sentimental side alone than any other relationship. Unless we have your full accord nothing will be done about this French loan. The whole thing is a misunderstanding; we started into it more or less as an evolution of an original proposition that we should give credits to individual French banks. In the beginning we had no idea of dealing directly with the French Government."

Now, what Rich said came from his heart. That was why it was important and for similar reasons it was important when Mr. Morgan walked up to Rich and in entire good humor slapped him on the back, saying: "We will get along all right."

We did get along, beautifully; and eventually the "prerogatives" that J. P. Morgan and Company had been concerned about took the form of an arrangement whereby they became the purchasing agent for the Allied Governments in the United States. In their establishment, for a long time, there was an almost god-like knowledge of what the future held in store for those American industrial corporations that were in a position to make goods needed overseas.

Photograph by Brown Brothers

HENRY P. DAVISON

Photograph by Brown Brothers

ANDREW CARNEGIE

CHAPTER XXV
FRESH FIELDS TO CULTIVATE

ALL during that critical time of a threatened break between the Morgans and the City Bank I was at home, ill. In the midst of the negotiations with Jusserand I had been aware of an unusual lassitude and an occasional dizziness. What I had was paratyphoid. At the end of a month in bed I was so weak I agreed to take the advice of my friend, Dr. P. N. Barnesby, and go far away.

There was a place out in California that I felt I ought to see, a 16,000-acre ranch that I had bought, with others, sight unseen as traders say. The property was situated on the seacoast, partly within the limits of Los Angeles. When I did see it I came to a mental halt: although I had become used to handling large projects I was overwhelmed by this possession. It was almost the size of Manhattan Island; but it was the complete antithesis of that swarming city where in mingled squalor and magnificence all the ancient problems of mankind can be seen to have survived with the virility of weeds.

I had grown up on a farm that was a mile square and in my boyhood eyes that was a broad range of land. When I encountered this new possession, which was equal to twenty-five of my boyhood farms, and found the opportunity of exploring it over ranch trails, it seemed like an empire. An exquisitely beautiful empire it is, too, with more than ten miles of seacoast, the whole surface in picturesque rolling hills and occasionally more picturesque canyons. Even the ocean view is more beautiful than ordinary, for the mauve and purple hills of Catalina Island make a central point of interest that adds as much to the picture as do the Palisades to the view across the Hudson; but it is an infinitely grander picture.

The road over which I drove as I filled my eyes with a first sight of Palos Verdes Ranch was the corridor of one of the most exciting experiences of my life. Before me lay a range of folded hills, miles and miles of tawny slopes patched with green, thrusting themselves abruptly from the Pacific. Above me were broad natural terraces, with here and there a little farm, backed by a range of taller hills. Wherever the road passed over a hillcrest I could see the shoreline of the ranch as a series of bold headlands spaced off by gleaming crescent beaches. I found myself reminded vividly of the Sorrentine Peninsula and the Amalfi Drive: Yet the most exciting part of my vision was that this gorgeous scene was not a piece of Italy at all but was here in America, an unspoiled sheet of paper to be written on with loving care.

At first I was nonplussed. I had grown used to tackling pretty large financial measures, but the problems of sixteen thousand acres of land in the edge of a great city cannot be condensed on a sheet of paper as neatly as can a very great financial undertaking. While the property was a ranch, it was in but a slight degree a problem in agriculture. The ultimate development would not be along agricultural lines, but as the sites of innumerable homes. It made every creative fiber in me cry out for expression, for those hills were not much altered from the day that Dana stood on them when he was accumulating those experiences that were preserved in *Two Years Before the Mast*. The coast of the Pacific in the neighborhood of Los Angeles has not been developed with an eye to the aesthetic amenities of the future. Far too much of it has been spoiled by greedy real estate operations and crowded architectural horrors.

For the space of my toiling journey to the ranch house I was a colonizer in my soul, a Raleigh. The property had been purchased in the belief that the price was so low it certainly could be sold for more, but, paraphrasing Omar Khayyam and his wine, I often wondered what the realtors buy, one-half so precious as the goods they sell. We did sell thirty-two hundred acres off the ends of the ranch, and under the skillful direction of the Olmstead Brothers, those acres have been developed into one of the choicest collections of modest homes that I know of anywhere in the world.

The war interfered with any immediate consummation of expensive plans, and the property still lies unharmed by architectural mistakes, in its original loveliness of winter verdure and summer browns. Hundreds of thousands have been expended in road-building and tree-planting. A story of California growth that is almost unbelievable is that practically every tree on the place, except the citrus orchards, we have raised there from the seed. An avenue of Italian cypress, now thirty feet high, came home in Mrs. Vanderlip's pocket as seeds from the Villa Palmieri, owned by my old Chicago friend, James Ellsworth, a name made more famous in the present generation by his son, the intrepid Arctic explorer.

As a boy I had been in a situation where, in common with all my neighbors, because of lack of roads and transportation, we were in effect serfs on the soil. The difficulty of transportation and the cost in time and money kept us from traveling. At that time, it was a great event to go as much as twenty miles from home. Fifteen miles was the range of the average individual's wanderings from the site of his bed. That was about as far as a horse could take him and bring him back in a day.

In certain seasons, notably in the early spring, every road was a morass through which wagons were drawn, hub deep, if at all. One of my vivid memories is of gazing at the strange lines of holes fixed in the road near our house by an overnight freeze. The previous evening a circus had passed and the impressions of the elephant's legs were left, each one like the matrix of a beer keg. We live in a totally different world nowadays.

With the early background I had, road building was naturally the first enterprise we undertook on the ranch. With easy access over good roads, the property for a time seemed in my mind a great asset. In the years since, it has contributed in the neighborhood of a million dollars of taxes. We experienced a rise from $13,000 to $100,000 of annual taxation, and I have since wondered whether it was an asset or a liability to own such a tract of land.

The automobile, the airplane and other gadgets of our times had not been developed in 1912 as we know them, but they were at least on the horizon of our minds; they were a part of my vision. It seemed to me that with my experience with that mysterious force with which banking is concerned I might bring to the land, specifically to that 16,000 acres of fertile Palos Verdes ranch-land with its equable climate and gorgeous scenery, all the benefits of our civilization filtered free of all the evils. I never worked out the details as to how that Utopia should be recruited. The vision was no more than a short dream and I recall it now because I have become aware in this changing world that too much ease does not necessarily make for lasting comfort, for contentment or well-being. Actually the toil which I performed as a boy and as an adolescent youth strengthened more than my muscles; it did things for my character. If I experienced hardships they were not the hardships of the gutter but hardships in connection with the maintenance of a home. Sometimes I wonder if there has not been a softening of American character as well as a softening of muscles in this high powered, mechanical age.

At all events I was diverted from my scheme at Palos Verdes by a rapid recovery and a quickened desire for the wider canvas of Wall Street. Today, when I go back to California I still can be thrilled by what we have there, by its possibilities; but I am content, for myself, to sit in a comfortable cane-chair in the open air. Six hundred feet above the ocean we have a villa, a pure Italian house flanked by groves and gardens and facing a large brick terrace furnished as an outdoor living-room. I cannot believe there is a better stimulus to the imagination anywhere than the view afforded on that terrace. Far below, the Pacific roars against a cliff. My friend Julian Street will have it that the Pacific's emerald surface is our lawn and twenty-five miles out—halfway to our horizon—the hills of Catalina Island are shrunken nicely to the proportions of a hedge.

Quite often after I possessed means anything that captured my whole-hearted interest was apt to take concrete form. The Scarborough School is a case in point.

One time when S. S. McClure was us at Scarborough he was on fire about the Montessori method of teaching. A short while before he had met Madame Montessori and his enthusiasm was boundless, as is usually the case with him. He is truly an extraordinary personage. He felt it would be a great thing to introduce the Montessori teaching methods into America. We were thinking in terms of primary and sub-primary education. Mrs. Vanderlip and I were eager to know more and McClure introduced us to a young woman, Miss George, who had been with Madame Montessori, and in a little while, down near our gate, she had six or eight pupils including one or two of our children. That was the nucleus of the Scarborough School.

After a year or more we saw that the Montessori system was not at all appropriate to the class of children to which we were applying it. Nevertheless, when we built the school we still were afflicted with some pretty radical ideas about the education of children. The school was not well designed, but that was my fault. It was built for classes of ten, to accommodate one hundred and twenty children. But classes of ten are too small, so some educators seem to think now, and anyway the school grew beyond that so that we had to add another building for the younger children and then a lunch-room and then a shop and a studio. As soon as some of our first pupils progressed to a point where they had to take entrance examinations in order to enter college we realized that our scheme would have to become more formalized. In the early days the children had been given so much freedom that there was an obvious and undesirable lack of discipline. There is still more than average freedom in the classrooms, but the teachers and the children know that examinations must be passed and I believe that hurdle is good for both.

I had some grand fun in that school. For awhile I carried on a course of lectures, of conversations rather, with the two upper classes of the high school.

FRESH FIELDS TO CULTIVATE

I tried to simplify political economy for them, and for myself at the same time. We imagined a group of young people cast upon an uninhabited but fruitful island; quite cut off from the world but possessing something of both political and technical twentieth century knowledge and skills. We more or less played Robinson Crusoe, or rather Swiss Family Robinson on that imaginary island. Some of us gathered berries; others collected supplies of shell-fish. Those that had berries wanted shell-fish and vice versa. What was to be the basis of exchange? At first it was expressed naturally in terms of a day's work. Soon, however, a complication arose in our play. Somebody found an abundant supply of berries. His day's work was more productive than the others. How was that to be adjusted in the island society? We experienced in play the development of capitalism. A man built a boat and thereafter was able to catch more fish than a dozen men could catch from the shore. He became a capitalist, using his first profits to build other boats which he hired to some of his fellows. As I say, that was grand fun for me and I hope it was beneficial to the students. I know that some of them after being graduated from Yale and Harvard came back to report to me that they got more fundamental economics from those imaginative discussions of ours than from much more solemn lectures in classrooms.

The truth is that I have no very high regard for political economists. I used to be quite puffed up when people referred to me as an economist; but I no longer feel pride in the label. I think that political economists have failed lamentably to develop into sound scientists. I have found as much stand-pat-ism among political economists as ever I have found among conservative bankers. I am certainly not suggesting that they should be red radicals, but they ought to keep their minds open and full of curiosity. They ought to be more alert to discover worthwhile inventions in this field. After all, every single one of the devices of finance is an invention; we lose sight of that fact and we rarely give credit to the inventors, yet in the long run of society they are going to do rather more for us than those inventors who are concerned simply with machines.

The conservative in financial circles I have often described as a man who thinks nothing new ought ever to be adopted for the first time. That attitude of inhibition toward new inventions in economics and finance marks the division between the Tory and the Liberal mind. We have accomplished miracles with mechanical inventions, but our social and financial mechanism has developed far more slowly. It is not as easy or as safe to try out a social or financial invention, and that makes a sound reason for the slower adoption of ideas and inventions in those fields, but in the age of plenty which the advent of power and mechanical genius has brought to our doors we have made slight progress with our understanding of the distribution of that plenty. When we do understand it, our capacity to produce will make possible a state of life which has as yet been outlined by few Utopians, but I am convinced that we will not reach that happy state either by resisting all change or by believing that wealth can be redistributed so that everyone can draw material abundance from an inexhaustible government treasury.

I am trying to tell a story of the past, rather than to comment on the present, but I cannot refrain from an expression of belief that much of our present trouble has come from a deterioration of national character. Some of us have found life too easy; many of us have been too greedy. When selfishness is unrestrained, the bad results react disastrously. Our present efforts in the direction of relief have broken down self-reliance and industry. I profoundly believe that society does not owe every man a living, but only a fair chance to contribute to the welfare of society sufficient effort to warrant his drawing back from society the elements of an abundant life.

CHAPTER XXVI
NEW PLANS FOR THE BANK

I CANNOT fix the precise time when I became aware that what I wished to do was to create a worldwide bank, but I am able to recapture my mood after my convalescence, as of February 12, 1915. To Mr. Stillman on that day I wrote:

I have been away from the office about three and a half months. I have, of course, by no means been out of touch with it, but the bank has been run by the staff and, to sum up a great deal that I might say, it has been run extremely well. Getting back gives me an impression of feeling as a farmer might; supposing he had done a good deal of hard work plowing and harrowing, and sowing his wheat; and then fancy him absenting himself from his fields until a day when the crop was just coming into full head, brilliant with promise and showing, beside the benefit of good planting, the effects of abundant rains and generous sunshine.

You will think I am getting picturesque to be talking like this, but really I have never felt as I do now about the future of the City Bank. Its limits cannot be seen.

That last statement was set down with the ecstasy of a prophet. A paragraph from another letter to Mr. Stillman gives a hint of the wide sweep of our schemes in 1915.

I feel [I wrote], that we have got the branch bank situation working better now than at any time before. The group of people who have directly to do with the branch banks—Gardin, Voorhees, Kies, Green of the International Banking Corporation, Jacobs, Farnham—now meet every day, and the whole scheme is being coordinated, and the combined judgment of all these officers is being applied to new questions. The plan is working capitally. We are giving serious attention to the matter of branches in Europe. We will not put a branch in Scandinavia, but Pyke returns there in a few days to open an office in Denmark, to be run on somewhat similar lines to the London office. I think we may open in Spain, Switzerland, and will make a study of Italy and determine later about that situation.

The bank was growing, growing, growing. As the war progressed our foreign branches (the first had been opened in 1914) developed faster than we could find trained men to run them. Something quite apart from the needs of the Allied Armies was tempting us into a fantastic expansion. The bulk of European exports had stopped and there was a correspondingly great world-demand for everything the fighting nations formerly had been accustomed to make and sell. The City Bank's great need then was for American men trained in foreign banking business; for cultured professional bankers able to speak and write and think in several languages—and such men were rare.

I scoured the world for the right kind of men. Actually, I was for a while negotiating with an Australian banker. In Texas the president of the First National of Houston had qualities we wanted. I went down to see him and Herbert Eldridge became a vice-president of the City Bank. He was just the man to supervise our foreign branches. But while crossing the Andes on his first tour of the South American branches, Eldridge's heart failed him; he died on the train. He was not easily replaced.

I remember being at a National Industrial Conference Board meeting up in the Catskills where I encountered a man named F. Charles Schwedtman, an electrical engineer, part Dutchman but German-born. He had never been associated with a bank, but I was captivated by his philosophy of life, by his intelligent, broad and fair-minded attitude toward industry and people. He had just concluded the handling of some industry out in Illinois for Chicago banks and was considering a position as an adviser of the Chinese Government. "This man," I thought, "would be useful to the City Bank." I made him an offer that he accepted and ultimately he became a vice-president. I counted on him heavily in the development of a scheme I had for the creation in the City Bank of a kind of West Point for the training of selected young men. We had fifteen of these college men in 1915; later we had sixty.

In explaining to Mr. Stillman my hopes for those financier-cadets I wrote:

They lived in a community house in Brooklyn and are being put through the different departments of the Banks; and in addition to their day's work in the Bank, have classes in practical banking that are conducted in a way that will really give them a broad insight into the business. We are paying them only $50 a month which is, perhaps, too low, but we are giving them a very extraordinary opportunity to learn.

NEW PLANS FOR THE BANK

The way banks have been run, in feeding their executive force with uneducated office boys, and trusting here and there to a development of some exceptional mind, is about on a par with the old-fashioned way of farming, where a man used the small potatoes for seed and sold the large ones. The modern farmer gives as much attention to his seed, to the careful selection of corn that has developed the best characteristics, to the selection of potatoes that have grown the most to the hill, as he does to cultivation after the crop is in the ground. That is just what we are doing now in the Bank and instead of having to trust to some boy here and there with only a grammar school education developing exceptional capacity, we are getting young men in with trained minds, of good families, and with a vision that banking is a profession instead of merely a job.

We have made arrangements with a number of the leading colleges by which they will present to us for selection some picked men at the end of the sophomore year. We plan to take one man each from perhaps a half dozen of the leading colleges, give them employment and instruction in the summers of their sophomore and junior years, and take them on permanently in the middle of their senior year. The instruction will be such that the colleges will give academic credit for a half-year's work and the men will be graduated after they have put in the last half of their senior year in the bank.... It will furnish a picked lot of men, particularly for foreign service, who are educated and will be adapted to that field and it will give the bank an unique position as being the training school for bankers.

In 1915 certain developments, one of which was the frailty of Mr. Stillman's health, made me conclude it was high time I took some steps to secure my own fortune. I was well-to-do, yes; but I wanted to be fixed to maintain myself in the job I had. It entailed an expensive life. Moreover, I had some excuse for

NEW PLANS FOR THE BANK

entertaining a notion of riches different from that of most; during fourteen years I had been associating with men who possessed gigantic fortunes; Stillman, Morgan, Frick, Carnegie, Baker, Harriman, William Rockefeller and others. I occupied one of the most conspicuous banking positions in the world and my salary was $100,000 a year. Does that seem an excessive slim of money? In six months of 1915 the enterprise under m_y command had net earnings of $3,406,000. Right now I am prepared to defend in debate the proposition that the one who is capable enough to manage successfully an enterprise like the National City Bank is worth much more than $100,000. To me it seems silly of Government officials to say that no railroad president is worth more than $60,000 a year. Some of this is beside the point. Here we have to dwell upon something else; a matter of the ego.

Consider who owned this bank to the service of which I was devoting all my energies, mental and physical. By far the largest stockholder was Mr. Stillman; he owned about 52,000 shares. The Morgan firm owned a big block of stock and so did William Rockefeller. There were some others who owned holdings considerably larger than my own modest interest. Among these were the Pynes. At intervals I had tried to buy some of the holdings of these others. But the first real success I had was when Jack Morgan told me he was disposed to let me have perhaps half of the Morgan interest in the City Bank.

A day or so after my conversation with him an assassin forced his way into the home of Mr. Morgan at Glen Cove on Long Island and began firing a revolver at him; one bullet struck the financier in the abdomen. That was when I determined to express my mind to Mr. Stillman, who I knew could live only a few years longer; he knew it too.

What I want to write about [I explained in my letter], I have had more or less on my mind for five years; but just as a drop of the right re-agent will precipitate a chemical compound from a glass of clear liquid, so the extremely narrow escape from a great tragedy which Mr. Morgan has had precipitates my conclusions in regard to what I am going to write to you about. I will take occasion in another letter to tell you all the details of the attempt to murder Mr. Morgan, and the chance in a thousand by which he escaped. My reason for mentioning it is that it has brought most forcefully to me the chances that go with my own responsibilities. They are chances which it is better not to think of at all, and ordinarily I do not think of them. I do not at all mean alone the chances of such an incident as an encounter myself with a hair-brained crank nor, I think, do I need to go into detail as to all the chances that one must take, of every nature, in such a position as this . . . . I only cite as my excuse for writing this letter, the fact that I have been having a flash-light revelation as to the responsibilities which I have in regard to a large family and a quite reasonable desire, which is very strongly upon me just now for definitely crystallizing the means properly to safeguard that responsibility for the future.

What I then asked Mr. Stillman to do was to give me an option running not less than five years on a big block of his City Bank stock. I made no argument whatever as to the price; the amount of stock was the important thing to me and I so explained.

I also reminded Mr. Stillman of a conversation in the previous summer from which I had gathered the impression that he would be willing to carry the Morgan stock for me if I could get it.

Now, I had no hope of owning permanently so large an interest in the City Bank as I was striving to get under option. I hoped to make enough on the transaction (I was fully persuaded the City Bank stock was the safest investment, and the biggest bargain, in the world) to be able to buy outright a smaller but substantial interest in the bank.

Shortly after I sent my letter I cabled Mr. Stillman that Mr. Morgan had given me options on 10,000 shares of City Bank stock. I had a difficult time buying those 10,000 shares; approximately $4,000,000 was involved, to be paid at intervals during about eight months. William Rockefeller thought I ought to divide that stock with himself; in a somewhat less vigorous degree Mr. Stillman thought I ought to divide with Mr. Stillman. There was some attempt to force me to their way of thinking. They were willing to help me carry the stock if I divided but, I was informed, they could not see their way clear to do so if I did not divide.

I had depended upon Mr. Stillman to carry that stock for me and when he did not I was left in one of the most embarrassing situations of my life. I had arranged to pay on a certain date $1,000,000 for the first 2,500 shares; unless I did so the options on the other 7,500 shares were forfeited. The day came and I did not have the million. However, Mr. Morgan earned my lasting gratitude by carrying the stock for me until I was ready to take it up. I took it all up, rather grimly.

However, I then owned 12,500 shares; more than Morgan, and what was hazardous, more than William Rockefeller. Frank Vanderlip had become the second largest stock-holder of the National City Bank. William Rockefeller was my neighbor; imposing Rockwood Hall (now a country-club) and Beechwood lie close together up the Hudson. He was in all circumstances a most polite man, and it is likewise in his favor that he had a sense of humor. He came to the bank in great glee one time after a walk about his North Tarrytown estate in the company of his namesake grandson.

"William," he had told the boy, "I am going to give you an acre of ground here on the estate. You are to own it and administer it. Pick out the acre you want."

"An acre, grandfather?"

"Yes, William. Which spot do you choose?"

"The one with the house on it!"

My favorite Rockefeller story concerned a day when that same precocious grandson was being guided through the Jekyl Island Club-house. The old gentleman showed the boy a display of stuffed and mounted birds all of which at some time or other had been shot on the island. "That's a wild turkey," explained Mr. Rockefeller, "and that's a quail and that's an owl." Finally they paused in front of the prize of the collection.

"There," he said impressively, "is an eagle."

"What?" exclaimed the smallest Rockefeller. "Why, grandfather, that's just an old bird. I thought an eagle was a gold piece."

Mr. Rockefeller was keen for money, but then it was pretty hard not to be in Wall Street. He came in to argue with me when I was engaged in organizing the American International Corporation. He wanted $5,000,000 of the stock and I would not let him have so much—but first I ought to tell how that venture began.

One day when I remained at Scarborough, Jim Perkins telephoned that he wanted to send out to see me two railroad contractors named Stone and Webster; they had fascinated him; he thought they might also fascinate me. They did, completely. These men had done well but were convinced there was not much more railroad building to be done in the United States. After looking over the world for a land that was thickly populated but lacking railroads they had come to the conclusion that China was the place. The next morning at the bank Stone, Webster, Perkins, Rich and I had another talk. It was all quite intoxicating but there came an interval of silence and Perkins looked at me.

"All right," I said, "we will shoot." And that was the way we conceived the American International Corporation. We had decided that what was needed was some kind of organization that could take a foreign business enterprise of great possibilities or even a good idea with management behind it and finance it into strength. Such an organization would be in a position to consider carefully some of the marvelous opportunities that a banker ordinarily would have to boot out of his path for sheer lack of time. For example, I, for $10,000 could have had a half-interest one time in an industry out in Toledo. The Stranahan brothers wanted that sum to help them get started with what became the Champion Spark Plug Company, and my $10,000 would have become millions.

Well, the American International Corporation had $50,000,000 of capital authorized; it was to be interested in all manner of promising enterprises in foreign lands, in the Orient, in South America; over the face of the whole earth. The very idea of the thing was exciting in Wall Street. We made C. A. Stone the president and had a remarkable Board of Directors; James J. Hill, Theodore Vail, P. A. Rockefeller, Stone, Edwin F. Webster, Otto Kahn, Ambrose Monell, James A. Stillman, Beekman Winthrop, Henry S. Pritchett, R. S. Lovett, Joseph P. Grace, Cyrus H. McCormick, Charles H. Sabin, W. E. Corey, J. Ogden Armour, and C. A. Coffin.

What days those were! One can be reconstructed from a letter I wrote to Mr. Stillman:

James A. Farrell and Albert Wiggin have been invited [on the board] but had to consult their committees before accepting. I also have in mind asking Henry Walters and Myron T. Herrick. Mr. Herrick is objected to by Mr. Rockefeller quite strongly but Mr. Stone wants him and I feel strongly that he would be particularly desirable in France. The whole thing has gone along with a smoothness that has been gratifying and the reception of it has been marked by an enthusiasm which has been surprising to me even though I was so strongly convinced we were on the right track.

I saw James J. Hill today, for example. He said at first that he could not possibly think of extending his responsibilities, but after I had finished telling him what we expected to do, he said he would be glad to go on the board, would take a large amount of stock and particularly he wanted a substantial interest in the City Bank, and commissioned me to buy him the stock at the market.

I talked with Ogden Armour about the matter today for the first time. He sat in perfect silence while I went through the story, and, without asking a single question, he said he would go on the board and wanted $500,000 stock.

Mr. Coffin [of General Electric] is another man who is retiring from everything, but has become so enthusiastic over this that he was willing to go on the board, and offers the most active coöperation.

I felt very good over getting Sabin. The Guaranty Trust is altogether the most active competitor we have in the field and it is of great value to get them into the fold in this way.

They have been particularly enthusiastic at Kuhn, Loeb's. They want to take up to $2,500,000. There was really quite a little competition to see who should get on the board, but as I had happened to talk with Kahn and had invited him first, it was decided he should go on. He is perhaps the most enthusiastic of any one. They want half a million stock for Sir Earnest Castle to whom they have cabled the plan and they have back from him approval of it.

I explained the whole matter to the Board [of the City Bank] Tuesday and got nothing but favorable comments.

Joe Grace had wanted $600,000 of the stock beside what he would get through his City Bank stock ownership; Monell wanted half a million and Corey,

Converse and the rest of the Midvale Steel people wanted large amounts. George Baker wanted $250,000, Frank Hine $100,000 and William Rockefeller tried, vainly, to get me to put him down for $5,000,000 of the common. He had something in common with a certain St. Louis grandfather who cut pie at the table in a slap-dash manner so that the wedges were of unequal size; but when he passed the plate the thumb of grandfather invariably was firmly sunk into the biggest wedge.

There was a lot of pie in Wall Street; every day tempting propositions were laid before me. I remember the Pynes and the Taylors asked me to see what could be done with Lackawanna Steel; they had 160,000 shares. I got in touch with James Campbell, then the head of Youngstown Sheet & Tube Company and we schemed out a possible combination of his company, with the Lackawanna, the Iroquois Furnishers in Chicago and the Cambria. It was like working a jig-saw puzzle out of squirming pieces. The one that got away that time was Cambria Steel. I had arranged to join with Mr. Frick, Mr. Mellon, and Horace Harding in buying 250,000 shares of Cambria owned by the Pennsylvania Railroad. Before we could act other interests closed a deal. Just before that I had arranged on my own account a $13,000,000 credit in order to accomplish the purchase and sale of Midvale Steel. At the same time I was trying to buy from J. B. Forgan control of the Haskell & Barker Car Works. In 1915, of course, those were the kind of industries that could make the most money. Peerless Motor was another that interested me just then; stock sufficient for control was tied up for ninety days under an option agreement given to Shearson & Hammill, who were conducting the matter. I had paid for a considerable amount of the underwriting.

I am recalling all this in order to explain something that I tried to make clear in my letters to Mr. Stillman in January, 1916. I believed that my chief work for the future was to be the coördination of the efforts of four organizations; the National City Bank, the International Banking Corporation, the National City Company and the American International Corporation.

"This," I told Mr. Stillman, "has brought me to the very clear belief that the time has come for me to retire from the presidency of the City Bank."

I desired to take the chairmanship of the other three companies and at the City Bank to become vice-chairman of the board. That was so as not to disturb Mr. Stillman in the chairmanship. In his reply he posed a difficult problem: who should become the next president of the City Bank?

CHAPTER XXVII
TROUBLE WITH A ROCKEFELLER

FROM the beginning of my career in the City Bank there were temperamental differences between William Rockefeller and me. We were so clearly fated to clash that the really astonishing thing is that I did not sooner come into conflict with him.

James Stillman, who truly enjoyed the society of Mr. Rockefeller, over and over warned me that the velvety politeness of his friend masked a character accustomed to work in darkness. Down the eighteen years of my association with the City Bank I knew that to be so, just as surely as I knew that a continued friendliness meant that much Rockefeller wealth would continue to be a part of our precious organism—the Bank. I wished to avoid giving offense to Mr. Rockefeller but I could not without wholly changing my character. Altogether, I was too lacking in compliance for his comfort. So matters for dispute arose between us. The first of these of any consequence was my refusal to divide with him the 10,000 shares of City Bank stock that I had optioned, and then bought, from the Morgans.

But there was another dispute that particularly galled Mr. Rockefeller. In spite of the fact that I had become the second-largest stock-holder I should say that he was, excepting Mr. Stillman, the most influential director. Besides his enormous fortune there was to be considered his family relationship with Mr. Stillman. The two sons of Mr. Rockefeller, William G. and Percy A., were married, respectively, to Elsie and Isabel, the daughters of James Stillman. Now, Mr. Rockefeller was also a director of the New York Central Railroad, and when we bought for the bank an issue of New York Central bonds he declared himself in on 25 percent of the profits.

I conceded this to him, because, after all, participations were spread around. However, as a director of the railroad he had agreed to sell those bonds; as a director of the bank he had agreed to buy them. He was, then, both buyer and seller. This dual role can be fulfilled with fairness to opposing groups of stockholders, but even under the best of conditions it is a difficult undertaking. As it happened, this sort of thing was the means of some of the worst abuses that occurred in Wall Street.

There "vas a time when he revealed to me that he was not habitually polite. It was not long after I had bought the Elliott F. Shepherd estate. It was a great place, on which about $2,000,000 had been spent and I picked it lip as a bargain, paying, I think, about $165,000. Mr. Rockefeller had wanted it for himself, but when I ha d it I discovered that Mrs. Vanderlip was unwilling to live there; it was too grandiose. So I made it into a golf-club, the Sleepy Hollow Country Club. I got Charley McDonald, a famous golfer, to lay out the course, and he decided we ought to have more ground. The adjoining property was owned by Mr. Rockefeller. I had bought it for him at a time when he did not wish to appear as the purchaser. I went to him and negotiated a leasing arrangement. I think it was the thirteenth tee that caused our difficulty. At any rate he went up there one day and, discovering that one of the tees had been built farther down the slope of the hill than he had anticipated, he became terribly angry. He came to see me at the bank, raging. That time our talk was really acrimonious. I thought he was making a great pother about a trifle, but the truth was, I guess, that he had a sort of line-fence complex.

I remember another time when we became concerned at Beechwood because a line-fence quarrel had broken out between Mr. Rockefeller and my friend Dr. P. N. Barnesby, who was my physician and the medical director of the City Bank. At Scarborough, Barnesby had become the squire of six acres, wedged in like Belgium between Beechwood and Rockwood Hall. The boundary between the Rockefeller estate and Barnesby's property was a broken-down fence and a ragged growth of scrubby bushes; really it was just a thin strip of soil that never had been cleared. The ugliness was a perpetual affront to the eyes of Dr. and Mrs. Barnesby; although out of sight of the Rockefeller home, it was close to the doctor's house. Unhappily, the bushes were all rooted on Rockefeller land.

One day as the Barnesbys stood in their garden, Mrs. Barnesby discovered that a heavy-set stranger who rested his elbows on top of that troublesome fence was no less a personage than the master of Rockwood Hall; also, she recognized the man's companion as the estate superintendent, Hawks. Urged by his wife,

Barnesby determined to consult his neighbor about the abominable scrub growth.

Strolling over, he said: "How do you do, Mr. Rockefeller? I am Dr. Barnesby."

There was no word, only a piercing look from the granite-featured gentleman. Dr. Barnesby cleared his throat and spoke his piece anyway: "Would you mind if I took down these scrub bushes and planted a nice row of trees in place of them?"

At that, Mr. Rockefeller, who was really tall, reared himself high above Dr. Barnesby. Not until he had buttoned his coat did he speak, and even then he simply growled: "See Hawks." After that, with yard-long strides he made his exit from the scene, closely dogged by Hawks.

A few days later, when Dr. Barnesby had become somewhat less choleric and his nostrils had ceased to flare as he breathed, he did take up the matter with the superintendent, Hawks, who told him, with what Barnesby felt was arrogance, that he must not touch anything on the Rockefeller premises; whereupon Barnesby got into a passion. Straight away he hired half a dozen Italian laborers and directed them as they cleared away the scrubs.

Well, then I was in a passion myself. I scolded Barnesby—a little, as one does with a dear friend. If Mr. Rockefeller's dignity had been too seriously affronted he might, I felt, salve it through some action against me or the bank. After all, he knew that Barnesby was my friend. However, the affair blew over and Barnesby thereafter was shielded from ugliness by a row of healthy young trees that were nourished by his own soil. I have wished often that I might as easily have acquired an effective shield against William Rockefeller.

Mr. Stillman, who in good health was all the shield that I ever would have needed, after 1915 was most of the time in a precarious state of health. Indeed, from then on, except for rather brief intervals, I cannot think of him as a banker at all, because sometimes for months on end he was completely an invalid, barred by the feebleness of his hold on life from receiving any news from the bank. Such news, his physicians had decided, would be too exciting for his diseased heart. Hypodermic injections of morphine were given to him so frequently during some months of 1915 that finally, so he told me, it became difficult to find space upon his legs where a needle could be inserted. Physically and mentally he was sore to the touch. Many of his letters from abroad contained pathetic appeals to me, his friend, to be careful not to wound him. Any unconsidered word was apt to fester in his mind long after the one who carelessly had uttered it had forgotten entirely that it had been said.

In spite of their respective crotchets, Mr. Stillman and Mr. Rockefeller seemed to enjoy each other's society. Apart they were unfailingly and harshly critical of one another, but when together they seemed to enjoy life. Sometimes they were really jovial. I remember how gleeful Mr. Stillman was when he arranged an audience with the Pope for himself and the Baptist, Mr. Rockefeller. At the very last minute it was revealed to Mr. Rockefeller that the strict etiquette of the occasion would require him to kneel and kiss the ring on the hand of the Pope.

"But I did not kiss his ring," said Mr. Rockefeller as they left the Vatican and he had bent to look ruefully at his knees.

"No?" said Mr. Stillman teasingly.

"No," said Mr. Rockefeller. "I squeezed his hand." And then he added triumphantly, "And he squeezed back."

Mr. Stillman had suffered so much in his illnesses that during the last years of his life the least little thing in the way of a symptom became something of the most alarming portent.

One night at Beechwood, Mr. Stillman—from his bedroom—sent forth word that he required the presence of Dr. Barnesby. He was to leave that evening with William Rockefeller for the Adirondacks. Saunders, the butler, opened Mr. Stillman's door and ushered Barnesby into the room.

Mr. Stillman sat in a big chair, quite motionless. A long cigarette-holder touched his lips. At intervals he puffed out a trace of smoke. To strangers his normal expression was forbidding, almost hawkish. Minute after minute he sat in silence without ever giving any audible reply to Barnesby's first greeting. Finally he spoke.

"What is the matter with my eyes?"

Barnesby's sensitive fingers, a brain in each one, tenderly seized the skin below one eye that caught his attention.

"A little bloodshot," he said after a moment. "Have you been coughing?"

"No. I am going blind."

"No, Mr. Stillman. Just a little hemorrhage of the sclerotic coat. You don't need to worry at all. It will clear up by absorption." Barnesby returned home, only to be summoned back. Mr. Stillman still sat with the long cigarette-holder at his lips.

"There is something the matter with my eyes."

"Just a little bloodshot, Mr. Stillman. It will be all right in the morning." This was followed by a brief medical lecture explaining the comparative unimportance of such a manifestation as was troubling Mr. Stillman. Barnesby returned home, but he was called back for the third time.

"What is the matter with my eyes?"

"Nothing. A little bloodshot. That is all."

A silent gesture with the cigarette-holder. Then: "Will it be all right for me to go to the Adirondacks tonight with Mr. Rockefeller?"

"Yes, Mr. Stillman. It will be all right."

"Very well. You go to the train with me."

They drove together to Philipse Manor, wordlessly. Far down the platform, abreast of where the baggage-car would stop, there was a great mound of luggage, twenty-five or more trunks belonging to Mr. and Mrs. Rockefeller and to Mr. Stillman. A tall Negro, probably the one in charge of transferring the baggage—seeing them standing under a single incandescent lamp's yellow glow, came over with a question.

"Mr. Stillman, is that you?"

"Go away from me. I don't know you. You don't know me."

The man went back into the darkness, and then a long train pulled into the station; two private cars were at the end. At the same time the Rockefeller automobile arrived, disgorging Mr. and Mrs. Rockefeller. She was quite deaf, and his sense of hearing was failing.

At the steps of one of the private cars Mr. Stillman spoke to Mr. Rockefeller:

"You know Barnesby?"

"Yes," said Mr. Rockefeller and climbed aboard the train. So did Mr. Stillman, saying no other word.

When Barnesby related this to me, with such emphasis as is not given to words as they rest coldly in type, he was so wrought up that our positions were quite reversed. I was for a little the physician and he was the patient. The fact is that when men dwell for many years in possession of tremendous riches, they are apt to be a little self-conscious in the presence of strangers; they are suspicious and their growls are defensive, like those of an old dog who rumbles in his throat when any one steps near the fireplace where he naps.

For me, for the members of my family, for each one of six exuberant children, James Stillman was always a tenderly considerate friend. My affection for him has been undimmed in the years since his death. I quite understand him, I think, in the attitude he took toward my request for an option on some of his City Bank stock. Of course he did not want to surrender any of it! It was a piece of himself that I was asking for. In a letter he did give me an option on 5,000 shares, but that kind of an option is something less than a contract. When the time came and I would have exercised it, Mr. Stillman's son, James A. Stillman, was unwilling to recognize the letter as something giving me a valid claim, and I can hardly blame him.

CHAPTER XXVIII
THE BURDEN OF A BANKER

OF COURSE, throughout my banking career I was, regarded as a radical by old-fashioned bankers. I was a banker publicist, but some of them supposed, I fancy, simply that I was a fellow who delighted at seeing his name in print. I made speeches, they thought, for the exquisite pleasure of hearing my own voice and for the sake of applause. Mr. Stillman knew better than that. Frequently he commented on the fact that I was making a reputation throughout the country, and internationally, that enabled the bank to cast a big shadow. A great deal of my success at the City Bank was due to the fact that I was, in addition to being a banker, a publicist. To be a publicist banker you have got to think, you have got to have something to say. It was because of those extramural activities of mine that the City Bank was taken out of the groove in which it previously had gone in comfort.

Yet the worldwide operations like those of the City Bank were no temptation at all to a conservative, old-time banker such as George Baker of the First National. I remember sitting next to him at dinner one night, when he quite opened his heart to me.

The old gentleman had every right to have a rosy flush on his wrinkled cheeks that night. Mr. Baker had just made one of his exceedingly generous and wise gifts of money to Cornell University, and at a luncheon the trustees of Cornell had given him an ovation. In referring to this as we unfolded our napkins, I said I supposed it had made him feel very proud.

"Oh, no," he said sadly, and shook his head from side to side. "There is no longer any meaning for me in things like that; not since I lost my wife."

As I fumbled around for a word of comfort, he asked me to recall a night at the Union League Club in 1907, after the panic. I remembered the occasion vividly; a host of men from Wall Street had stood and cheered Mr. Baker for the part he had played in saving the country from a worse economic disaster.

"Well," he said to me, "that night at the Union League Club I could hardly get away fast enough. I was wild to get home to tell my wife all about it. But whom can I tell now?"

Thereafter, I always thought of Mr. Baker as a lonely, sorrowful man; never as an aloof one.

That night he had told me how Mr. Stillman once had proposed to him a merger of the First National and the City Bank; Mr. Baker to become the president. He had declined, he told me, because he had no ambition at all to broaden the field of the First National. He said he had enough work as things were. He understood domestic banking and did not want to have to apply himself to a study of the intricacies of foreign banking. In his own field of banking, Mr. Baker was a master. I was astonished that night to discover completely he was posted about the railroad properties with which he was connected. Not only could he quote the figures of earnings, but he was familiar with the statistics of car-loadings right up to the day before.

That was in January, 1916, and as I talked with Mr. Baker, who was many years older, I was quite sure I never could go on and on in my job as he had in his. A day or so before, I had informed John Sterling that I was getting away for a vacation, as I was about as thoroughly tired as a man could be.

"For how long?" he asked.

"Six weeks; California."

"What?" He was really alarmed, and began to chide me. "Suppose something should occur? A panic! Suppose we lost $100,000,000 in deposits. What then?"

"Is that your notion of the worst that might happen?" I asked him.

"Yes," he said, and drummed his fingers on his waistcoat.

"Well, Mr. Sterling," I said gaily, "be quite easy in your mind. The City Bank could pay $100,000,000 back to its depositors without a quiver." Then I recited figures to prove my case until he was chuckling with relief.

I had then reached a time when my work for the City Bank was even more like drudgery than that work I had done in overalls before a lathe in an Aurora machine-shop. When the novelty had worn off, there was considerably less zest to the exercise of power, I found; and I grew weary of the repetitions involved in work that could not be delegated. Each problem that was laid before me I had to understand right down to its roots before I could make a sound decision. If I had not possessed a physique of extraordinary vigor I could not have stood it. Remember, I had been going at top-speed in the City Bank since the summer of 1901 and there had been no let-up, except as I was occasionally permitted to enjoy an illness.

My days began early and lasted long. After 1914 I really did get a bit of exercise; as late into the season as Thanksgiving I would start the day by plunging into the lovely blue of the outdoor swimming-pool that Wells Bosworth had designed for us at Beechwood. Consequently, I would be wide-awake and steaming with energy as I arrived at the station and entered a private club-car hooked to the rear of the 8:26 train. By the time we had left Tarrytown behind on the run to New York we would have an interesting company of passengers on that car. Occasionally, as guests, were one or more of the Rockefeller clan aboard; sometimes John D., Jr.; also John D. Archbold of the Standard Oil; James Speyer, Andrew Mills, Dr. Barnesby, Edward Harden, Currier, and enough others so that there was always a poker game. I never played, but I remember looking up one time to watch John D. Archbold with extended fingers raking in a pot that he had won. Mr. Archbold who, when he did not travel with us, floated down the Hudson on his yacht, was talking loudly. I saw that the eyes of John D., Jr., had stopped their swift travel back and forth on the page of his newspaper; he was listening.

"Fourteen cents in that pot," Mr. Archbold was boasting. "Well, after years of association with Mr.

THE BURDEN OF A BANKER

Rockefeller, I can tell you something: save your pennies and they become nickels. Save your nickels and they become dimes. The dimes will become dollars, and Mr. Rockefeller will look after the dollars." Then he chortled and his paunch shook.

Young Mr. Rockefeller's eyes once more focused on the print and I heard Mr. Archbold ask for "three cards."

I could rarely spare the time to chat on those trips to town; that was the time to digest the newspapers and pore over documents that Currier would place in my pockets or hand to me from a briefcase.

Every morning at the office I would find on my desk a card about a foot in depth, and it was numbered with the minutes of the day. There were never fewer than four engagements to the hour during the periods I was at my desk; but as a director in about forty corporations, frequently I was obliged to go out to attend meetings. Some of the directorships were in such a group as the Harriman roads, so that I might get through a number of meetings at one sitting. However, I was on the executive committee of practically all those boards on which I sat. Between meetings I had to move swiftly to keep pace with a schedule that in time began to be a kind of slavery. It was no simple knapsack burden that I carried. I could not put it down. Indeed, that on rolling, overpowering mass of work was far too much for me. It was a frightful load.

My job followed me wherever I went. I remember that when I was going to California for that 1916 vacation I offered this as an excuse when I was "regretting" my inability to make a speech at some dinner in New York. The gentlemen who were urging me returned with the information that they had arranged for a telephone wire from Los Angeles to New York and that each guest would have a telephone receiver beside his plate. "That," I wrote Mr. Stillman, "is certainly startlingly up-to-date." I also wrote him that I was never more ready for a vacation; however, on my way West I felt obliged to go by way of New Orleans in order to deliver a speech—I prepared it on the train—before the Foreign Trade Association. It is no wonder to me now that I was quite exhausted at the end of each day. I was paying an impossible price for the bank-account I was building up in the black; physically, I was going swiftly into the red. Although I did not know it until three years later I was, as early as 1917, developing diabetes. Still, even in my most extreme moments of weariness, I did not want to quit; rather, I should say, I wished to mold my job into some kind of proportions that would enable me to regard it with active pleasure. Again and again in my letters to Mr. Stillman I brought up the question of a successor.

I was on the lookout for the right man all the time. There was a feeling on Mr. Stillman's part, and I shared it, that because I had seen the bank grow from $200,000,000 until it had increased five-fold that it would not be easy to get a man sufficiently young to make a change desirable, and yet capable enough to be master of our friendly monster. That was precisely why we were disposed in favor of a plan to have me keep on, probably as vice-chairman. It cannot be said that I was blind to the presence in the bank of some men of great capacity. I have repeated the prophecy I made in 1914 about Perkins. In 1916 Currier, on my behalf, wrote to Mr. Stillman: "The City Company a few months ago acquired a man named Mitchell. He is about 38 years old and has had valuable business and banking experience. He is a very well set-up, intelligent man with a good eye and a keen mind. He is undoubtedly going to prove of real strength to the whole situation. Mr. Vanderlip believes in him strongly, as does Mr. Perkins, who is working closely with him." Charlie Mitchell truly had an astonishing capacity to generate energy; in 1921, when some of the troubled directors of the City Rank asked my opinion, I endorsed Mitchell. They elected him to the presidency of the City Bank in place of James A. Stillman, who had resigned. But that is going far ahead of my story.

The excitements, the pressures, the chaos of the war-days added much to the load of a Wall Street banker. All of us down there had to readjust our mental attitudes toward money. We had to calculate utterly unpredictable forces and weigh terrifying hazards. What was the Russian situation in the middle of 1916? We had two vice-presidents over there closing up an important piece of financing amounting to $50,000,000 or $75,000,000. The Government wanted saddles, harness, shoes, ammunition, cloth and food; and every piece of leather, every pound of cotton, every morsel of food they bought helped to derange the American farmers' sense of values. At the same time as we negotiated with Finance Minister Bark of Russia, the City Bank was closing a renewal of a $50,000,000 loan to London banks for one year at 5 percent. We found it significant that they preferred this as against our offer of the money for six months at 4 1/2 percent.

I remember when a joint British and French commission arrived to negotiate a private loan to pay for still more goods from us. The figures they had in mind sounded appalling when uttered in New York beyond the rumbling sound of the guns faintly heard in Threadneedle Street. They talked about a billion dollars. Finally a group undertook the handling of a $500,000,000 Anglo-French loan and it went like a breeze. As bankers we had given careful consideration to the matter of repayment, and those private loans were repaid, that is, excepting what Russia borrowed. It was the loans made by the American Government that piled up into an unpayable debt.

Those Government loans, after we got into the war, were first negotiated on the theory that they were to pay for goods purchased here, and the Allied buyers did not hold to that theory too closely. They bought, to some extent, all over the earth with borrowed American dollars; they used some of the borrowed money for the quite necessary purpose of sustaining their credit in other countries. The British, for example, were being hard put to sustain the pound against the Argentine exchange and used borrowed American Liberty Loan dollars to do the trick.

Long before we got into the war there were spies in the bank, and possibly afterward. Poor Mr. Stillman's codes were of no avail against the British censor's crytographers. The censors opened all our letters and cables, and whenever they read anything that might be of value to an English merchant or banker, it was, we strongly felt, passed along to interested parties. The Germans did not overlook us, either.

One day just before America got into the war, secret agents of the United States and a British agent of some kind came to see me. They reported that they believed they had tracked a spy into the bank.

"What could he do here?" I asked.

"The Ships' manifests that pass through your foreign department reveal what ships are carrying munitions. Those are the ones their subs are most eager to get."

"What shall we do?"

"May we put a man in the bank to ferret him out?"

"By all means," I said, and assigned an officer of the bank to make the arrangements.

Soon afterward one of our German employees was caught in the very act of dropping out of a window a roll of paper. A man on the sidewalk below who caught the paper was promptly seized and so was the bank's employee. The paper contained excerpts copied from ships' manifests. We found out that for some time similar information had been delivered to an official of the Hamburg-American Line in New York, and he, in some devious way, conveyed it to Germany so it could be relayed to the German submarines. Our ex-employee before very long was in an internment camp.

During the Liberty Loan campaign of May and June in 1917, I found, somehow, new sources of energy. I suppose I could find enthusiasm for that work that I could not produce just then for the heavy routine of the City Bank. I was a member of the Liberty Loan Committee appointed by the Federal Reserve Board for the New York district, and I was made chairman of the sub-committee on publicity. Week after week I had a schedule crowded with speaking engagements. Then Congress passed a War Savings act. No clear scheme had been worked out but it was intended that a way should be found to capture the small change from the pockets of the nation for the purpose of helping to finance the war effort. I was invited to take the chairmanship of the educational committee for the sale of War Savings Certificates; I accepted as of September 25, 1917.

Mr. Stillman had returned to the United States and was in his office at the City Bank daily. He gave his consent for me to take a leave of absence and soon afterward, having relinquished my salary of $100,000 a year, I set out for Washington, to become a dollar-a-year man. There were a lot of us.

CHAPTER XXIX
DOLLAR-A-YEAR MAN

MY office in the Treasury Department was a small one that was entered directly from the public corridor. I shared it with the man who had been my private secretary at the City Bank, H. E. Benedict. Soon after I was established there a visitor who had come down from New York to help me opened my door. This was Julian Street and he was astonished and indignant to find that he could walk right in upon me.

"This is the kind of an office they'd give a chief clerk," he complained bitterly.

I did not share my friend's indignation. With a grin I told him I cherished the hope that before many days I would get a chance to talk with an assistant secretary. I wanted to raise some money to help finance the war. Street fumed and then pitched in to help; everybody was helping in those days.

On the committee of which I had been made the chairman were a number of distinguished persons—one, I remember, was Henry Ford—but really our committee never functioned. I do not recall that the whole committee ever met. I was rather happy on that account because it gave me a freer hand. However, there was one man who joined wholeheartedly with me; that was Frederic A.

Delano, a former president of the Wabash Railroad who had become a member of the Federal Reserve Board. He is an uncle of President Franklin Delano Roosevelt.

Together we worked out a scheme whereby anyone could lend money to the Government by purchasing a 25c Thrift Stamp at a post-office window. Mr. Delano was the inventor of the tri-fold cardboard on which purchasers could accumulate their war thrift stamps. We had wanted a device that could be carried conveniently in a man's breastpocket. Eventually we had the mechanism in such a form as entitled the project to survival in peace times. It was an admirable arrangement for the promotion of saving among persons who ordinarily let their money trickle through their fingers.

I wanted McAdoo to calculate the interest on War Savings Certificates on a basis at least as attractive as Liberty Bonds, but he would not listen to that; we had to be content with an arrangement for 3 percent. Throughout our effort we were conscious that we were competing—often it was unfriendly competition, too—with those persons who were endeavoring to make the greatest possible sales of Liberty Bonds. We competed mighty effectively, nevertheless.

Our selling organization was brought together swiftly and functioned so as to make me proud. I had organized the thing in this way: I selected a man from each of the twelve Federal Reserve districts and invited him to come to Washington and serve in a sort of thrift stamp cabinet. We then appointed a chairman for each state and to each state chairman was delegated responsibility for the appointment of county chairman and the county chairmen in turn appointed lesser chairman until not a single election precinct had been overlooked. That was our system and it worked.

I wrote an explanation of the thrift stamp program in the form of questions and answers and tried to make it simple enough for a child to understand. This information was printed as a circular and mailed to 20,000,000 persons in the United States. Now, how could we mail so many? We simply sent bundles of circulars to all post-offices; the postmasters were directed to see that mail-carriers distributed the circulars as they made their regular deliveries. We had contests among artists in order to develop some stirring and attractive posters. Plays were written for presentation in schools. There must have been developed a thousand schemes for getting our project into the public mind and conscience. Eventually we succeeded so well that in all the schools a large proportion of the children were saving their pennies, nickels and dimes by lending them to the Government. Housewives and clerks were saving and helping the Government. In one year from the day that the first stamp was sold the people purchased one billion dollars' worth of thrift stamps. Eventually a total of $4,000,000,000 worth were sold. I deeply regret that the project was not kept alive into peace times as was done in England.

However, I kept pondering on that astounding revelation: There had been accumulated in the space of a single year, from the loose change in the pockets of the American public, money enough to create an institution as great as the nation's biggest bank. As the president of the City Bank, I was required to have a pretty astute understanding as to the meaning, the power, of a billion dollars. I began to wonder if some financial engine could not be invented that would make that loose change in the pockets of the people serve them better than it does when they drop it into all manner of thriftless, catch-penny devices. Now, all my life I have been aware of and interested in the instinct common to us all to gamble, to risk little in the hope of winning much. I began to wonder whether the gambling instinct might be used as a motive power to overcome the normal inertia of the mass of the people which resists efforts made to improve their status.

Since it is pleasant to take a chance and dream of getting something for nothing, why would it not be worthwhile to make all the human grasshoppers become ant-like through their most extravagant instinct, their natural habit of gambling? Now, what are the objections to gambling? After the primary objection on behalf of the individual, that he is rather more apt to lose than to win, there is another, on behalf of society, that if he wins it is at the expense of another or others. These objections have never loomed large in my mind, I must admit. I began to wonder whether a lottery could be devised that would promote thrift. My own objection to lotteries has been that very rarely does the winning do the winner any good. It is easily established that the ordinary winner of a lottery prize fritters his money away and at the end of his experience is rather worse off than he was in the beginning.

Well, how could one meet that objection? What I devised was a Government lottery to provide old age security. It was and is my idea that the Government should place on sale in every post-office in the country a type of postal-card that could be bought for one dollar. It would have attached to it a coupon that would become the purchaser's receipt. After writing his name and address on the postal-card he would drop it into the post-office receptacle. Every day in Washington there could be a drawing as carefully supervised as, let us say, the Irish Hospital Sweepstakes. One winning card would be drawn for each thousand cards in the wheel. That would designate the winners of the prizes but what would those prized be? An old age annuity beginning at sixty. It would be a simple matter for Congress to make it impossible for any winner to sell or by any sort of contract otherwise to dispose of his Government annuity. Consequently, no winner could fritter away such winnings. Furthermore, as a prospective beneficiary of Government finds he would tend to become a strong advocate and supporter of a conservative financial policy in the Government.

I believe this scheme if put into operation would bring in an enormous amount of money. Unlike any other lottery I ever heard of it would give the participants all of the money involved. There would be no jack-pot for a little clique of gamblers or Government insiders. According to my idea the money would be invested only in bonds of the United States purchased in the open market. This would create a great supporting demand all the time for Government bonds and there would be no question of wisdom in making investments. The enterprise should and could be conducted with no expense to the partipants and no expense to the Government, except for the birth certificate and registration of the winner's identity. Of course, I am aware that some persons might be so unfortunate as never to win while others would win repeatedly. It could be arranged that any man who vainly persisted until he had bought one hundred cards should be permitted to file his one hundred coupons with the Government agency and that upon attaining the age of sixty he would receive back all, or a portion of his $100, depending upon certain age factors.

When I first publicized this idea the response was uniformly favorable. Indeed, some congressmen were interested but none had the nerve to further it. Someday I should like to see the people given an opportunity to express themselves for or against this scheme, as they did on prohibition, through a straw vote.

Security is the one thing that people all around the world crave. I believe that by this sort of thrift lottery the nation could easily begin to devote a billion dollars a year toward old-age pensions.

The money would come out of myriads of pockets in such a way that none would feel any loss and in the course of ten years we would have built up a staunch body of endowed citizens. That is the great need in America; indeed, it is the great need throughout the world, economic security in old age to all who work. If the Government were to adventure into my lottery scheme I believe that almost inevitably it would proceed more widely into the field of annuities.

MR. AND MRS. FRANK A. VANDERLIP

CHAPTER XXX
I LEAVE THE BANK

OUT of the scores and scores of speech-making episodes of the war, there is one that I like to recall. It is a sort of high-watermark among all the incidents of my career that tell of friendships long retained. A banquet was given to me in the Gold Room of the Congress Hotel by the Bankers' Club of Chicago. All the men of LaSalle Street into whose offices I had trudged when I was a reporter on the Chicago *Tribune* were there, and happy on my account. It had been twenty years since I had left Chicago, a newspaperman, and my old paper measured the change by reporting that there was about $3,000,000,000 of money-power represented by the audience that faced me as I began to speak. James B. Forgan was there, and John J. Mitchell and many others. Proud? Of course I was proud.

I spent most of the winter in Washington, but every now and then I traveled back to Wall Street and into the bank. I knew there was something wrong with my health and late in February, 1918, I started once more for California and the ranch. I wrote to Mr. Stillman during my first week.

"My present idea," I wrote, or rather dictated, "is to take a month at the ranch, if everything moves along so there is not much of a call for me to come

I LEAVE THE BANK

back, and see if I cannot get back my ambition to ta.ke hold of things. I am entirely well and can only diagnose my case as one of being thoroughly tired, or temporarily lazy, all of which is probably super induced by feeling very much depressed over the world in general. The human family is really a pretty poor lot."

I had not the faintest idea then that my whole trouble was a diabetic condition. I was constantly tired. Yet I reported to Mr. Stillman that I had seen quite a little, at Santa Barbara, of Edward P. Ripley, the president of the Atchison, Topeka & Santa Fe Railroad. "He seems," I wrote, "inclined to take government ownership philosophically and never expects to see the railroads back in the hands of the stockholders."

Then I finished: "I trust I shall feel more in the letter-writing mood from now on, and if so you will hear from me much more frequently." But, as it happened, this was the last letter of mine that Mr. Stillman ever was to read. His answer to it did not reach me until I had received from his son, James A. Stillman, a telegram: "Father passed away peacefully this afternoon."

Mr. Stillman had been in fragile health for so long that the news of his death came to me without shock; but there was, nevertheless, profound sorrow. As I boarded a train for the East on that March day in 1918, I was feeling very keenly that I had lost something precious. This friend who had gone was the one who had singled me out to take his place in

I LEAVE THE BANK

an institution that was dearer to him, I think, than life itself.

You are bound to love one who compliments you so flatteringly and so sincerely year upon year. But to James Stillman there ran even heavier obligations. During that four-day journey to New York I lived much in the past, recalling, oh, so many instances of his long-range judgment that had been revealed to me in the form of wise counsels. If I say he was great, I do so calmly, after measuring the word and him to whom I apply it. All the years that I knew him he was concerned much more with the generation-to-come than with the one about to die. When such a concern is coupled with extraordinary capacity, surely it may be called greatness. Eccentricities? I suspect that all of us have them. I can smile now as I recall Mr. Stillman and Mr. Sterling passing judgments on men. I remember that Mr. Stillman would not place his confidence in any man who wore his hair pompadour, and Mr. Sterling was habitually croaking warnings against men whose smiles faded too quickly. Such rubbery quality in a man's smile, he held, was evidence of insincerity. Well, the funeral was over when I reached New York.

Mr. Sterling was an executor of Mr. Stillman's estate. Jimmy Stillman, at the next meeting of the board, was elected chairman. It was in that period that he confided to me that his father had cautioned him never to aspire to the presidency of the City Bank. At that time I am certain that he did not.

I LEAVE THE BANK

By this time I had to deal with a William Rockefeller who no longer masked his unfriendliness. Indeed, after the death of Mr. Stillman he was quite willing that I should see that he was, to use a school-boy phrase, "after me."

During my stay in Washington there had been set up an executive committee of which Mr. Rockefeller was a member. At an executive-committee meeting one morning in 1918, Mr. Rockefeller spoke to me with a good deal of harshness, of petulance. "You're trying to run the bank on one day a week," he said.

Mr. Sterling heard him and James H. Post. They rather gasped at the behavior of the old man. I did not reply; it was unnecessary that I should, because for eighteen years I had given to the bank all that there was in me. Of course, my work in Washington on the war-savings effort had taken time, but during" that period I had been on a leave of absence without salary.

Well, I went to Europe as soon as it was possible to travel after the war. Over there I gained a view that was contrary to the beliefs of most persons. I did not believe that Germany was going to pay her debts. I did not believe that we were going to be the financial center of the world. I believed quite positively that we were going to have to struggle to hold onto any foreign trade whatever. Once more there was stiff competition in the world from all of its people. As a matter of fact, among Americans, I found myself in accord only with Herbert Hoover, with whom I had long and interesting talks in Paris, and with Colonel House, who had fallen mysteriously out of favor with President Wilson.

I had not thought of writing a book until I went on board the *Olympic*, homeward bound. Then, realizing that I would have five uninterrupted days, I began forthwith to dictate. By the time we had reached Halifax—our ship was ferrying thousands of Canadian soldiers back to their homes—I had produced the script of a book that I called *What Happened to Europe*.

Currier came aboard my train sometime after I left Halifax. He was my assistant by that time, and as he sat down with me behind the closed door of my drawing-room, his face was full of concern.

There was, he told me, a kind of movement—"plot" was what my loyal friend called it—to get my resignation from the presidency of the City Bank. He had learned that Jimmy Stillman had said he now proposed to become president; moreover, that William Rockefeller was behind Jimmy. I felt chagrin the moment Rockefeller's name was mentioned. I wanted to get out. I did not want to be put out.

Well, I came on back to Wall Street and saw Jimmy. It was quite true. He did want to be president. We exchanged only a few words and thereafter I let it be known that I would get out gladly.

That transaction was arranged by a go-between, a friend of the Stillman's named William Kiernan. He

I LEAVE THE BANK

had never been in the bank but I had known him for a long time. When I got Jimmy's check for my stock I was ready to abdicate. I could have made a fight; but I cannot say too strongly that I welcomed the chance to get out.

I came back from Europe on May 19th. In the interval between my return and the announcement of my resignation on June 4th, I had sold my stock and I had made several speeches. Those speeches were not well received in Wall Street, because I said that the country was facing a period of business depression. That sort of information, however true, never is well received in Wall Street. Consequently, many persons erroneously jumped to the conclusion that my speeches were the cause of my resignation.

On June 4th I attended a meeting of the board. I simply stated that Jimmy wanted to be president and that I was entirely agreeable, which was absolutely true. Some of the board wanted to discuss the matter. Stillman and I left the room. There was some discussion; a few voices were raised. But it was settled. I resigned, packed up and walked out of the National City Bank for good.

It took me about a week, I think, to discover that if it suited me, I might sleep as late as I cared to. Let the old world spin! I could sit around and talk with my children or even, if I liked, go on a picnic. As a matter of fact, I did go on a picnic. For twenty years I had received every year an invitation to attend a reunion of former pupils of the Oswego school who had been there during the days of Christopher Duffy.

I LEAVE THE BANK

Could that Civil War veteran still be alive? He was, indeed! After ten years as county superintendent of schools, he had been elected clerk of the appellate court, second district, of Illinois. I went to Ottawa and shook hands with Mr. Duffy, and wandered about looking into aging faces there for eyes that I could recognize. I saw Gus Voss, and Harry Vanevra, now a postmaster. Harry and I were sent out of the room one time for misbehaving. As we were still pretty exuberant we climbed to the roof of the outhouse and with our antics attracted the attention of the children. For that we were properly caned by Christopher Duffy. His rattan pointer, when he got through with me, was all in splinters. I had a sore back and was a good deal ashamed. But, if you want to know the truth, there is very little else in my life of which I am ashamed.

It would not be fair of me to look backward and say how I might have behaved had I remained in a place of authority in Wall Street; however, I sometimes find myself wondering how James Stillman, if he had lived, would have conducted himself in that period of almost universal madness that we speak of as the boom era.

I well know that Mr. Stillman would have brought great wisdom and therefore sharp restraint to many expanding operations. It never was his way to think in terms of this year's profits or the profits of the year to come. What he was concerned with from moment to moment was the solidity of the bank's position from generation to generation. Yet fairness

I LEAVE THE BANK

impels me to add that what happened in the years after 1919 was confusing to the wisest and most experienced minds. Even a wise man is apt to lose faith in his judgment when the disasters he foresees repeatedly fail to occur.

My own fortune increased after I retired from the bank, but I was not so much smarter than others that I would care to boast about it. Repeatedly I sold stocks I had been holding because I felt they were selling for more than they were worth, only to buy them back at a higher price. Prices were being driven lip to a point where they had an absurd ratio to earnings. Stocks sold for ten times earnings, then twenty times and even thirty times. I sold repeatedly as did many of my friends, but when the market by advancing seemed to prove us to be wrong, we were not disposed to argue with the barometer. We were all in the same boat; we are all of us in the same boat now.

One night a few years ago I sat in front of the first in my library at Beechwood in the company of another farm-reared boy, Herbert Hoover. I commented on the fact that his career was the clearest kind of proof that in America the way from the bottom to the top was wide open.

Mr. Hoover stretched his legs a little closer to the fire. Then he began to talk; he said that for some hundreds of years the Western world had been fighting against a system whereby political power passed by heredity, grooved in channels of paternity. He reminded me that there were now only a few sons of true monarchs who might look forward with any degree of certainty to the succession to their father's thrones. Mr. Hoover advanced the thought that the people might in time object to the inheritance of economic power, in line with their having rejected the inheritance of political power. That did not mean the abolition of property inheritance, for the motive of laying by enough to take care of one's dependents must not be decreased. It would mean that after the economic needs of dependents were fully provided for, any excess that amounted purely to the inheritance of economic power would be taken by the State.

One does not have to pursue the thought far to see that it is fraught with enormous problems. Leadership and statesmanship do not always follow hereditary lines and in a greater degree, inheritance of economic power falling into untrained hands of widows, daughters and playboy sons does not make a promising industrial heritage.

There is the further important point that an inheritance tax is a levy on capital and that capital should not be dissipated through Government expenditures. The question might well be raised as to whether the Government would provide men who would administer wealth more fairly or as efficiently as the business men who are frankly actuated by a profit motive. I am well aware that there are men in Government jobs who have abilities that would have carried them to the top in commercial life, men who are diligent watch-dogs of the people's rights; but I question whether such men ever have or ever will be found in Government in a larger proportion than they are to be found in business.

The solution of our problems is not going to be easy. I am convinced that it does not lie in Government commissions nor in control of all jobs by the Government.

The older I get the more strongly I am persuaded that what we are lacking in our nation and in the world is not economic leadership so much as moral, spiritual leadership. Our greatest need is a philosophy of morality so widely indoctrinated that no man could rise to power among us who was not dominated by that morality.

INDEX

Ade, George, 46, 47
Ailes, Milton E., 117, 227, 236, 237, 238, 239, 242
Aldrich, Senator Nelson, 210, 211, 212, 213, 214, 216, 217, 218, 219
Andrew, Abram Piatt, 214, 215, 217
Archbold, John D., 284, 285
Armour, J. Ogden, 268, 269
Armour, P. D., 62, 63
Arthur, Chester Alan, 22
Axson, Margaret, 138

Baker, George F., 111, 126, 183, 184, 194, 195, 208, 214, 263, 269, 281, 282, 283
Barnesby, Dr. P. N., 249, 274, 275, 276, 277, 278, 284
Barnesby, Mrs. P. N., 274
Barney, John T., 164, 176
Barrett, Lawrence, 28
Benedict, H. E., 291
Booth, Edwin, 28
Bosworth, Welles, 284
Bowles, Samuel, 29
Brown, James Stanley, 66
Brown, Molly Garfield, 66
Brown, William C., 197
Bryan, William Jennings, 184, 245, 246
Burlingame, Edward L., 104

Campbell, James, 270
Canman, Leo, 43
Cannon, James G., 171

Carnegie, Andrew, 38, 139, 142, 263
Carter, Mrs. Leslie, 48
Castle, Sir Earnest, 269
Coffin, C. A., 268, 269
Conway, Mrs. Norton, 134, 222
Corey, W. E., 268, 269
Currier, Edward, 96, 97, 114, 150, 183, 227, 229, 233, 234, 237, 239, 240, 241, 284, 285, 287, 302

Davison, Henry P., 126, 132, 171, 180, 191, 192, 193, 194, 195, 196, 211, 213, 214, 216, 217, 227, 240, 246, 247
Delano, Frederic A., 291, 292
Dewey, Admiral George, 85, 86, 87, 88, 89
Dillingham, Charles, 46, 47, 48, 51
Duffy, Christopher, 16, 303, 304
Dunne, Finley Peter, 46, 47, 49

Eastman, George, 118
Eldridge, Herbert, 260, 261
Ellsworth, James, 252
Evans, Clinton B., 62
Evans, Rudulph, 1

Farrell, James A., 268
Ferguson, Elsie, 48
Field, Marshall, 33, 58, 59
Flower, Elliott, 42
Ford, Henry, 291
Forgan, James B., 270, 298
Frew, Walter E., 171

INDEX

Frick, Henry Clay, 141, 142, 150, 263, 270

Gage, Cornelia, 67
Gage, Lyman J., 52, 53, 64, 65, 67, 69, 71, 72, 74, 75, 78, 80, 81, 83, 84, 93, 94, 96, 97, 116, 117, 125, 137, 151, 228, 230, 231, 237
Gardin, John, 228, 260
Garfield, James A., 20
Gary, Judge Elbert, 28
Gould, Jay, 140
Grace, Joseph P., 268, 269
Grant, Ulysses S., 16
Green, Richard, 68, 69, 70, 138

Hall, David, 16
Hall, Frederick, 38, 39, 40
Hallinan, J. P., 158
Hamlin, Frederick, 129
Hanna, Senator Mark, 72
Harden, Edward Walker, 79, 80, 85, 86, 88, 89, 198, 230, 284
Harding, Horace, 269
Harriman, Edward H., 110, 142, 144, 145, 150, 157, 183, 184, 191, 199, 202, 203, 204, 205, 206, 207, 263
Harrison, Benjamin, 169
Harrison, Carter, 48
Harvey, George, 225
Havemeyer, Henry O., 154, 155
Hayes, Rutherford B., 22
Heintze, F. Augustus, 176
Henry, Philip W., 157
Herrick, Myron J., 268
Higgins, Ambrose, 17, 25
Hill, James J., 144, 154, 163, 268
Hine, Francis L., 235, 236, 240, 269

Hitchcock, F. C., 157, 158
Holden, Sir Edward, 187
Holtz, Von, 61
Hoover, Herbert, 301, 305
Hopkins, Mark, 37
Horner, Errol, 241
Hoyt, Moses, 3, 17

Ingersoll, Colonel Robert, 59

Jekyl Island, 210, 213, 215, 216, 217
Johnson, Joseph French, 29, 33, 34, 37, 38, 51
Johnson, Mrs. Joseph French, 51
Jusserand, Jules, 246, 249
Kahn, Otto, 206, 268, 269
Keeley, James, 44, 45, 63, 85
Kiernan, William, 302
Kruttschnitt, Julius, 202, 203

La Shelle, Kirk, 129
Lamont, Thomas, 247
Langdon, Woodbury, 191
Laughlin, J. Lawrence, 61
Lawson, Thomas W., 99
Leaf, Walter, 187
Leon, Maurice, 246
Loeb, James, 146, 187
Long, John D., 80
Lorimer, the Rev. George C., 43
Lovett, Judge Robert Scott, 203, 204, 268
Lydston, Frank, 59

Marlowe, Julia, 48
Marston, Edwin S., 172

INDEX

McAdoo, William Gibbs, 225, 235, 238, 240, 241, 242, 292
McAllister, Ward, 67, 69
McClure, S. S., 254
McCormick, Cyrus H., 154, 268
McCutcheon, John T., 50, 80, 86, 87
McDonald, Charles, 273
McEldowney, John H., 228
McGarrah, Gates W., 171, 240
McKinley, William B., 65, 70, 71, 80, 81, 82, 84, 85, 96, 98
McKinley, Mrs. William B., 82
McPhelan, Theodore, 44
McRoberts, Samuel, 229, 246, 247
Medill, Joseph, 58, 59
Mellon, Andrew W., 270
Meredith, Wynn, 23, 24, 25
Metropolitan Club, 130, 131, 146, 154, 240
Miller, Adolph, 61
Mills, Andrew, 284
Miln, George C., 18
Mitchell, Charles, 287
Mitchell, John L., 298
Monell, Ambrose, 268, 269
Morgan, J. Pierpont, 1, 2, 11, 84, 97, 110, 126, 144, 148, 149, 168, 169, 173, 174, 175, 183, 184, 189, 191, 192, 194, 195, 196, 208, 230, 234, 240, 265
Morgan, J. P., Jr., 119, 146, 148, 191, 192, 193, 194, 195, 196, 231, 240, 247, 262, 263, 264, 265
Morrison, William, 232
Morse, Charles W., 164, 174, 176
Morton, Paul, 169, 191

Newlands, Edith, 67, 68
Newlands, Senator, 67, 68

Patti, Adelina, 44
Perkins, George W., 146, 147, 148
Perkins, James H., 301
Post, James, 229, 230, 267, 287
Press Club, 59, 61
Pritchett, Henry S., 76, 138, 208

Randolph, Epes, 201, 202
Read, Opie, 59
Revelstoke, Lord, 187, 234
Rich, Charles, 230, 231, 247, 248, 267
Ripley, Edward P., 299
Roberts, George E., 117
Roosevelt, Franklin Delano, 292
Roosevelt, Theodore, 80, 81, 82, 93, 98, 125, 162, 163
Root, Elihu, 83
Rockefeller, John D., 148
Rockefeller, John D., Jr., 148, 212, 285, 300
Rockefeller, Mrs. John D., Jr., 213, 273
Rockefeller, Percy A., 268, 273
Rockefeller, Mrs. Percy A., 224, 273, 278, 279
Rockefeller, William, 108, 111, 134, 148, 194, 195, 198, 207, 234, 263, 264, 265, 266, 272, 273, 274, 275, 276, 277, 279, 300, 301, 302
Rockefeller, William, Jr., 148, 266, 269, 273
Rockefeller, Mrs. William, Jr., 94
Ryan, Thomas Fortune, 148, 149, 150, 192

Sabin, Charles H., 113, 132, 240, 268, 269
Scheff, Fritzi, 48
Schwedtman, F. Charles, 261

INDEX

Scudder, Moses, 33, 34, 35, 38, 54, 74, 29, 30
Shaw, Leslie M., 2
Shepard, Elliott F., 273
Shibusawa, Viscount, 105, 106, 107
Shiff, Jacob R., 144, 145, 146, 150, 183, 191, 192, 231
Shuster, W. Morgan, 143
Sloan, Samuel, 137
Speyer, James, 284
Stanford, Leland, Jr., 37
Sterling, John, 95, 110, 111, 150, 151, 152, 153, 154, 182, 184, 194, 207, 283, 300, 301
Stickney, Joseph, 86, 87
Stillman, James, 93, 94, 95, 96, 97, 98, 99, 100, 101, 102, 103, 104, 105, 106, 107, 108, 109, 110, 112, 113, 114, 115, 118, 119, 121, 125, 126, 127, 130, 131, 134, 135, 136, 140, 141, 142, 143, 146, 147, 148, 149, 150, 153, 155, 159, 160, 168, 172, 173, 178, 179, 182, 183, 184, 185, 187, 188, 189, 192, 193, 196, 197, 198, 205, 207, 208, 209, 211, 212, 213, 223, 224, 229, 230, 231, 232, 233, 234, 240, 242, 245, 259, 261, 262, 263, 264, 265, 268, 270, 271, 272, 273, 276, 277, 278, 279, 280, 281, 282, 286, 287, 289, 290, 298, 299, 300, 304
Stillman, James, Jr., 184, 229, 280, 287, 299, 300, 302, 303
Stolp, Myron, 24, 29
Stone, C. A., 267
Stratton, Samuel, 77
Street, Julian, 165, 166, 167, 254, 291
Street, Mrs. Julian, 127, 222
Strong, Benjamin, 132, 181, 179, 80, 213, 214, 215, 216, 217, 218, 227

Taft, Howard, 184, 218
Talbert, Joseph, 229
Thomas, Augustus, 91, 129
Thomas, Edward R., 174
Thomas, Orlando F., 174
Thompson, Thomas, 232
Thorne, Oakleigh, 176
Trumbull, Frank, 215

Union League Club, 59, 130, 131, 282

Vail, Theodore, 268
Van Benthuysen, 44
Vanderbilt, Commodore, 205
Vanderlip, Charlotte Woodworth, 3
Vanderlip, Mrs. Frank A., 124, 125, 252, 254, 273
Vanderlip, Frank Arthur, Jr., 222
Vanderlip, John Mann, 222
Vanderlip, Kelvin Cox, 222
Vanderlip, Ruth, 125, 222
Vanderlip, Virginia Jocelyn, 198, 222
Vanevra, Harry, 304
Vokes, Rosina, 28
Voss, Gus, 303

Wallace, James N., 240
Walters, Henry, 268
Warburg, Felix, 145
Warburg, Paul, 146, 180, 213, 214, 215, 216, 217, 181
Webster, Edwin F., 267, 268

INDEX

Webster, H. T., 102
Whitechapel Club, 59
Whitson, G. S., 160
Wiggin, Albert H., 132, 171, 235, 236, 268
Wilkie, John, 38, 39, 78, 91
Williams, John Skelton, 211, 238, 240, 242
Wilson, Woodrow, 8, 207, 208, 212, 218, 224, 225, 226, 227, 244, 301
Wilson, Mrs. Woodrow, 138
Winthrop, Beekman, 268
Wister, Owen, 129
Witt, Sergius de, 123

Wolff, Abraham, 145
Woodward, William, 235, 236, 240

Yerkes, Charles T., 54, 55, 56
Young, Arthur, 11

www.ingramcontent.com/pod-product-compliance
Lightning Source LLC
Chambersburg PA
CBHW020628220526
45464CB00001B/57